PRAISE FOR TOUCH THE SKY

"Tess takes on Kilimanjaro – but reading this uplifting book makes you feel you can take on the world!"
Chloe Hayward, BBC journalist.

"This story brings to light the way to reach high places. Just don't say no!"
Doug Scott CBE, first Briton to summit Everest (and survive!).

"As you join Tess on her challenging climb, you will I am sure, be with her in spirit and want to add your voice to her Peace Messages. As I have. Reading her very personal, touching and illuminating story, you will know indisputably the pen is mightier than the sword."
Virginia McKenna OBE, actress and founder of Born Free Foundation.

"This inspirational writing helps me access my own inner strength."
Margaret Coles, journalist, presenter and author of 'The Greening.'

"As a mountaineer, I well know the tremendous efforts undertaken here. It will touch your heart."
Neville Shulman CBE, explorer, philosopher, author of 'Zen in the Art of Climbing Mountains.'

"Tess's work is a truly inspiring initiative, enabling many people to make a real difference to our environment... to our world. I've been a keen supporter for many years, and I urge everyone to read this book."
Sir Jonathon Porritt CBE, environmentalist, founder of Forum for the Future and author of 'The World We Made.'

Other books by the author:

Cry from the Highest Mountain
Cold Hands Warm Heart

TOUCH THE SKY

Tess Burrows

eye books

Challenging the way we see things

First published in Great Britain in 2014 by:

Eye Books Ltd
29 Barrow Street
Much Wenlock
Shropshire
TF13 6EN

www.eye-books.com

Front cover image taken by Jackie Hau
Back cover author picture taken by Brendan O'Sullivan
Cover design by John Clarkson

British Library Cataloguing in Publication Data.
A catalogue record for this book is available from the British Library.

Printed by CPI Group (UK) Ltd, Croydon, CR0 4YY

ISBN: 978-1-903070-89-5

With love
For my grandson Bodhi
That the expression of the name he carries may shine
for Peace across our world

CONTENTS

INVITATION

Dear Reader

What are you PASSIONATE about doing? What makes you feel truly ALIVE, just at the thought of it? Let's assume your intention is for the good of all, then whatever it is, surely it's important to GO FOR IT.

Isn't it?

But suppose it involves something physical and say you're a granny with a creaky body and wandering mind, definitely in the latter part of life and should be at home knitting, what then?

And just imagine you want to pull a tyre up a mountain to 6,000 metres and everyone says, "You're bonkers ... You'll never do it". Instead, should you listen to that voice inside that says "I can do anything if I want it enough"?

Who should you listen to?

I suppose if we had listened to others in 1998, my partner Pete and I would never have started raising sponsorship to finance the building of six schools in Tibet. And we wouldn't have set out on missions to send off Peace Messages in the Tibetan manner from the high-flung, far-away places of the planet, on journeys that made us broke and threatened our lives. Having struggled to the ends of the Earth ... Himalayas, Andes, Pacific, North Pole and South Pole, surely we could now say enough was enough?

The trouble was, we'd fired up five zones across the globe and to do just one more would complete a figure of perfect harmony, a six-pointed star of Peace. Wouldn't that be great?

So we should really collect Peace Messages and take them to the highest point in Africa. We should tackle it head on, putting in effort, and have an appealing focus for Peace.

Yes, I had the belief to attempt it, but would our old bodies be able to cope? And pulling a tyre, for goodness sakes, that's ridiculous! What about the altitude? We'd experienced that before ... the pain and the insanity. Could we bear to go through that again?

The voice inside shouted at me. "It's important to try!"

"Follow your passion!"

"It's important to try!"

So we did.

I invite you to share my journey.

It might save you having to do it!

EAST AFRICA

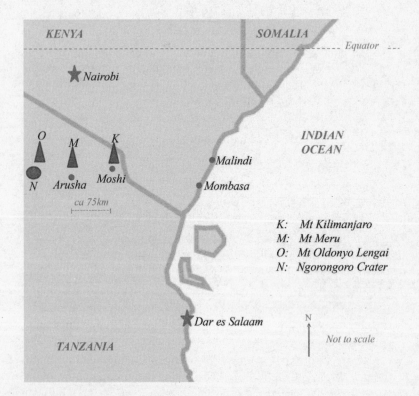

Hakuna Matata

4th September, 2011

The talisman spoke to me. It was merely a white bone trinket, shaped like a shield painted with a rough face, and held by a brown-beaded cord on a piece of old string. I found it in a souvenir shop that – in the traditional manner – was roofed with elephant grass. On either side of the shop were brightly coloured paintings, rows of bongo drums just waiting to be tapped and dusty wooden carvings of scary head-masks.

The young shopkeeper's face spread into a grin. "Jambo, Mama. See, this is Maasai."

I was charmed; the necklace had to come with me. So I started bargaining. Having promised myself that because of the poverty in Africa I would always bargain upwards, we agreed on 7,000 shillings. Twice what it was worth.

I turned to my cousin Nicholas, who in spite of his long shorts and boots still looked like the staunch, upright English businessman that he was. "D'you happen to have any Tanzania shillings on you?"

Clearly impressed by my bargaining skills, he put up the money. "Well, maybe it'll protect us," he said. "We're certainly going to need it with three major mountains to climb." Nicholas looked distinctly nervous. At the age of almost 68 he'd virtually never been on a mountain before.

Maybe it was foolhardy, but he believed in the importance of our mission for Peace.

"Oh, you'll be fine. It'll be a piece of cake," laughed Pete, coming up to hurry us into the waiting vehicle. "It's only the altitude you have to worry about." This was typical of his let's-go-for-adventure attitude, which I knew so well. Pete was my long-time partner, knight in shining armour and highly experienced mountaineer. When he was around I always felt that everything would be okay.

It was the altitude that worried Nicholas the most. We'd all heard what happened only the day before yesterday. About the man, exactly his age, who had come here to East Africa to climb Mount Kilimanjaro, as many inexperienced people do. He had reached the summit, then died on the way down. Presumed heart attack. He had died daring to climb to 6,000 metres, just like we were about to do ... or hoping to do. And our plan included two reckless additions: to spend a night in the summit crater and to pull a tyre up the highest mountain in Africa containing Peace Messages from every nation on Earth. Whatever had we signed up for?

"C'mon," said Pete putting a reassuring hand on Nicholas's shoulder.

As we joined the others in the vehicle I showed Pete my purchase.

"I bought it from that African from the Chagga tribe whose homeland is Kilimanjaro. He said I had to buy something today because today is special. It's Sunday."

Pete's eyes crinkled with amusement. "He saw you coming."

But I was convinced it was a good buy. I put the necklace on, tightening the little screw clasp. Idly I rubbed my right forefingers and thumb up and down it, feeling its hardness, but a hardness holding life. I wondered where the bone had come from. It was at that moment that I heard the voice:

"We are one spirit, you and I."

I knew it wasn't a physical voice but an internal one; even so I looked around to see if anyone else had heard it. Everyone was, however, hanging onto any bit of vehicle they could find as we turned out of the Nkake Jambo campsite and rock and rolled down a rusty brown high street, charging over speed bumps like a bucking bronco, already coughing and trying not to inhale the dust-laden air.

Hmm, I thought, fingering the bone. What was this 'one spirit' thing about?

I tried to absorb what I could of the little town Mto wa Mbu, which attractively translates as 'river of mosquitoes'. We bounced along behind a pick-up truck with around twenty people with sad resigned faces standing squashed like cattle on the back, past stores which were battered collections of tin roofs, some held up by packing cases. Groups of locals wandered along the dry dirt; women in long skirts and vivid coloured headscarves, pretty against their black faces and arms, many carrying loads on their heads or babies on their backs. The men were mostly in jeans and T-shirts, some wrapped in reddish checked cloaks.

This was only our third day in Tanzania, a place I'd always wanted to visit. We were on the way to the first part of our Peace Climb, and I still had the new awareness of being thrust into a different country. My eyes had had a lifetime of western civilisation; I had always lived in a land of plenty. Here we were watching life happening on the streets. People walking through the dirt, cycling with heavy loads of wood, pushing carts that looked too heavy for the human body. It was hard to see past the poverty.

A loud bang made me turn. Jackie was in the back seat trying not to cry and rubbing her head, which had made contact with the roof of the car. She was being comforted by her cousin, Ann. They were very close, like sisters, from a Chinese family who had emigrated to the UK from an ancestral village in Hong Kong where the elders were still in touch with the Earth. But Jackie and Ann had never really been adventuring before. Hmm, I thought, I bet they're thinking they never will again. And we hadn't even started the physical stuff yet. Any exercise beyond walking up the stairs was quite alien to their bodies. In spite of the excitement of being part of a vital mountaineering journey it was going to be tough for them. Now, it didn't feel like our first-class tourist vehicle was actually much better than the local version we were following.

"Sorry!" shouted Marco, the driver. He flashed a devastating smile from his full handsome face and slowed down over the next speed bump.

"Hakuna matata," we shouted in chorus, practicing our Swahili lingo. 'Hakuna matata' means 'no worries'. It was the easiest phrase to remember and, as we were to learn, the most useful.

Marco was from the Iragw tribe, one of 122 different tribes in Tanzania, each one having its own language as well as Swahili and English. Wow, I was having enough trouble just trying to remember the tribe names.

Ann pointed at the sticker on the back window which said 'One Human Family'. "That's so right," she exclaimed, her gentle, loving nature picking up on things that were good and true.

Jackie, quiet and thoughtful – perhaps as she was the youngest of our team – now spoke, recovered it seemed by some of Ann's homeopathic pills from being bashed on the head. "Why's that sticker there, Marco?"

"Well, we're all one family aren't we? That's how we see it in Tanzania. All the tribes intermingle now and there are lots of mixed marriages. Our country is a good example for the rest of Africa."

"So why is Tanzania peaceful now when so many other African countries have tribes still killing each other?" Nicholas asked.

"We're a nation of brotherhood because of our first president, Julius Nyerere," Marco declared proudly. "He was an idealist, going for peaceful change. Since independence in 1961 he worked hard for the 'one human family' principle. He was a light for Africa and the world."

Aha. So we're definitely in the right country for our Peace Climb.

"Marco. We've got a quote from Nyerere as one of our

Peace Messages," I said. "It's about shining a light from the top of Kilimanjaro." At this his face lit up. His eyes shone.

I felt that human attributes are somehow very close to the surface here in this ancient land where man began. People aren't all shut down beneath the hard skin of civilisation. This fitted in with our philosophy.

And I thought how lovely that we had such a caring warm-hearted Peace Climb team. Pete and I smiled at each other. I bet he was thinking the same thing. The rest of our team, the other six with little mountaineering experience between them, would be arriving in the country later, but we were so happy to be getting to know our core team – five including us – each one out to help the world.

Was this more important than having a team of fit expert climbers who had a better chance of reaching the top of the mountains?

Hmm ...

Time would tell.

For us to be at the summit of Africa's highest mountain, Kilimanjaro, was crucial to the fulfillment of the dream I'd been carrying for thirteen years. My dream was to collect thousands of Peace Messages from individuals and speak them out in the Tibetan manner from high-flung, far-away places around the world. Pete and I, working with our charity organisation Climb For Tibet, had already undergone Peace Climbs in five zones: the Himalayas, the Andes, the Pacific, the North Pole and the South Pole. To fire up the Africa zone now in this way would mean that we had symbolically drawn a figure of a six-pointed star of Peace across the planet. I believed that this would help, not only those who conceived the Messages, but also at a subtle level creating something far greater for Peace in their coming together.

Did we have a hope of doing it?

To reach our first mountain we had to skirt up the edge of the Great Rift Valley, which sweeps 10,000 kilometres down Africa from Jordan to Mozambique, crossing the Ngorongoro Crater, which is famous for its wildlife.

We were in Maasai country. These widespread semi-nomadic tribal people have grazed cattle sustainably here for generations, cattle being fundamental to their way of life. This was their land. It must be extremely tricky to hold the harmony of wildlife conservation and tourist needs alongside that of the Maasai. Somehow though their presence made it feel more real, as though the natural order of things was in place. But it also made me realise that it was us who were the interlopers. Instinctively my hand touched the bone talisman at my throat and I asked in my mind "Permission to enter this land?" Again I heard, *"We are one spirit, you and I"*. All was well.

We passed many animals including warthogs, elephant, antelope, giraffe and hippos. Zebras seemed to be the most common, though, along with buffalo who we learnt gore and kill over 200 people every year.

Then – wow! We were suddenly aware that we were with the king of the beasts. We stopped maybe 20 metres from a male and a female lion. They were magnificent. A pale biscuit colour, sleek and muscular; the male adorned with a fine tawny mane which made him appear much bigger than the female. A powerful presence. I felt excited that interaction was taking place, as lions are very often nocturnal hunters. They appeared to be deep in conversation, so Pete ad-libbed some dialogue:

"How about you and me, Lioness?"

"No, sorry, not now. I've got a headache."

With that the king lion turned his large proud head towards us and opened his mouth into a yawn, showing an array of teeth, two large canines up, two large canines down, that could tear any one of us to bits in seconds. Watching from the roof, feeling set apart and safe, I held my bone talisman and tried to reach an age-old connection, *"Hello, King. We are one spirit, you and I"*. Perhaps it wasn't the right moment for such an approach. It seemed he had other things on his mind, in particular another younger male threateningly close. The king tried to stare him down.

"Looks like life in the lion world isn't a lot different from the human world," Nicholas laughed.

"Even the highest king or master still has to find a way to live in the world at a practical level," chimed in Ann.

"Don't we all ..."

We moved away reluctantly. I would have liked to have lingered longer and honoured the lion. I've no idea how. Certainly it did seem that as observers, the lions took little notice of us. It surprised me. But I suppose they were all used to us weird creatures coming along in noisy clunky things, smelling of oil. Decidedly untasty. Nor did we emit hostile signals. But Marco warned, "Take one step out of the protection of the vehicle and you'll be history ... or dinner, depending on how you look at it."

A cheetah posed serenely in the distance. Definitely dinner.

The special magic of Ngorongoro held me in a concentrated focus that expanded my awareness. In a very natural way I knew that I had been joined by the presence of my mother, who had passed over a few months previously. This made me glow with an intense inner joy. She used to love watching the TV safari programmes, especially the ones about the cheetah and its young. Now she was somehow watching them for real through me. I'm not sure how the mechanics work; maybe like tuning into a different frequency on a radio, she was able to tune her vibration into that of mine which enabled her to sense as I sensed. Anyway, I knew beyond a shadow of a doubt that she was there, and my heart was touched by her happiness.

She is part of my journey. I am part of hers. In the same way I am sure she is connected to the rest of her loved ones. Are we all intertwined in this way? Do journeys never really end?

I smiled at the thought. As we left the fantastic wildlife haven, I realised that Africa gave my heart wings.

Here an estimated 25,000 large animals live closely together in harmony, mostly concerned with basic survival: food, sex, child-care, real-estate and not being preyed upon, but they were all interacting in a way which uses the least energy and results in the most Peace. It appeared to be an ecosystem held in balance, but how fragile was this? Surely vulnerable to too many tourists, overgrazing by cattle, wildlife population explosions and climate change which could easily, like the precarious environment of the Earth, be tipped over the edge.

We all voiced our concerns – and that we would try and make a difference – as we headed up through the umbrella trees to the rim of the Ngorongoro Crater bowl. Our shared experience was making for good team bonding for the work ahead.

We continued northeast across rugged volcanic highlands where scrubland dropped away and open grassland took over.

There was no mistaking that this was Maasai home-land. Cattle were all around, herded by tall, slim young men in checked scarlet and blue traditional cloaks wrapped like robes around their bodies. These cloaks, known as *shukas*, were made of cotton cloth having replaced the original animal skins half a century or so ago. They were also worn by girls as skirts and shawls as they herded the goats and sheep, adorned with beautiful coloured beaded jewellery. Maasai homes were clusters of little round thatched mud huts, held mostly in enclosures known as *bomas*, protected by thick thorn hedges against desperate predators.

Smoke patches clustered around where the Maasai had lit fires to encourage new grass to grow for their all important livestock, which provided not only most of their food, but also dung for the walls of the huts. I hoped it would rain for them. It felt like it never would here, with all the dust, brownness and lack of trees.

I watched out of the window fascinated, wishing I could observe without being seen. The people smiled and waved to us but I still felt like an interloper in their world. I held my bone talisman and somehow that helped a little, but it was all so entirely different from my world. The only time that my life had been touched by the Maasai was three years ago when I'd run the London Marathon with six warriors. Me and 35,300 other runners!

The warriors had come to London to try and raise some funds to build a bore hole for clean water at their village. Two out of three of the children in their village died from water born disease before the age of five, and some were killed collecting water from a dam they shared with wildlife. Imagine having to send your children to collect water shared by hippos, lions, buffalo and crocodiles! They were struggling with famine, the effect of forty years of drought, climate change, deforestation and the needs of conservationists. Against all the odds they were trying to hold onto their traditional way of life.

Londoners had thought it strange that they ran in rubber sandals made from car-tyres, did amazing standing jumps straight up into the air, were decorated with ceremonial beaded jewellery, carried heavy shields made from buffalo hide and long spears in case they met up with lions. And that was before even mentioning sharing property such as wives, and drinking blood from the jugular veins of live cattle.

Now here in their world I understood why they had thought aeroplanes, flushing loos, moving staircases and the London Eye so strange, as well as eating processed food loaded up with salt and sugar and the manic rushing about of London office workers. I hoped that they had been given some black pudding, the only blood-food thing I could think of in Britain.

I knew then that I'd be a useless Maasai. Even though their cattle are considered so sacred that to eat or drink from them is an expression of Divine union, I don't like eating meat or drinking milk, or even blood for that matter! But surely there is much to learn from their ancient way of life living in harmony with the land, especially dry lands, respecting our Earth.

The Maasai warriors had bravely faced the terrors of our western culture and managed the challenge of our marathon with ease. Could we now approach their ancient culture with an open mind and manage the challenge of their mountain? Their special mountain was to be our first mountain.

We didn't have to wait much longer to find out. Passing a few shrubby bushes we came into the village of Naiyobi, a collection of bomas and huts that made me feel we'd turned back time a few millennia and moved through to a little patch of higher ground on the other side. This was the end of the road.

And there before us was our mountain. Oldonyo Lengai, translating from Maasai as 'Mountain of God'.

You only get to have a first meeting once. It's in that first moment of recognition that you connect and understand. It's then that you know if there is love, if it's something special to you or not. You can grow to love in a different way, but that first moment ... that's when you know.

I knew Oldonyo Lengai. It was a perfect symmetrical shape, like a pyramid, with a bit of an extra lip at the top and coloured in an almost uniform greyness amidst lava striations. There was a sense of timeless, endless strength. Perhaps this stemmed from the eruption barely three years ago, so its covering was newly arrived from the heart of our Earth, connected like a baby, and yet carrying the energy of millions of years with it. And maybe it was all the worship by the Maasai people, climbing up generation after generation to speak to the Sky, to the Divine – known as Engai or just Ngai – who resided there. Though still fifteen kilometres away, Oldonyo Lengai completely dominated the skyline. There was no way the mountain could not be important to them here.

Somehow, I could feel it all deep within me. But it didn't look easy to climb. Not one little bit.

This first mountain was the beginning of our Peace Climb. Whilst the plan was to speak Peace Messages out and pull the Peace-tyre up Kilimanjaro itself, we wanted to build up over three stages from Oldonyo Lengai at 2,989 metres, to Mount Meru at 4,562 metres, to Mount Kilimanjaro at 5,895 metres. The build-up was crucial for us. Many people rush up and down Kilimanjaro in five or six days and barely have time for their low-oxygen adaptation to kick in. We wanted to do a slow climb of Kilimanjaro over eight days with time to speak out Peace Messages and then spend the night in the crater at the 6,000-metre summit. This was pretty unusual and widely considered crazy. But to give ourselves the optimum chance of success, acclimatisation was the key. Ideally we'd go for five months living here at altitude for our bodies to be well adapted. But with our busy lives we were doing better than most to have found a month. The rest of our team members yet to arrive would find it even harder with less time to acclimatise.

Our bodies needed time to become used to the altitude, to adapt physiologically to cope with the lack of oxygen. In the process the build-up would help our fitness and give experience to our team's mountain novices.

This early part of the journey was also giving us the chance to be with the land, to get the feel of Africa. We had come to do something important to help the Earth and humanity. We needed to feel welcomed and accepted by land and people for it to work. I knew we needed to come humbly and in the spirit of service. Only under these conditions would the process of our work for Peace take on its optimum benefit for the greater good.

Now, at the meeting of our first mountain I felt greatly humbled. I was sure that the others would also see that there was a big struggle ahead. Well, Nicholas, Ann and Jackie. Not Pete of course.

Marco unloaded us and the gear, before speeding off back along the track.

"We are to have some sort of a show in the village," said Nicholas. "By then our kit will be loaded onto donkeys and we can set off on foot with them. Justin here is to be our guide."

By the backdrop of the great mountain I saw Pete talking to a striking looking Maasai about thirty-five years old in western jeans, boots, expedition jacket and a thick black balaclava. I wondered at the headgear. Hmm, not too many banks to rob around here! He led us down into the village to a small boma enclosed by wooden stakes and thorn bushes. An old man was already sitting wrapped in a thick blue blanket and woollen cap with youngsters cuddling up close. This was Chief Landeipa. We were introduced and, not knowing the proper Maasai greeting, shook hands. He gave out the sense of being a kindly and gentle soul. I felt excited at the thought of an authentic show, which would demonstrate more about the Maasai culture. We waited eagerly, feeling rather like celebrities.

However there seemed to be a problem. Discussions were taking place amongst the Maasai men. Justin approached. "What's going on?" I asked, looking up into a face that startled me. There was something about the way he was that I just knew. Like his mountain ...

"We can't do the show," he said. His words were slow and deliberate, with a lilting African drawl, but mostly easy to understand which was surprising considering English was his third language.

"Oh no. That's disappointing."

He pointed to a mud hut a mere two metres to the outside of the boma. "A baby is being born."

"A baby is being born?" I repeated in disbelief.

"Yes, right at this minute. We must respect the new life arriving."

I stared at the hut. I could hear no sounds through its thick mud and stick walls, just agitated chatter around us. "Wow. Of course. Please could you convey our blessings to the mother?"

"Yes, yes ... and as the chief's son is not here, it falls on me to do the ceremony."

"What ceremony?"

"I must climb onto the roof of the hut to welcome the baby, so that its guardian spirit may enter."

Without further ado and ignoring the coming and going of women through the darkness of the doorway, he shook his boots off and scrambled up to stand on the apex of the little hut, the shape almost a mini-replica of the mountain behind him. Arms out, he shouted in Maasai, "Hey woman. You got baby. Well done!" Then he sat down and sang "Thank you, Ngai, for this new day and for all the miracles, and also for delivering this beautiful baby."

"Hey!" I turned to the others. "That's so amazing. The beginning of our Peace Climb, representing a new birth of Peace. You know, a new way of finding Peace in the world, by the opening of the hearts of thousands of individuals writing our Peace Messages ... And what do we get? A real, physical birth. How symbolic is that? We're here in this village for only a few minutes and that's the time the baby decides to be born."

I high-fived Justin through the boma fencing when he came down. "It's so auspicious," I told him. "New birth! We're climbing for a new birth of Peace. That's why we've come to Africa."

His smile spread over his entire face. I knew he somehow related exactly to what I was talking about.

"I shall ask that the baby girl be called Peace in your honour," he said. "The chief will name her in a few days. The name is Sakimba."

"Sakimba."

"Yes. Actually it's my name too."

"But I thought you were called Justin."

"When we go to school, we are given Christian names which are used by white people. My real name is Sakimba."

"Can we call you Sakimba?"

"Of course."

So. We were to be guided by a man named Peace. How wonderful.

Being near the equator twilight came suddenly. The low evening light sent the long shadows of our donkey cavalcade across the dry grassland and picked out the ruts in the rough tracks over which we walked. The wind blew fiercely from the west bringing dust to our faces and every nook and cranny of our clothes. From the other direction came herds of cattle, lowing melodiously with cowbells ringing, being brought home by young men in their red robes along with donkeys carrying wood. The dying sun sent golden rays of light skyward, silhouetting the animals and picking up their dust like trails of glory. The mountain drifted nearer. Thoughts floated ...

My senses filled up ... I feel so much joy ... as though I'm flowing in a river of light. What type of deep magic is this that makes me feel so uplifted?

I looked at Ann. She smiled sweetly, knowing. "I'm experiencing it too," she said.

The mountain must be to blame.

I turned to Sakimba, "Is the mountain welcoming us?" I asked.

"Of course."

Then he continued, "Oldonyo Lengai is our sacred mountain. Ngai is there. He is the sky. Also the rain, the lightning, the clouds, the moon ... He is life, a living God." Then he patted his heart. "And we know He is here also. We can pray by looking up to the sky, but when we are in trouble we go to the mountain and pray to Ngai there."

I nodded. It sounded familiar. But there was something more that I hadn't experienced before. It was the sense that this young man was the land. He was the mountain. He, his land and his mountain were one and the same.

"We will have special Maasai prayers on the summit of our mountain," he promised.

"Thank you. That's completely perfect," I beamed. "Lengai is the first of our three mountains. After that we must climb Meru and finally Kilimanjaro where we will speak out thousands of Peace Messages. It's a way of pulling together the prayers of many people to help Peace, to help the Earth."

The concepts were difficult in any language, but I felt that he understood. He understood because his heart knew.

So I figured he'd have the answer to the question that was bothering me. "See this," I said, holding up my bone talisman, "does this connect up with the Earth?"

"Ah," he said, "that's a Maasai warrior talisman," and nodded as if that explained it all and there was nothing more to be said.

We walked in silence for a while until he offered, "I'll tell you the story of how I became a warrior."

Jackie and Ann drew in closer to listen.

"I was nineteen years old when the time came for me and

my brothers in my age set to go for initiation. It's quite a long process, but we were all excited. First was the sacred ritual of circumcision. This was painful and we had to undergo it without flinching. But we had been looking forward to it from the time we could first talk. It was our stepping into manhood."

I listened, not wanting to imagine the knife or the dirt ...

"Then my brothers and I had to go out into the bush for six months and survive on our own."

Hmm. On their own meant with nothing but a spear, a knife and their wits ... nowhere to sleep, nothing to eat.

"Then all that was left was the killing of the lion."

Oh, was that all.

"This symbolises the protection of our sacred cattle and our people. It used to be that every man could kill a lion, but now of course there just aren't the numbers. The elders allow only one representative from each age set. I was the chosen one. When the time came my brothers and I chased the lion for a long time, then we encircled him and sang to his spirit."

"Weren't you afraid?"

"I trembled at the thought of it, but no, when the time came, I wasn't afraid."

"Why not?"

"Well, I was going to be a warrior and so be highly respected, particularly by the girls of my tribe," he replied, a smile in his voice.

I turned to Ann and Jackie who were walking open-mouthed beside me and we exchanged glances.

"So," he continued, "I threw the spear and hit the lion, but in the heat of the moment the lion clawed me on the neck and shoulder and a brother also threw his spear and hit me in the face."

He pulled down his black balaclava to reveal a long scar reaching from his forehead, down the bridge of his nose, to under his right ear. "And since that day I've been blind in one eye."

I said nothing. I was too busy trying to digest his story. Obviously great importance was afforded here to being a warrior. And it went with the strong sense of the others in the tribe. Pondering this I thought about the riots and looting that had been going on in the UK just before we left and how initiation tests of strength and courage in any culture could really benefit young men and give them a sense of purpose and pride in their community. But killing a lion! I wasn't sure how to fit this concept into my thinking.

I had always abhorred the old colonial way of hunting for sport and ego, but the Maasai had lived in balance with lions for a very long time and like all native peoples never took more than was necessary. I suppose if the lion was to threaten their god-like cattle there was justification, but it seemed to be a lot more than that. Did the spirit of the lion that Sakimba had killed come with him now, in the same way that I was experiencing that my mother came to me? Was the lion spirit sharing his warrior lion-heart attributes? Had he become a brother?

My unanswered questions only emphasised that the Maasai people seemed to me to be drifting between two worlds. What was their way forward? Could they bring with them into the new world the positive ways and understandings of their old world? For of course life cannot stand still.

It was gratifying to see that this young man from a mud hut who had barely left his homeland had something quite knowing about him, carrying as he was the innate wisdom of an ancient native people. It was as though he was in touch with a higher purpose.

None of us could doubt his sincerity when he said, "I would be honoured to come with you on your other two climbs as well. It may not be possible to be taken on as a guide so would probably be for no pay, but my heart is with what you are doing."

So it appeared our Peace Climb Team had gathered a Maasai warrior.

However, try as I might, I couldn't work out how the courage of a warrior could give me the answer to the matter of my bone talisman.

That night we camped alongside the donkeys after a scarlet sky turned black to welcome a thin slither of moon. I held a torch for Sakimba wrapped in his warrior shuka, so he could write a Peace Message in Maasai, Swahili and English: "As a human being we have a responsibility to keep Peace in the world."

Like most of our Messages it was a simple expression. I wondered how a young man from a mud hut could have acquired so worldly an attitude. Was it just in him, or in all of the Maasai people? Or was it common to the whole of humanity?

I didn't know then just how much his beautiful belief in harmony was to be challenged.

In the morning we followed Sakimba to the top of a ridge and stared at his mountain in awe. A white-necked raven squawed overhead. The only other sound was the wind battering our clothes and rucksacks with hot volcanic ash.

Nicholas was the first to speak. "I wouldn't have thought anyone'd be mad enough to walk up there." He laughed uneasily, ignoring Pete's mumble of "piece of cake."

"You are a strong warrior," said Sakimba, "and we'll take it gently. Remember it's a sacred place. We'll be protected. No one's ever been injured on the mountain. Not counting the boy who fell into hot lava in the summit crater and burned his legs."

No, of course we wouldn't count that ...

"It'll be better in the dark when it's cooler."

At this Ann looked horrified. "We climb in the dark?" She turned to me. "Have you climbed in the dark?"

"Oh, yes", I replied, "don't worry, our group strength will carry you. Anyway in the dark it's easier to connect with the inner energy."

She and Jackie exchanged grim glances. Even without their inexperience and unfit bodies there was no doubting that this would be the toughest thing they'd ever tried to do.

The mountain was a forbidding sight. There was nothing to break the steepness of the climb, some 1,800 metres of vertical ascent the entire way to the summit. It looked like a huge pile of grey ash, with deeper grey channels gouging their way randomly. Nearing the top there was something of white colouration, almost like a snow covering, and just a faint hint of a plume of smoke. Yes, this was one awesome volcano.

So this was it. The first giant step of our Peace Climb. At last it was about to happen. Could all of us climb efficiently and stand at that sacred summit by our Maasai warrior?

I was hopeful.

But we were about to learn that things here are not always as expected. This is Africa. Things work in the African way.

Oldonyo Lengai

The blistering heat sapped our energy. It came from all sides, not only the fiery ball above but also the bare volcanic material at our feet, which was absorbing the sun's radiation. We had been walking for eight hours to reach the foot of the mountain, and coupled with the heavy, dust-laden wind, were being dried to a cinder. It seemed entirely right that it should be hot held in the reaches of an active volcano. Wow, this is an active volcano, the only one left in East Africa, and uniquely, the only carbonate one in the world. This meant that it was not a common red-hot silicate volcano, but exclusively one that emits cool fluid black lava of the constituency of molten chocolate, which solidifies and turns grey within hours. Geologically cool implying temperatures as low as 600°C. So really cool then!

It had been only three years since Oldonyo Lengai's last big eruption, so this was geologically very much a live volcano. Not dangerously so (we hoped) but still ticking over, busy in its ongoing job of shaping the form of the Great Rift Valley.

Sakimba found us respite in a shallow cave on the edge of an empty water-course. It was good to give our weary bodies a chance to sit down as we drained the last of our water bottles. I listened on my MP3 player to an inspirational song about a group who were together carrying a flame. It had been recorded by our friend Sheila, who worked with the World Peace Flame. This special light, born in the lead up to the Millennium as a gathering of six flames lit by Peace-makers around the world, was flown on military aircraft and united together to burn eternally in North Wales. Now candles and lanterns lit from it are sent out around the world to be a focus and hold a light for Peace. We were honoured to carry it now on our African journey.

The song reminded me that however tired we might feel we must always remember our mission as we stepped up our three mountains, onwards come what may, and it gave me the energy boost I needed.

We were led through more dust and heat across an open plain with tussocky grass clumps to see a distant welcoming sight, the car. Marco had driven as far as he dared off the road to meet us. We collapsed gratefully into the vehicle, only to be asked to stand in the sun again whilst a flat tyre was changed assisted by some herders who appeared it seemed from nowhere. There were young boys too, who stared at us with pleading eyes. The wind now felt different. By the safety of the vehicle it was almost cooling on our fair skins. Drained of vitality under the intense sun I was beginning to see the usefulness of the dark skins of all those around us who seemed to be full of energy.

We drove towards desolate Lake Natron. This is the world's most caustic body of water clothed at times in bright red micro-organisms like algae and braved almost exclusively by flamingos. Near here was the Mikuyu River campsite where we would rest and sleep before continuing the climb.

We were the only visitors in a compound which consisted of little more than trees, a few shacks and one dining shelter with tables and chairs. One of the bags of food had mysteriously disappeared off the back of the vehicle, but it was a bit late to discover that this area had a reputation for bandits.

There was more. Our personal bags, which we had left in the vehicle yesterday, had been dropped at the campsite where we would be the following night. But we needed them now. Oh no! In my weary state this felt like a complete disaster. It's just a little test, I told myself. Keep strong, all is well. I would be without all my kit so carefully prepared in England. All my vital glyco-nutritional supplements, two little sachets for morning and night, which I believed kept my body going and held my energy together. And the go-faster Empact sports drink. Then there was the power food I'd packed: the salted peanuts and nuts that Pete likes and the high carbohydrate energy bars, as my own body works best on nibbling little and often. I had also prepared little survival packs of dried fruit, dates and seeds. Now suddenly I was dependant on what the Universe would provide. As were the others. Pete was concerned that, critically, he had no head-torch batteries. Ann and Jackie were upset about no spare clothes. Nicholas was keeping a stiff upper lip.

We hadn't eaten since breakfast, a long time ago. I usually feel wonky if I haven't nibbled for three hours. Now I was into a low blood sugar level state, dizzy and shaky. We put up the tents and I went and pleaded with Laurah, the cook, for something, indeed anything to eat, feeling that I was being annoying as he had also had a long day trekking. Indeed he had trekked with a box of eggs in his hands. Under a little open-sided tin roof shelter he was lighting a gas bottle and starting to prepare a meal for us. He washed and cut up some carrots, cucumbers and tomatoes; I could have hugged him!

After this I felt almost human again and tackled the dribble of cold water which came through, from time to time, in the shower hut. Wonderful, except everything we touched was so dusty that it wasn't long before I felt I hadn't had a shower. Now all we needed to do was eat quickly, which didn't look like happening for ages, and then have some sleep, the length of time for which was becoming shorter minute by minute.

Marco drove off to pick up a guide from somewhere locally. This surprised us. It meant that Sakimba was presumably now to be assistant guide. We waited. The fierce hot wind did little to relieve the sense that things weren't quite right. Marco returned with a large bare-chested man named Bora Bora. He wore a brown leopard skin over one shoulder and carried a machete. My idea of what a Zulu warrior might look like. Obviously he was experienced at climbing Oldonyo Lengai.

He looked us up and down assessing his job of dragging a motley collection of tourists up a mountain. Somehow I couldn't warm to him.

"I would normally leave at midnight to make the most of the cool hours," he said, "but with a less fast group I think we should go earlier. I'll return at 11pm. Be ready then. And carry three litres of water each. I shall bring my brother Julius with me as my assistant guide." And he was gone.

Sakimba was told that he couldn't be our guide after all, wouldn't get paid and could now walk home again.

We tried to work out why these changes were happening, but tired and confused as we were, and knowing the efficiency of our tour company, we could only put it down to tribal politics. It was in a dazed and down-hearted state that we eventually sat down to eat, the table dimly lit by candles. Laurah had prepared soup, rice and vegetables, not easy under the circumstances, and there were small silver foil parcels of fried bread as supplies for the climb.

As we finished eating Sakimba came into the little circle of light to talk to us. He had struck a chord with all of us, as our very own Peace Climb Maasai warrior. No theatre performance could have moved us more as he expressed how he felt in his slow deliberate drawl as though tearing out each word from deep within, his voice quivering, "I feel so much a part of your team. I so wanted to come with you ... to climb to the sky for Peace and send onto the wind my Peace Message from the top of our sacred mountain Lengai ... for all people. A Maasai warrior does not break a promise. But I shall have to break this one. It is heartbreaking to do."

What had happened? All had seemed so perfect just a little while ago. Tears were streaking my cheeks. I could hear Jackie sniffing beside me. Ann was all choked up.

"You will be okay. Bora Bora is a good guide; yes, I have worked with him before. But his heart is not with the spirit of the mountain."

I knew instinctively that this was important, that this was the difference between the two men. My eyes welled up further as

I struggled to say, "We'll do it for you. We'll read your Peace Message for you."

"We're so sorry you're not coming," said Pete, standing to give him a hug. "I'll talk with Marco and say that you need to be paid whatever." Nicholas tried to give him some money from us all, but he wouldn't take it.

"I'm not sure what I'll do now," he said. "Maybe I'll try and get a lift to Arusha and see if I can come on Meru and Kili with you ..." He was too upset to continue.

We retired to our tents. There were two and a half hours before we had to get up. Pete snored so I knew that he slept a little. It was a happy sort of a snore, but still I couldn't settle. The injustice of the situation went round and round in my brain. And on top of that was the worry of setting off on a major climb with no sleep.

At 11pm we crawled out of our tents. My body felt shattered, my mind scattered. I missed my pills and powders. But Pete's closeness as always made me feel that all would be well. Nobody in the team spoke. As we left for the car, Sakimba appeared and gave me a parcel. "It's my Maasai shuka cloak," he said. "Red, the colour of power. Please carry it and wear it on the summit. You are now the warrior. I make you an honorary warrior."

I was too taken aback to reply.

"And these are Peace words for Ngai." He thrust at me a brown piece of cardboard with words written on it.

I hurriedly rolled it into a Maasai wood-smoked container from his Maasai village, in the summit-bag in my rucksack.

"And here five red-bull drinks for energy and a packet of biscuits. It's all I've got."

"Thank you for giving us all you've got," I managed to say. "We'll do it for you." And I wondered then if by doing it for him it would help us each find more inner strength than we might have ... help us give more of ourselves than we might have. It wasn't until much later that I reached some understanding about this.

The vehicle bumped and swayed along a track and then wove

35

between scrubby bushes on loose skidding ground. Marco was driving us back as near to the mountain as possible. I fiddled about with my gear, wondering if there was anything I could chuck to lighten my load, but the movement was making me feel sicker. Eventually I decided to leave some water behind. Pete reckoned that two litres was plenty. Water was the heaviest thing to carry and taking too much would certainly slow us down. Then I drank the red-bull. It was the first time I'd tried it. It made me feel even more nauseous but at least it was liquid that I was carrying inside – rather than outside – of me.

It was 12.45am, much later than planned, by the time we stopped. By the headlights we could see that we were in tall dry grass. I laced my boots on and looked up into the dark. There was nothing but black, timeless black. No red glow from the summit direction, so all quiet there. No visible stars; no moon gracing the sky. It had been stifling in the vehicle, but now we were hit by a wild hot wind loaded with ash. The air had the feeling of lead as though there was a storm brewing. I pulled on my windproof jacket, leaving the front undone but the hood up over my windproof hat and head-torch, the best protection I could think of against the battering ash ram. I couldn't wear my sunglasses as it was pitch dark, so I would just have to pull the hood well down and screw up my eyes. Rucksack on, grab sticks and we were off.

Now that we were actually on the way I could relax a bit. I loved the feeling of setting out into the unknown, in the middle of the night, in the middle of nowhere. It was like giving up trying to be in control and handing everything over to the Universe. And I loved following the little pools of light from the head-torches of our team as though we were going into battle. Two of the guides and five of ours, no four really as Pete's was pretty much too dim to be counted. But he coped without a murmur, accepting that there were no new batteries and nothing he could do about it.

I slotted in behind Bora Bora, who had looked so at home in his Zulu clothes last night but now wore shorts and an old thin jumper with a purple shuka wrapped around his shoulders.

His boots had holes in them and no tread. He carried a very small rucksack with a picture of Bob Marley on the back. Certainly not enough room for more than a litre of drink at the most.

It took an hour or so traipsing across dry grass and ash trails before the nausea and light-headedness left me. For some reason the elephants at Ngorongoro came to mind and I thought of their steady plod-plod energy, which helped me settle into the rhythm of the climb. We left the grass behind at a place where there was a deep molten rock fissure and Bora Bora helped Ann and Jackie across. From now on there was only loose ash, brittle lava and hard angular lava. Shortly after there was another deeper fissure. Here the gradient changed dramatically. We had reached the mountain itself. There would be no more easy stuff. Only steepness and more steepness.

Our pace slowed. It wasn't long before we stopped altogether. Ann was in trouble.

"This is crazy. It's nearly vertical ... I feel awful," she said and promptly threw up.

I negotiated the narrow gouge of soft ash which we were following to rest by her side. Her face was ashen grey, like the volcanic world around us. I put my hand on her back and held healing thoughts.

"You're surrounded by love," I comforted. "You'll get through this, like you did practicing in Wales."

"I'll do it," she mumbled bravely. "It's just this uphill stuff."

Bora Bora took her pack and gave it to his brother Julius to carry.

"We could split the team ..."

"No, no," we all responded. We wanted to do this together. So we drank water and then after a little rest continued, slowly on into the night.

We were wading our way up through loose sand-like material which collected in small channels. It was like tackling sugar snow, stepping up and sliding back. At least it meant that we could stand upright even though the gradient was severe. The alternative was crawling up on hands and feet across the hard crumbly lava on either side which had easier footing but an increasing feeling of exposure. Often we had to go for this alternative when the channels ran out.

"Mountaineering term for this is a 'heap of slag'," said Pete, mildly amused at what we were putting ourselves through. No one else shared his good humour.

I glanced up and became aware of a change. The cloud had shifted and the sky was alive with a million sparkling stars. Orion was low on the black horizon, quite different from how we normally see him in our British latitudes. Nor do we see so many stars. But here we were in the equator lands. The latitude of the bulge of the Earth. Awestruck, I moved into the awareness of how small and insignificant the Earth is. Beyond was too great to comprehend. But I couldn't stay in the night sky. The wind battered into my eyes, reminding me that my concentration needed to be at my feet. On the next step. Place each foot carefully. Sometimes on sharp lava, sometimes loose shingle, sometimes deep ash, often a mixture. All crumbly and unstable. Sometimes upright, sometimes on all fours. Little to hang on to and dark, dark, dark.

We tried to stay close together, in particular to help the girls. But it was frustrating being behind and taking two steps up and then waiting, three steps up and then waiting. For a while I position myself behind Pete. This is the place I like to be best on a mountain. It's where I always feel safest, stepping where he steps. Now it became hazardous as his sticks kept flailing out and striking me. But his methodical ascent steadied me and I could fall into a gentle rhythm, set the focus of my body and use the time for mind work. I went through my daily meditation and repeatedly asked the mountain for our safe passage. I felt such a warm welcome as though there were presences all around looking after us.

Bora Bora stopped us to put his jumper back on, "I'm freezing cold," he said. "We go so slow. It's not good." He obviously liked to nip up and down quickly.

"One year," he continued, "before the eruptions of 2007 and 2008, I climbed up twice in one day. It was all grass and vegetation then ... a much easier climb. Now it's become hard."

That was when it dawned on me. All the information I'd read about ducking up Oldonyo Lengai prior to breakfast and it being easy-peasy had been written before the recent eruptions! Nothing had said 'really tough climb' or 'hairy', or 'might explode'. Ah, so I wouldn't be asked to book trips again ...

This was certainly an unexpectedly rough initiation test for Ann, Jackie and Nicholas. Ann seemed to have recovered a little, but Jackie was struggling. "Please can you take her pack?" I ask Bora Bora, wondering why he hadn't suggested it before. The girls were being gutsy, supporting each other and doing amazingly well, all things considered. Nicholas was going well at our snail pace, never once losing his composure or his smile.

As we set off again Pete moved to just in front of Ann to help her. His head torch was now useless, but he must have checked his watch to know of the impending dawn. Within a few minutes there was a definite line to our left where the edge of the mountain was. Behind it the eastern sky tinged pink. And as suddenly as the sun dances into being in the equator lands we could see where we were. Wow! How magnificent!

But with the light, the reality of the picture hit me. We were small and vulnerable, perched precariously half way up a huge steep mountain covered with unstable material. "Dear spirit of the mountain," I prayed, "please keep us safe," and I tried to hold myself strong. Behind us unfolded a landscape of a raw Earth dominated by volcanic footprints. No place for man.

It was easier to climb now, but Bora Bora called us to a halt again. "Let's eat and drink," he said. It was difficult to find safe sitting spots which wouldn't slide away under weight, so we all spread out to perch on the scattered solid bits. I drank water; even though I was really hungry I just couldn't face fried bread. I missed my energy bars. Maasai tradition has it that those carrying up the sheep to sacrifice shouldn't eat on the mountain, but instead rely on Ngai to fill them. Well, I would do that, too.

"We have to split," said Bora Bora. "Now it's light I need to get the two girls down and off the mountain." I was sad at this but realised that it was a good call.

"I think I'll quit whilst I'm ahead and go down too," said Nicholas.

So that was it, then. Pete and I would represent the Peace Climb team. We turned and faced upwards again, Julius leading the way. We scampered on at a good pace and it seemed in no time at all the others were tiny dots far below us clinging to existence. We moved out onto the more solid lava for faster movement and I enjoyed the scrambling flow using all of my body. It would have been like a nice rock climb, except that holds frequently coming off in our hands didn't instill much confidence and the gradient became even steeper. "Mountaineering term for this is 'dodgy'," I said to Pete. "Good decision not to bring the girls up." Then I looked down. This was a bad idea. Things looked possible going up. Things looked impossible going down. A worry worm came in and started wriggling. How were we ever going to get down this? Think of something else, I told myself. Every bit of concentration is needed to find stable foot and hand placements.

There was a distinct sulphur smell by the time we hit the snow-white lava which was a steep concrete-like ramp, known as the Pearly Gates. Why was it so white? It seemed to mimic big brother Kilimanjaro with its topping of snow. I remembered then Sakimba telling me about his childhood memory of his mother coming out of their hut on a clear day pointing to the distant Kilimanjaro and describing it as the venerable old man with his snow-white beard.

"Not far from the top now. That's 45 minutes," called Julius, looking down at us from a lava perch, but I wasn't sure if he meant 45 to a rock wall which we saw looming on the skyline high above us or 45 from the rock wall to the summit. Like many Africans we'd met he tended to say yes to everything when not quite sure what we said. Even though it was always accompanied by a big smile it didn't take away the fact that details were sometimes hard to ascertain.

In the event it was double the time. The sun was rising higher. Stopping precariously, we stashed our windproof jackets in our rucksacks which gave us weight to carry but a better sense of freedom. Feeling exposed except when there were narrow gullies of ash to retreat into, we crawled our way up the steep ramp, carefully keeping balance on the loose gravel which worked like marbles to unbalance us. However would they carry up a live sacrificial sheep on this, I wondered. Maybe knowing Ngai was going to speak to them makes all things possible.

It was with great relief that we reached the rock wall. I breathed deeply. For a short while I felt protected and safe. There was a run-out of only two metres behind us instead of nigh on two thousand. But we couldn't hug the wall for long and headed out again with a sickening sense of exposure. This was the steepest part of the climb. We crept on and up past small vents of sulphur smoke coming out of bottomless holes which filled our nostrils with the smell of rotten eggs, but I didn't dare lift my eyes. Hold the focus. Hold the focus.

We were almost at the top when I started shaking. I'm not sure what started it off other than the feeling of vulnerability, but I was definitely wobbly as we finally clambered out onto a narrow ridge and stood upright. We made it! Yeah! Empty space above us. Here we were – touching the sky. Just for one fleeting moment I understood that mountain, sky and the Divine are one and the same thing. And then it was gone. I was left feeling lost. Great Ngai, if this is your abode then I'm quaking in your presence. At the sight before me now I felt only smallness, helplessness and trepidation.

I had read that it was possible to walk in the crater of this volcano, unique with its peculiar chemical composition, and see weird lumps born in the boiling caldron and rapidly cooled. But since the eruptions, vast amount of material had been blown away. Now beyond a narrow skirt there was just a straight drop 150 metres to the crater floor . You'd need to be a base jumper with a death wish. Looking down into the shadow of the bowels of the Earth, I gulped. I could see a grey solidified and cracked lava lake, with round plop holes and lava blobs and what appeared to be only a couple of small steaming vents. But up here on the rim any gases were dissipated on the wind. Happily, Ngai provided only a light breeze for us. This was no place to be in the sort of strong wind that we'd had eight hours ago when we had set off, which already seemed like a lifetime ago. Though it was now only 9am.

"The highest point is over there," said Julius pointing to the far side, maybe 300 metres away. "C'mon."

Oh no! We had to go further.

I took a deep breath and followed on behind Pete, trying all I could to be steady. My mouth felt dry. My head in a dizzying haze. There was a tiny path, just wide enough for feet along the crater rim. On our right side was the steep slope down to the Rift Valley floor. On the left the crater throat. Everything was loose and unstable. I could see where a large chunk of the rim we were standing on had fallen inwards. Yes, unstable.

C'mon girl, I told myself. At ground level this would be no problem, but with sheer drops on either side things were different. I tried to push out my awareness. Please protect us, mountain God Ngai, I prayed. Then I remembered that we were doing this for Ann, Jackie and Nicholas, and we were also doing this for Sakimba. I had been entrusted as a carrier of the Maasai spirit, because at some level it was him that was the sacrifice. I could not let him down.

Julius and Pete nonchalantly marched along; I gingerly followed. There was a sense of tiptoeing along a cloud.

The circle of the crater rim brought us around to a wide bridge connecting with the extra lip to the south. Thankfully this meant a considerably lesser drop to the outside, though to the inside the angle had become vertical. Julius headed for a spot which looked little different from any other. "Everyone uses this as the summit," he beamed. We hugged.

It was good to take off rucksacks and drink water and find some of Sakimba's biscuits to eat. We'd forgotten we had them. Ah, Ngai had been doing his job. I had no idea how I'd survived so long without food and now he had provided for us!

"To Kilimanjaro and beyond!" we shouted. This had been our training battle cry for weeks. We had hoped to see the great mountain from here, but though we were in sunlight there was now heavy cloud to the east and a general haze. This meant no view of Kilimanjaro nor of Meru, our second mountain.

But there was also sacred work to do. These were our offerings for Ngai. I opened the summit-bag and laid out the United Nations world flag. Pete fixed it down with pieces of ash. I placed a little candle which had been lit from the World Peace Flame. Then put six quartz Peace crystals blessed for our work with the six-pointed star, each crystal representing one of our zones of the Earth. How exciting it was to be in the sixth and final zone.

Pete rolled out the new Tibetan prayer flags which had been given to us on our expedition to the South Pole on condition we fly them somewhere special. Well, here we were. Couldn't get much more special than this. And we both wore our Tibetan caps. Bringing out the wood-smoked container we read Sakimba's Peace words for Ngai. They were simple: "Peace and Love." Ngai would know of their value, even if humanity did not. In honour of the sacred Maasai mountain we chanted the word 'Sakimba' six times and followed this with 'Om' twenty times in reverence to all that is. Finally we asked Julius to read the Peace Message that Sakimba had written way down at the Acacia camp, oh so long ago: "Kijeu naleng Sakimba."

Beautiful! Sacred jobs completed. Ah, except for one.

I had to put on the Maasai warrior cloak. It became all muddled. Julius helped me straighten it and lent me his stick. I stood holding it, feeling slightly silly but deeply honoured.

"Great Ngai, we ask for blessings on our Peace Climb."

Glancing behind me to check that I wasn't too close to the edge, I clasped my bone talisman, shut my eyes and allowed my awareness to open in meditation.

An energy surges through me. Again and again I hear, "We are one spirit," until it resonates through my very being. I am Maasai. I feel the power of connection to the Earth. I feel harmony and balance and am part of that spirit.

There is the sound of the vibrating of a drum. Though I don't know if it's blood throbbing through my temples, or periodic gas release of the volcano, or the rumbling of a passing sky storm, or Ngai himself. It makes no difference. All is one and the same.

Quite disorientated and no less shaky than when we had arrived I packed everything away into my rucksack. I was happy that, here in this most sacred Maasai place of worship, we had honoured Ngai and would be forever grateful for the privilege.

"We'd better go back now," said Julius starting to retrace our steps. "Polé, polé!" This is the Swahili phrase widely used over East Africa which means 'slowly, slowly'. Never had it sounded more apt. Sure, I would take it gently. I just wished my body would stop trembling.

We reached a place on the perimeter where there was a sulphur smoke vent that I hadn't noticed on the way over. Here, amazingly, I felt the presence of my mother. Of all the places to choose! As clearly as if she had been standing there, like someone had changed the channel on TV, I heard in my mind, "You can keep your mountains. Let's go back to the game parks." Mum, I thought, I could do without that sort of advice just now. But the smile it brought helped steady my nerves along the sky path, holding the focus until I caught up with Pete, who had stopped at the point where we had to come off the ridge.

"One slip here and we're a goner," he stated. "There's a heck of a run-out, with nothing to stop us." The comment wasn't particularly meant for me. It was just his standard assessment of a situation before he got down and dealt with it.

"It's really scary," I said, longing for a hug or to sit and chat, anything that meant we didn't have to do it.

I looked down and the lava ramp from this angle seemed to be made of glass.

I froze.

Space was drifting. The aliveness of the recent volcanic eruption held me in its grip; it held a power that I didn't want to face. I held out my dust-covered hand and tried to see it steady. But beneath it the rock seemed to be moving in waves.

Breathe deeply, I told myself. All is well. But my mind – which usually responds to this command – had other ideas. If I slipped and fell, nothing would stop a headlong descent into oblivion. But then the work that we had to do would be lost. The all-important last piece of the jigsaw. We had to find a way to complete it. Our destiny.

It's only fear, I heard myself say. Only fear ...

Involuntarily my hand moved to the hard bone of my necklace and stroked it. I heard the voice: *"We are one spirit, you and I."*

And then I saw the vision. *It's the warrior cloak. Bright red. As red as the sky that we had seen. It gently touches me on the shoulders and enfolds me.*

That was when the strength came.

And I knew ...

I knew I had inner warrior strength. The vision of the warrior cloak wrapped around me was a cloak of courage. All the strength I needed was within me. This was my lesson. I exhaled the tension. My shoulders went down and back. I felt my heart open. This was my gift from the mountain.

And Sakimba's journey, in tune with this land, this Earth, had been to make sure that our hearts were open. With an open heart was the way to visit Ngai. This was the preparation needed for the work ahead, the next mountain, and the next. Thank you, Sakimba for your sacrifice, given lovingly. It helped open my heart to Ngai and find my inner warrior energy.

All this happened in a flash.

"Polé, polé," Julius said again. We crawled on our bottoms off the crater rim, ignoring holes in trousers, hands flat, spreading the force. Slowly, slowly. Safely, safely.

"Never done this before," said Pete, excited at discovering a new technique after a lifetime of mountaineering.

From time to time we were able to stand upright, but mostly we did the bottom shuffle diagonally across to where there were good footholds by the wall and then out onto the face again, until the sulphur smells were left behind and we hit the volcanic ash rivulets. At first we took these carefully, but as the hours went by I found that I was getting the hang of it and speeding up. At times it was like surfing on rivers of ash. As I wiped dust out of my eyes, I thought how brilliant that I'd had my eyes lasered and didn't have to wear contact lenses any more, which would've been impossible in these conditions. In the end we were almost running down the steep slope, spitting dust and yelping in fun, yeah!

Down, down and past steep precipices looking straight into cavernous ravines which we had climbed close by in the dark. I felt glad not to have known their whereabouts then, and able to trust the route of our guides.

The distant dot of the waiting vehicle seemed to take forever to grow, but eventually we reached the end of the steep terrain and then off the grey into the delicious tawny colour of dried grass. A large bird soared overhead as we reached the vehicle. My pensioner knees felt like concrete and the rest of my legs jelly that would never walk again. There were dust-ridden hugs from Ann, Nicholas and Jackie.

We couldn't thank Julius enough for guiding us. He'd been a lovely relaxed presence. And we all thanked Bora Bora. In spite of our misgivings he had looked after everyone, guided us safely and made the important decision that enabled everyone to happily survive the experience.

At the campsite, Sakimba was asleep under a tree. Ann, Jackie and I decided that we should give him the quartz Peace crystals for safekeeping. It was the highest honour we could think of. We woke him up and presented them to him. He accepted them in a daze, and fell back to sleep. I was sure he'd have no recollection of it when he finally woke up properly. It was a dreamtime gift. I laid his warrior cloak beside him. I had no more need of it. I knew that whenever I was facing fear in my mind I just had to imagine the warrior cloak around me and there it was. Bingo. Courage! For me it was a key to the door that had been stopping me access the inner strength that was there all the time.

A young man was selling Oldonyo Lengai T-shirts. I bought one, the colour of sand. In Africa, it almost seemed wrong to wear un-earthy tones.

"Did you get to the top?" he asked.

I nodded.

"Wow," he replied, "you are very strong Mama ... and Bwana, too?"

I nodded again. I could see respect in his eyes, which touched me.

Marco was urging us into the car, when suddenly I was grabbed by the arm. It was Sakimba. "Come, come," he said and took me to the gate of the compound where a group of Maasai women had their shop.

"I have no money," I said shaking my head.

"No, these are gifts for you. Hold out your arm," he said clipping a beautiful white beaded bracelet onto my wrist. "The colour white represents Peace."

Then he placed a multi-coloured star around my neck and gave me an exquisitely beaded knobbed stick. "You know what this is. It's a warrior stick. You are a warrior."

If Marco hadn't been calling us to get going I might have been too embarrassed to accept it. Later I understood that it was from Ngai, the great sky, honouring all Peace warriors.

The large bird was still circling overhead as we drove away. We speeded along the fourth side of the mountain so we'd been all the way round, done the kora as it's known in Tibet, where it's the correct way to honour the sacred. I turned and gazed with a mixture of relief and incredibility. "Farewell great sacred Maasai mountain and thank you," I whispered silently. Then between the bumps of the track I placed my hand on Pete's.

"One down. Two to go," he said. That's the way he is.

My goodness, if our first little acclimatisation climb has been this tough, however are we going to go on Mount Meru? Even the guidebooks say it's no picnic. And that will be with most of our team of inexperienced climbers. That's even before we look at the big one. And for Kilimanjaro we'll be pulling the Peace-tyre. Oh help!

Pete saw my expression. "Don't worry," he said. "We'll just get on and do it. It'll be a piece of cake."

I knew he'd say that. I used to be normal before I met Pete ...

Back in Time

I'm sure I was normal for anyone brought up in the south of England after the Second World War. As a child I used to daydream about being an adventurer, a way to rebel against the safeness around me that my parents' generation had fought so hard to achieve. This continued into my university days in the 1960s, times of idealism and blowing in the wind. I was studying ecological science which stirred in me a fascination with whether things were separate or interconnected. Never mind realism. Were we made of star-dust?

After a down-to-earth period in Australia growing trees I found myself back in England with three young sons to bring up by myself. They meant everything to me. Motherhood gave complete purpose of being. I suppose it's an unconditional love thing.

When my children spent time with their father I missed them so badly I started rock climbing to occupy myself. I became involved in protest climbs, which gave me a realisation: Yes, motherhood was all-consuming , but I also needed to help the Earth. I liked the idea of climbing to make statements, to make a difference. It's a medium where a small number of people can wave a banner about and people take notice. Like hanging for eleven days on the face of Sugarloaf Mountain in Rio during the first Earth Summit when the police were shooting street children. Our presence helped make this known and it became an international issue.

By the time my sons were teenagers I was speculating on ways to change the world. I wanted to involve thousands of individuals. I imagined reaching out and raising masses of money for charity. I yearned to help wherever there was a need.

That's when I met Pete. I was an idealist, a dreamer. He was a pragmatist, feet-on-the-ground logical thinker. Whilst most people were busy talking about things he was off actually doing them. Making them happen. There was an unassailable attraction.

Like I said, I was fairly normal before I met Pete. From then on he would make my dreams a reality. Before, I had been riding the wave of life. Now we would be out there actually giving it direction.

I'd always had a hunger to help occupied Tibet, so we gave birth to our charity organisation, Climb For Tibet. The Dalai Lama became our chief patron. He's my inspiration. He says that we are each first and foremost part of the human family, so must love and respect our brothers and sisters, leaving no one out, not even the oppressor.

He advised that one of the best ways to help hold the structure of Tibet together was to build schools actually located in Tibet. That this would help prevent the tide of youngsters being sent by parents secretly out over the Himalayas in search of education and freedom, many dying along the way.

So this is what we did. We raised funds for the building of six schools for little nomad and farming children who, without western help, would have had no chance of being taught to read and write. It was important to have that practical purpose behind us.

We raised these funds by being sponsored on various Peace Climbs for which thousands of individuals sent us Peace Messages and we undertook to speak them out. All sorts of

Messages came in including prayers, wishes and pledges for Peace or the environment, the important criteria being that they were expressed lovingly from the individual.

We were inspired by traditional Tibetan ways. Peace Messages have long been written on prayer flags and flown from the highest and furthest places possible. This is believed to be a way of sending out Peace and harmony to all beings. It seemed to me that taking up this method was a way of making a difference, not only at an individual level with the conceiving and writing of the Peace Message, but also at a wider level, by bringing together and expressing the Messages which would create something greater than the sum of the parts.

Anyway, I liked the idea of collecting the highest aspirations of people's hearts and expressing them from the highest places we could find. Somehow it just felt the right thing to do.

Our first Peace Climb, the subject of my book *Cry from the Highest Mountain*, was in 1998 to the 'Point furthest from the centre of the Earth'. This is a mountain in Ecuador named Chimborazo, which although only 6,310 metres above sea level is actually 2,150 metres further from the centre of the Earth than Everest is. "Whatever are you on about?" was the usual reaction to this information. "Ah," was my response, "Well, you see it's all to do with the shape of the Earth, which bulges at the equator. But this has to be the highest mountain as it's the bit of our Earth which sticks out most into space." Many people shook their head and signed the sponsor form just to get rid of me.

Also in the Andes was our Peace Climb to the 'Place nearest the sun at the turn of the Millennium'. Another interesting Earth point that took a bit of explaining. The place on our Earth nearest the sun varies on a day-to-day basis between the tropics, due to the tilt in our orbit. Over the 24 hours of the Millennium change the point nearest the sun was on a latitude of 20°30´South. Following this round we found the highest point to be right on the Chile-Bolivian border, a mountain named Aucanquilcha at 6,176 metres. Thousands of square miles from anywhere. It was the point nearest the sun for the duration of 17 seconds. We had actually been invited to Millennium parties a bit nearer to home, but hey, where else could you feel quite so high? And anyway, sponsors felt like they were getting their money's worth.

By now it was accepted practice in Britain that people would raise money for charities by asking folk for sponsorship and putting in considerable effort in one way or another. It felt to me a nice way to do a little bit to balance out the inequalities of the world's resources.

Whenever anyone gave us money, mostly friends as it turned out, we'd always put one hundred per cent towards the charity funds, so of course we had to pay for the journeys themselves. In one way or another each one made us broke. The next one was no exception.

It was time to head for the Himalayas and go into Tibet to visit our schools. We took Peace Messages to Mount Kailas, the most sacred in all of Asia; to Mount Shishapangma, the highest in Tibet; and to mighty Mount Everest, the highest mountain above sea level.

We weren't sure if we were going to be allowed into Tibet as we had been blacklisted by the Chinese as pro-Tibet activists. From our point of view all we wanted was, following the lead of the Dalai Lama, to help find a way forward for everyone to live in Peace without oppression. We were delighted when we were allowed to cross over the white line painted in the middle of the Friendship Bridge over the gorge leading from Nepal into Tibet. After all, we were bringing in useful western money. Now we could experience first-hand the heart-rendering sadness and the time-honoured beauty. It felt good to quietly speak out our Peace Messages on the three parts of our journey, as though we were bringing Peace-energy like water to a parched desert. Though it wasn't so quiet on Everest just below Camp 3 when we shouted at the tops of our voices:

"Long live the Dalai Lama."

The extreme risk was not so much for our own safety but for any possible reprisals on our Tibetan team and for whom any connection with the Dalai Lama can bring at best a gaol sentence and at worst torture and death. We considered that it was worth the risk to imbue the land with that Message which so many Tibetans yearned to shout but were unable to do. We were doing it for them.

We returned from Tibet with added determination to make known the dreadful oppression, to continue raising funds for Tibetan schooling and to do the work with the Peace Messages expressed in the Tibetan way in order to help the whole world.

So where else could we go? The answer came as I was reading Geographical Magazine. An article stated: "Everest is not the tallest mountain on Earth. That honour goes to a mountain in the middle of the Pacific Ocean, Mauna Kea. It's a volcano that starts 5,000 metres below the ocean and rises 4,205 above which makes it 357 metres taller than Everest." Ah just what we needed! So we headed off to Hawai'i. It sounded a restful holiday sort of a place. It would have been if we hadn't decided to run the 55 kilometres from the ocean to the summit.

By now our loyal sponsors were becoming quite broke too, or at least over-approached. "For goodness sakes, how many more times can Climb For Tibet find a highest place?" But we soldiered on. What about the tallest building in the world? We headed to Toronto in Canada to the CN Tower at 553 metres (now superseded in height by taller buildings). We clambered up the 2,579 steps to the top and just managed to speak out our Peace Messages before an irate warden decided it was time to throw out disruptive activists.

Being in Canada prompted us to realise the inevitable. Of course: we needed to send Peace Messages off from the Top of the World. Why hadn't we thought of that before? All my life I'd longed to experience the frozen North. So how were we going to do that? Might be a bit chilly. Might need a lot of dragging the body into better fitness. I have always believed that when there is a need, the Universe will provide an answer so long as you are open and look for it.

The answer was the Magnetic North Pole, not quite how we'd expected it, but we managed our Peace ceremony there. We were honoured to speak our Peace Messages with a group of Inuit children at Resolute on the Northwest Passage. During all the collecting of our Peace Messages over the years I think none have quite touched my heart as much as the ones that these children wrote. Though they could barely read, they wrote the most profound thoughts about all the world working together as a team, and all nations being one people.

I was humbled and returned from the Arctic determined to keep the work going.

I bet that anyone who endures the North Pole is going to think, "Well, I wonder what it's like at the South." Were we predictable? For sure!

Particularly as there was a very important reason. I discovered that our Peace Climbs in the Himalayas and the Andes were opposite and balanced on the globe. Hmm ... If we carried out one opposite and balanced to the Pacific and one opposite and balanced to the North Pole, then we would have drawn on the Earth a symbolic figure of a six-pointed star. Now that would be harmony, indeed.

The only problem with this exhilarating plan was that it meant that somehow we would have to reach the South Pole. Pete and I were now becoming pretty ancient, so we would have to get on with it. It's all very well saying we're going to take Peace Messages to the South Pole, but however do you get there? The answer was to join the South Pole Race. It was the first race to the South Pole since Scott and Amundsen almost a hundred years ago and billed as the toughest race on Earth. Perfectly fitting then for a couple of pensioners. So we signed up. It's important on these occasions not to think about things too much or you'll never do anything!

Now we were talking serious money. When we couldn't find corporate sponsorship we just had to go into loans and mortgages. Well, even if you're in debt for the rest of your life you have to do these things, don't you? I mean, how often do you get a chance to walk to the South Pole?

So after coming through this, there we were. We had 'fired-up' the fifth zone of our six-pointed star of peace. It was exciting. There was only one piece of the jigsaw left. Africa.

I felt as though I was doing exactly the work I needed to be doing. It was my passion. I was touching the stars.

But then life sent a harsh reminder that stars can sometimes implode ...

August, 2009.

The diagnosis came a few weeks after we returned from the South Pole.

"I have an aggressive prostate cancer," Pete informed me. "Early stage, but it's spreading."

The news numbed me. A trembling fear tried to creep in.

Cancer.

What now?

All my life I've had a tendency to ignore things I haven't liked, hoping they'll go away. This one was going to be hard. I decided I would just be there for him with optimistic encouragement. And most of all, always be in that place of knowing that all is well for him.

Pete's world collapsed. This was the sort of thing that happens to other people, not to him. It was as though suddenly everything had been taken away. All his normal means of defence against life's problems were gone. He had faced risk and death all his life as a climber, but there had always been his own experience to fall back on. Now he was stripped bare. What was the way forward?

He updated his will and put his affairs in order, whilst watching a neighbour – also struck with prostate cancer – go rapidly downhill, having done little about it. The neighbour died within a year.

Pete, true to form, took action. Having researched his options, he decided he would work his way out of it by fitness, diet and attitude. He set to with vigour.

Being forced to look at his life brought him very much into the present. Now he appreciated every little thing, from a bird tweeting to a hug, from a talk with one of his kids to sitting in the sunshine. Every moment was precious. And he became even more giving. If there was the remotest chance of someone needing help he was there. Fixing things, being a listener, lifts in the car ...

Health shocks can be gifts in disguise. In our advanced society we need reminders to see the beauty all around us, to enjoy nature and simply to just be. His attitude was an inspiration.

Then one day he suddenly said, "I'm going to go for surgery, in spite of the risks. I just want to be free of the cancer as soon as possible."

It was a brave decision.

I couldn't help worrying if he would live to regret it.

All thoughts of our next project had evaporated now. Gone was the plan for the final part of our mission, the sixth point of our star. I spent the time doing talks and author signings of my new book, *Cold Hands Warm Heart*, which tells the story of Pete and me going to the South Pole. People would invariably ask, "What are you doing next?" and I would think to myself with a heavy sigh, well, that all depends on Pete.

After the surgery came the pain, the anxiety, the weakness, the discomfort and coping with a body trying to adapt to a new road map. To cap it all he had to sit still for a while, though the doctor's definition of 'sitting' may have been different from his. "C'mon," he said. "This recovery process is not going to stop me doing things. I'm going to grab life and do as much as I can. Let's go skiing."

My knight in shining armour was back!

Around this time I was witness to more courage in overcoming adversity.

Our friend Gautam, who started life with polio in one of Mother Teresa's orphanages in Calcutta and needs crutches to be his legs, undertook a stunt to raise funds for his charity 'Freedom in the Air' which allows disabled people to learn how to pilot planes. "Just because you can't walk, doesn't stop you flying and being free," he said, agreeing to take my mascot penguin Gaius with him. Gaius is a smart black-and-white Emperor penguin with many attributes and achievements, including helping me pull my sledge to the South Pole, but flying had not been one of them. There was a possibility for a penguin first here!

"Stiff upper beak, Gaius. You can do it!"

They were both strapped to the top of a plane and flew off high into the sky, Gaius' flippers streaming behind. And so it was that a record-breaking penguin wing-walk took place.

It all goes to show ... you think you can't do something, because everyone always says you can't. "You can't fly. Penguins can't fly. "But what about listening to your own inner truth? With enough guts, you can find your way around difficulties. Courage will rise to the need.

Bravo Gaius ... and Gautam too!

Witnessing a demonstration of courage always made me think of the Tibetan people, and others living under oppressive regimes. Having to live with all that they value – their very life-blood – taken away: religion, land, culture, means of livelihood, beloved leader and any chance of educating their children. They are left with no dignity. And to live in fear of being beaten up, put in gaol and tortured. Still. Still it goes on after half a century.

Whilst in Tibet we ourselves witnessed Chinese military police use their tools of torture – electric batons. I can still hear them laugh. The stories of brutality against Tibetans touch me so deeply I am often reduced to tears.

One of the schools we had funded in Tibet was in a major earthquake area where an entire city of a hundred thousand people was wiped out. At least two thousand Tibetans died. The British Tibetan charities were able to help the immediate needs of survival and to assist the difficult process of rebuilding in a manner that would benefit the Tibetans and their culture. Schools were high on the list. We were able to donate some funds but so much more was needed.

So, we were eager to raise money for Tibet, to reach out to people and again be part of the great tide of charity-giving, encouraging heart-opening generosity and helping to rebalance the world.

Pete also wanted to collect for the Prostate Cancer Research Centre as a thank you for his life-saving surgery and to help other men come through the same problem in the future.

The time had arrived to gather thoughts for our climb and start bringing in sponsorship.

We needed to send off Peace Messages from the final zone of our star, from a mountain in Africa.

It didn't take long to pinpoint the mountain. Whilst Mount Kenya was a contender because it was enticing as a challenging climb with few people on it, its altitude was only 5,199 metres. No, it had to be Mount Kilimanjaro at 5,896 metres. We always promised that we would carry people's highest aspirations and so it had to be to the highest place possible. Not only is Kilimanjaro the highest mountain on the African continent, but it has the greatest distance from base to summit of any mountain on Earth, a measurement of 4,600 metres (Everest only has a measly 3,840 metres). Most of the world's high mountains are in ranges and their bases are at a high level. As such, Kilimanjaro is ranked as the world's highest free-standing mountain.

Sounded like our sort of ascent.

The first question was when to do the Kilimanjaro climb.

I went to take advice from Master Advarr, an ascended spirit master, channelled by our friend Ivy Smith through whom he spoke. It sounds curious to those who aren't used to this, but together they do much important work for the healing of the planet. We had been guided in this way for many years on the work of creating the six-pointed star.

"It needs to be before 2012," I told Pete, "so that the final zone is fired up and there can be a pulling together of all the six zones into the star of light. This will help the bringing in of light to the planet at this crucial time of change."

Pete nodded with his 'I'm-not-really-interested-in-angels-and-all-that-stuff' face. He knew better than to question my somewhat unusual source of information but now after many years accepted it as though it was no stranger than finding information on the internet. And he knew that when I spoke of light in this way I meant the kind of high frequency love which I used often as a way of sending love, healing and positive vibes to people by putting a thought bubble of light around them.

Seeing the practicalities of the climb he said, "Well, we must do it during the dry trekking months. We don't want to hit the rainy seasons and have to wade through deep snow on the mountain."

"Simon, the astrologer at the White Eagle Lodge, says that July 6th would be an auspiciously harmonic time. It'd be nice to do this Peace Climb on the Dalai Lama's birthday, like we've done before."

"Wrong season to climb."

"How about the 11th of the 11th of 2011? That would be fun and a powerful time."

"Wrong season."

"Well, it has to *feel* like the right date ..."

It wasn't until later that it came to me. Of course: we had to do it on the 21st of September – United Nations International Day of Peace. A cease-fire on fighting all around the globe. The people of the world focusing on Peace. We fitted right in. Kilimanjaro was one of the few high mountains that was possible for people with no mountaineering experience to climb. It was open to all, always crowded. It was the people's mountain. Perfect. I let the idea settle overnight and woke up with that high-energized feeling inside that always says to me 'yes, this is the path to follow'.

So 21st September, 2011 was the date.

But still something simmered that I knew I had to look at. All our previous Peace Climbs had been in wild, far-off places that had involved heavy training and planning, and effort on our part. It had been very much us carrying the Peace Messages, putting in the supreme effort required. Somehow they had been our journeys. There was something very different about this Peace Climb. Okay it was the completion one, the one that would pull all the others together to make one whole greater than the sum of the parts. But this was the people's mountain. Maybe what was trying to get through to me was that we had to be more open to include everyone. As the Dalai Lama said (and come to think of it Michael Jackson, too) we have to include each and everyone to make the world a better place. For it to work, no one can be left out. We are the family of man.

So how to do this? How to include everyone across the globe? It wouldn't be possible to collect a Peace Message from every person, but ... aha ... what would be feasible would be to collect and carry with us a Peace Message from every *nation* on Earth.

If I had known then how hard it was going to be, I may not have felt quite so exhilarated.

Preparing for Peace

The year 2011 dawned. As with every passing of a year it was a time to reflect, to take stock of life. Perhaps, I thought, as time is apparently increasing its frequency I need to take stock more often, every month or every day, to recognise the purpose of my life. To find what it is that is important to this one little me in particular. To do what is worthwhile.

My New Year resolution was clear. It was to obtain a Peace Message from every nation on Earth. I had no idea how I was going to do it. But I knew that the important first step was the stating of the fact that it will happen.

I shared my resolution with my mother as we lit a candle at midnight. It was precious time with her. She had reached the stage in life that she always called 'in my bath chair'. Her body had mostly given up, though her mind was still as sharp as ever. She knew that after a long good life her time to move on was approaching. My brother and sisters and I were delighted that she was still able to be in her own home; this was so important to her.

Eleven days later she died.

It was an experience that I shall always cherish.

I held her in my arms, enfolding her like a baby. I stroked her forehead repeating over and over "Love you. Love you ..." I held her in strong light, knowing this gave the strength she needed. I called for help and immediately there was a circle of angelic beings carrying her essence upwards with ease. I was aware of her being met by my father and other family members and a host of joyful beings. There was a wonderful sense of welcome and a feeling of the change from density into lightness.

It was her time to go. I was so privileged to be able to be there for her.

Being present at my mother's passing helped me cope with the loss, even though there was a gaping hole at both a physical and mental level. I would often think, "Ah, must tell Mum that," or "Mum, can't wait to show you that photo". But the gap was to some extent filled by a new immediate closeness. I had been reminded that she was now just a thought away. Yes, I did believe that and it gave me strength. Also, there were other things to help fill my mind. It was less than six months before we had to leave for Africa.

"There's a lot to organise for the climb," I said to Pete when he declared that he had to go ski-mountaineering in Canada.

"You sort it out."

Okay. I would. And if it turned out slightly hippy without his usual efficient organisation and common sense, then so be it.

But first I needed to pull myself together. My body was feeling sad and soggy. I decided to do a detox at all levels. You know the sort of thing. Cut out junk food, sugar, wheat and cheese, eat lots of fruit and vegetables, vacuum the house (now this was getting serious!), be mindful of holding beautiful thoughts and most importantly, exercise. Running made my knees sore, but overall I felt better.

I knew that I had to hold what we were going to do not only in clarity but also in the right intention. Then it would all flow well. I lit candles in my sitting room, breathed deeply to relax, found a stillness within and opened my awareness to Africa. To Mount Kilimanjaro.

"Great mountain spirit, I humbly ask permission that we may come to your land, climb your slopes and bring Peace Messages and sacred gifts to your summit. We come in the spirit of healing and Peace for our Earth."

I sense a gathering of energies around the mountain itself, and a presence that fills this room, safe, steady and strong.

I feel the word, "Welcome". I know it is so.

I hear, "Remember to come in unconditional love".

As I opened my eyes I caught myself thinking – oh no, not more unconditional love stuff. I seem to have been working on that for years. I suppose it never really stops. I sighed, but felt ready to start work on the preparations for the climb.

First, I narrowed down the search for a trekking agent. It's Tanzanian law that tourist can't climb Kilimanjaro without a locally based agent who uses local guides and porters. So even though we would have preferred to just go and climb we had no choice but to book through an agent. However, it was a great way for one of the world's poorest countries to bring in foreign exchange and employment for its people. So I was delighted when I found the friendly and easily contactable UK based Henry Stedman of 'Climb Mount Kilimanjaro', working together with the Tanzanian-based 'Team Kilimanjaro', who said that one of his priorities was to make sure the local porters were paid well. To top it off, Henry had written the Trailblazer guidebook so there was a good chance he knew a thing or two. Yup, he would take on organising our Kilimanjaro Peace Climb to include Oldonyo Lengai, then Mount Meru and finally Mount Kilimanjaro itself.

He recommended that we get on and book our flights. I had previously suggested to Pete that it would be more environmentally friendly to go by boat, train or even walk. I was told in no uncertain terms to be sensible. So did I feel that our work to help the Earth outweighed any detrimental environmental effects our plane might have? Yes, hugely. There were three airlines that went to Tanzania. The most dodgy-sounding one was Air Ethiopia. It meant changing at Addis Ababa. With a magic, swashbuckling name like that, obviously we had to go for it. Where was Addis Ababa anyway?

It was unclear how many people would join us, so I tried to reel in those interested, of which there were many. It was good that this was a climb that anyone with reasonable fitness could do. Coping with the altitude would be the main drawback. But there was also the problem of finance. Our full programme looked like having no change out of £3,000. Even though friends were keen to be part of carrying the Peace Messages, most reluctantly fell by the wayside.

Rima, we knew, was up for it. She was our special friend who'd often supported us in ways that made a difference. She had helped us train for the South Pole race a couple of years ago. We had wanted her to join us for that but she hadn't been able to raise the cash. However, she'd promised that she would come up Kilimanjaro with us.

Then there was my cousin Nicholas. There was something about the tackling of a tough adventure in the form of a vision quest to help the Earth that struck a chord with him.

And then there was Ann who worked for Ivy and Master Advarr. She had watched for years as they had advised and inspired us. She'd also been part of their collecting and programming of special crystals which we had carried with the Peace Messages to the ends of the Earth, and longed to be a part of it. "Can I bring my cousin Jackie, too?" she had asked. "She's an accountant. Might be useful!"

So it looked like we'd be a team of six. I had a feeling that we'd be six as when I visualised us on the summit, I saw six people. But then it was understandable, I suppose, due to the importance of the number. This was our sixth zone of the Earth. It was the sixth and final point of our star of peace. It was the sacred number for us, so of course we would be six.

"It's all happening," I told Pete when he phoned. "The most important thing now is to gather Peace Messages, particularly the Nation Messages."

For the first time I felt really excited about the climb.

"There's also the kit to think about," he said in his down-to-earth way, "and the crucial matter of fitness for everybody."

"Fitness ... yes of course. Well, I am going to meet up with Rima for a tyre-pull."

"Why can't you just meet up for coffee or lunch like normal people?"

"'Cos it's sort of training. You see, there's something I need to tell you about. We have a wonderful idea ..."

There was an ominous silence. I could imagine his expression of what's-she-trying-to-do-now.

I continued, "We're going to pull a tyre to the top of Kilimanjaro. Don't you think it's great? Just think, we can put all the Messages in it. A fantastic focus for Peace! We can drag it between us and the sign can be 'Pulling Together for Peace' ... How symbolic is that! Anyway it's so boring just to walk up."

There was a groan on the other end of the line followed by grumbling mumblings, "I'm not doing that! You won't be able to get a tyre on the plane. You'll never be allowed to drag it up the mountain ..."

Where was my go-for-it man? It was a perfectly abnormal sort of suggestion. I wasn't talking about a huge tractor tyre, which come to think of it would look macho and amazing, no, just a normal sort of car tyre, friendly and round.

I emailed Rima. I knew she wouldn't be put off. It appealed to our sense of fun. Even though she was of Chinese descent from Singapore, we were on the same wavelength. Soul sisters.

"Pete's going to take some persuading about the tyre," I wrote. "Don't worry, he'll come round ..."

It was actually a job to catch him. In true knight style he propelled himself from one adventure to another, determined that no cancer operation was ever going to slow him down. "I'm just so grateful that I had a check-up and caught the cancer in the early stages. I'm alive!"

No one would ever guess the crisis he had been through.

The summits of North Wales were next. Pete wanted to make sure that the novices of the team gleaned some mountain experience. Ann and Jackie couldn't make it. Well, we would initiate urban-man Nicholas. He'd never been on a mountain before, nor had he camped. Age 67 seemed a good time to start.

In brilliant Easter sunshine we took him up near-vertical Pen yr Ole Wen, the steepest slope we could find, followed by one of the toughest routes up Snowdon. We were impressed that he plodded through it all without a murmur of discontent, though he had considerable problems with his blow-up bed. I thought I'd keep quiet about my excruciating knee pain going downhill, with the worry worm shouting at me, "if you can't manage this how're you ever going to cope in Africa?"

We did learn something new while there. We visited our lovely friend Sheila who works with the World Peace Flame and was organising the African representative Paul to lend us his lantern to carry the flame on Kilimanjaro. Her husband Sam, ex-chief ranger of Snowdonia National Park, told us, "If you're going up to 6,000 metres you really need to use the Welsh method of altitude training. It's tried and tested. The trick is to be drunk as often as possible so that the hangover state of nausea and head-banging exhaustion simulates altitude sickness. It's great practice for the body being deprived of oxygen." They breed 'em tough in Wales.

Pete, though, decided that for real toughness Scotland was the place. Following Wales and after a couple of measly short rock climbing days he saw that he'd been at home too long (well, it was almost a week) and undertook a challenge to walk from the west to the east coast of Scotland, marching happily through freezing temperatures, gales and continual downpours.

I thought I'd better show willing and do a little bit of fitness too so went out on a tyre-pull around the common by my house. I built up the weight a bit by sitting granddaughter Elsie in the tyre. She thought it a lovely way to travel! At last the muscles seemed to be building up around my knees which helped them but I was suffering painful night cramps in my calf muscles. I spoke about it to Andy who runs the excellent circuit training sessions in my local town, Haslemere. Andy said, "Muscle cramps are all to do with hydration." He was right. Drinking more water in the evenings sorted that problem. Of course it created a new one, that of having to get up in the middle of the night anyway. Ah the trials of a granny body ...

At circuit training I often chatted with my pal, Maureen. "I have a friend who's wanted to climb Kilimanjaro all her life," she said. And so I met Mary, an attractive South African. I liked her immediately. Even though busy running (or possibly being run by) three teenage daughters she was sensitive to the Earth at a greater level and particularly driven to make a difference to help Africa. She had been prevented from doing Kilimanjaro last year by illness and so yes would love to join us. She would also bring her boyfriend Nick. And her two young cousins, Jacob and Gideon. Great, now we would be a team of ten which would make the whole process more powerful, not to mention cheaper per person.

So: on to the Peace Messages. Over the last couple of years I had collected over two thousand from various talks, street stalls, the Climb For Tibet website and generally everyone I met. The originals were too bulky to take so they all had to be put onto file. Night after night for weeks I sat at my little computer. It was a beautiful but poignant job. Whilst the international media told of earthquakes and tsunamis ravaging the world, tearing open our hearts, compounded by nonsensical killings between packs of humans, I typed out precious deeply-felt thoughts for harmony.

Some were in the form of prayers: "I pray for Peace and Justice for people in all nations of the world, that they reach out in love and respect for each other and care strenuously for creation".

Some were pledges to respect the Earth in individual ways: "I promise not to step on flowers".

Lots were positive guidance: "Even the severed branch grows again, and the sunken moon returns. Wise men who ponder this are not troubled in adversity".

A large number from children were simple pleas: "I wish for no more wars because it's horrible".

It's so obvious but why, I wondered, do we have to wait for the children to say it? And how many more children will it take to shout: "I wish for no more wars" before we will listen. How many more children?

I kept working on bringing in the Peace Messages. One day I had a little table at a local school fair. I was also selling my South Pole book so Gaius the penguin came along to help. A small boy came bounding up and asked, "How can I win that penguin? I really would like him."

Oh, help. I wouldn't want to part with Gaius. We'd been through far too much together. "I'm afraid he's not for winning," I replied. "You see, he's one of our team members for Kilimanjaro." Hmm, that was news to me! Gaius obviously was to have an important part to play on the Africa journey. Now we had a team of eleven, one of whom doubled as a nice soft pillow.

I was excited about the preparations for the journey, the Peace work that we were doing and the unknown adventure of it all. But there was one thing that was holding me back. Actually, it was wonderful news. I was to be a granny again. My son Scott told me that his beautiful Nella had had a scan and the baby was to be a boy. A brother for Elsie and Bess. My first grandson. Yippee! But I was desperate to be with them for the birth. And I wouldn't be; I'd be half way up Kilimanjaro. I couldn't change the date of the UN Peace Day and Nella emphatically wouldn't change *her date*. So there we were. I just felt sad at the thought of missing the arrival. Nothing lesser would have stopped me.

Then one Thursday, my day for being part of the healing work at the White Eagle Lodge, the healing guide Jan asked me how my grandchildren were. "I shall be on the Peace Climb for the birth of my grandson," I said sadly.

"It's no coincidence that he will be born around that time," she said in her wise and gentle way.

I looked at her, puzzled.

"I believe he's coming to carry on your Earth healing work."

With that a huge whoosh of confirmation went up and down my back.

"But I won't be there ..."

"That's not the important thing," she said. "What is important is his arrival during that time of Peace focus."

So, if he and my other grandchildren and some of their contemporaries were to be inspired by our Peace Climbs in some way, that would be wonderful. Perhaps a nudge to their souls. Of course, future generations have to do things in their own ways, which may be quite out of my comprehension. I can be their wind to blow in a particular direction, but they have their own wings ...

However it manifested, we were to be blessed with a little Peace warrior. I felt better about missing the birth after that and resolved to be more open to the bigger picture.

Collecting the Peace Messages continued and I was able to pull out quite a few from specific countries. So the 'nations list' began. There were 194 member states of the United Nations, which were on our base list of countries to obtain. Then there were the few dodgy not-always-recognised ones like Tibet, Palestine and Taiwan. Basically we wanted to represent all the peoples of the world leaving no one out, so would gather every extra race and group we could. It was a question of finding someone from each country. Shouldn't be a problem I thought. Wrong! Whilst there were always people wandering around from European and western countries, how many times do you bump into those from Sao Tome & Principe, Moldova, North Korea, Suriname, Guinea-Bissau, Vanuatu ... ? Oh I'll try all the embassies I thought. Then I discovered that not all countries have embassies in the UK or even in some other easily contactable country. My phone bill started to rise into the hundreds. My language skills struggled beyond a little bit of French and made up Spanish. My hours of sleep shortened as I tried to catch people in different time zones.

When I looked at it rationally, with the resources and time available, it was an impossible task. I frequently felt waves of panic coming over me. *However* were we to collect all the Nation Messages we needed? I kept having to bring myself back to the thought that this was a really important thing to do and that I believed it would happen. Concentrate on having them, I told myself. Never think of the lack. Know they will come. We shall climb the mountain with a Message from every nation on Earth. It was blind trust.

I learnt to rely more on this as I went along. One day as I was sitting at my desk the phone rang. It was one of those annoying tele-sales calls. A lady with a heavy accent started her sales spiel so I interrupted with, "Where are you from?"

"The Philippines," she said.

"Tell me the good things about your country."

"Well, it's hospitable, hardworking, welcoming ..."

"Would you like to represent the Philippines for us by writing a Peace Message for the world?"

"Hmm ... how about ... 'May the warm hospitality of our country be experienced by all nations?'"

"Lovely. Thank you."

She hung up, having forgotten the reason she phoned.

You never know who's going to call. It just might be the Universe, trying to provide you with what you need.

I learnt to research countries before asking for a Message. I found some had a useful national ethos or motto in the spirit of Peace. Some an important leader, like Haile Selassie, Emperor of Ethiopia, who had inspired millions, including Nelson Mandela and Martin Luther King with his work for social justice and freedom for the oppressed. His quote to the UN in 1968 " ... until that day the dream of lasting Peace, world citizenship and rule of international morality, will remain but a fleeting illusion ..." not only motivated a Bob Marley song, but also the Ethiopian Airlines lady I eventually tracked down and spoke to at length. Her Message was, "*Now* is the day for the dream of lasting Peace, world citizenship and rule of international morality." Yeah! Sometimes there was a feeling of history moving along.

My knowledge of geography improved no end, along with my networking skills trying to reach friends of friends who might just know somebody of an unusual nationality. Lots of people helped. Rima was pushing it hard collecting some on her website and using her IT skills; Sheila was a wonderful support with World Peace Flame contacts; and my beautiful daughter-in-law-to-be Chloe found obscure international colleagues.

There were few shortcuts; I found I had to bring them in slowly, one country at a time. Find a representative of a land, negotiate an opportunity to speak to him or her, which sometimes took days, and then explain in a way that might inspire that specific person. It was necessary to touch the heart of each one. Most embassy personnel told me, "I certainly wouldn't be qualified to write a Peace Message!" Eventually I plucked up the courage to reply, "Well, if you're human, you qualify." Email was hopeless as few responded. What we were doing generally had to be explained personally. I suppose people respond to the enthusiasm, sincerity and love for what you are doing in a voice. Anyway, emails carry their own problems. Like the embassy of Guinea, I phoned requesting to speak with Amba whose email address I had acquired, only to find that no such person existed there, in spite of my insisting there must be. It wasn't until sometime in the middle of the night that it suddenly came to me. I sat up, rigid with the realisation ... oh my goodness, 'Amba' means 'ambassador'.

It was always easier when talking to people face to face. One day I came across an international food market in London, with lots of opportunities to speak with different nationalities. To do this I had to buy a plate of food from each stand. Fine until my stomach decided it'd had enough of going global. As always it was a matter of drawing people's thoughts away from the mundane business in front of them, in this case stomachs, to see the bigger picture of the oneness of humanity and our Earth and the realisation that each individual makes a difference.

Often I would try for days to find someone of a particular nationality then suddenly be speaking to a person who was wildly delighted to be part of the work with one beautiful simple Message from the heart: "I wish all the nations Peace and harmony and lots of love," from Angola. That's all that was needed. And it was powerful.

I reached a point where I understood what this climb was all about. I had ended up like a fulcrum bringing the world together, country by country. This was the energy of pulling together for Peace.

Through the long hours and stresses of collecting the Messages, fitness training was not one of my priorities. It should have been, with a big mountain climb on the horizon, but I just hoped I could rely on my general fitness and build up whilst in Africa. But I did think about some preparation for altitude. This I knew was going to be the biggest problem on Kilimanjaro. Having experienced altitude sickness before, indeed so badly in South America that death was imminent, this was important for me. Also, I had watched Pete suffer on several occasions. I knew if there was anything that I could do that would prepare my lungs for coping with less oxygen then it would be useful. Ideally spending time at altitude is the solution. We were addressing this to a large extent by planning the two acclimatisation climbs in Africa.

But before then I thought I'd try an experiment. I knew my granny body, not to mention my granny brain, wouldn't survive Sam's method of being as drunk as possible. And besides, mine was cheaper: deep breathing. Not being disciplined enough to do it properly at home, I figured holding my breath underwater would prevent my body taking an extra breath whilst my brain wasn't watching. So I took to visiting the swimming pool a couple of times a week and gradually building up the length of time I held my head underwater whilst moving. I discovered that the more relaxed I was the longer I could hold my breath. I'd never heard of this method of acclimatisation before but it made sense to me.

Lifeguards at the pool must have thought it slightly odd having a little old granny gasping for breath all the time, but one of the things about reaching pensioner age is that you don't care what other people think of you. (Actually I'm not sure I cared that much before, but there have to be some advantages in being so ancient). Anyway, the frequent swims gave me the added benefit of always having clean hair.

Then along came some useful and happy walking training. Pete and I were invited to a Tibetan wedding in the middle of France. The traditional way to honour a bridal couple in Tibet is to walk long distances to the wedding. Okay. We would walk to the wedding. On closer inspection we didn't have time to walk the entire way, so came up with a plan to just walk from the Atlantic coast 150 miles or so up the Loire River and then a couple of days further northeast.

Along the way we celebrated Pete's 65th birthday. I gave him a bag of sweeties. It wasn't much of a present, though it had been lovingly carried. It's said that Queen Victoria gave Mount Kilimanjaro as a birthday present to her grandson, the German Kaiser in 1886. Still at least mine could be eaten, an important consideration on a long walk. After nine days, encouraged by French locals shouting "Bon courage!" and having survived losing our only map, being chased by flesh-eating fish whilst trying to sneak through a nuclear power station and being bitten by a pack of dogs, we finally arrived at the wedding site. Our close friend Migmar who'd been on our Andes Peace Climbs and his bride Kunsang were delighted that they had been honoured in this way. All their Tibetan friends had come by train or car!

After this I wondered if we could squeeze in one more little training session. A very important one. "How about we do something along the Greensands Way? It'd be only three or four days from

Haslemere to Leith Hill, the highest point in southeast England."

"Excellent idea," said Pete.

"We have to do it as a tyre-pull."

"Oh, well ... okay."

I had him! Excitedly I phoned Rima. She was the only one of us from our tyre-pulling days of polar training who had kept this sport up by doing marathons pulling a tyre. Sadly she wasn't able to join us on this measly seventy miles (well, not everyone is a retired pensioner) but she was delighted that we now had Pete back in the tyre-pulling fraternity.

His practical mind was soon busy organising the adaption of a tyre for Africa. If he drilled the right sort of holes he could fit clamps to hold two metal tubes for the Peace Messages and additional rope handles so everyone could help pull the tyre together. And a trailing rope would also be useful for a person behind to assist on awkward terrain. We would have to screw on securely the all-important 'Pulling Together for Peace' sign. And a sunny coat of yellow paint would be brilliant. Then all that would be needed was to hide it in one of our luggage bags cunningly disguised as a toiletry and we would be ready to go. Sorted!

Sorted that was, assuming we didn't hear back from the Tanzania Parks authority who we'd emailed asking for permission to pull a tyre up their favourite mountain. I'd heard that Tanzania was in the middle of problems with no petrol availability and on the edge of riots so no doubt there was more important things to think about and our request was sitting in the pulling-tyres-up-mountains file or even the whatever-do-we-do-with-this-one file. And we weren't about to remind them. Anyway, in my mind the mountain had given us the okay. That was the important thing.

There was just time after the tyre-pull to fit in another couple of days in North Wales to initiate Ann and Jackie in the same manner as Nicholas. Only this time Ann really struggled on Pen yr Ole Wen. As soon as things became steep she collapsed and threw up. Jackie was very tentative. Oh dear, we thought. It didn't bode well for Africa. Rima joined us and helped to coax them along. She'd brought a friend too. "This is Jess," she said introducing a smiley blonde. "She's going to join us on Kilimanjaro. She's with the US Air Force, you know 'fly, fight and win' motto and all that!" Jess looked fit and capable as though she'd do just that. We wouldn't have to worry about her, unless it was to keep the African men at bay from her all-American good looks! Now we were to be a team of eleven. It sounded a good number. But let's not forget Gaius penguin. He made us up to a nice round number of twelve.

In the last couple of weeks before leaving I connected up with Mary who was coming out a little after us. "Be prepared for life in Africa to be different," she said. "Things are slower and work in their own way. People take time to greet one another, particularly making eye contact to show respect. People time is important." Hmm. Sounded good to me. And I could do with slowing down a bit.

We swapped ideas on kit. She gave us some useful-looking water bottles with filters attached. Certainly, drinking enough water was going to be crucial to the success of everything. She'd managed to track down a school that we could fundraise for, in particular for facilities to bring water in. I was reminded that we were heading to a part of our world which was a dry land, where resources could never be taken for granted. We added to our fundraising list the charity African Initiatives, which assists the Maasai pastoralists in land rights and girls' education. And also the charity Tree Aid. It seemed to me that planting trees in Africa was a big part of the long-term solution to this tragic problem of drought and famine.

Pete had already had every immunisation possible. I like to do mine homeopathically so started on a combination of pills, making sure of a programme to cover malaria.

The collecting of the last Nation Messages looked like it was going to go down to the wire. I somehow knew it would. I was trusting that the Universe would help me get them all. How nice it would be to have them finished two weeks before leaving. But oh no, the Universe doesn't waste nice trusting energy like that. And of course I was left with all the hardest ones, which involved traipsing round the world on the phone searching for a clever solution to impossible looking countries with a language that I might be able to communicate in. South Sudan declared itself a new country. Most inconvenient of it.

Sometimes the exhaustion of the chasing got me down and I'd have to say to myself, "I can do this," over and over again. Then an email would come in: "You are a tower of strength and light. Let the light shine," from Beverley at the White Eagle Lodge. Or "You're nearly there ... keep trusting," from Sheila. And I'd think what a difference it makes to have the support of friends. Then a wonderful Nation Message would come in that would bring tears to my eyes and I'd remember how worthwhile it all was.

The last few I gleaned from the UN in New York, which is when it dawned on me that we should be asking the UN Secretary General, Ban Ki-moon, to also write a Peace Message. Forty-eight hours later the deal was done. There was just time. Time that was, before Hurricane Irene hit the US with $19billion worth of damage and New York City shut down.

In the midst of all of this, my little pussycat Kitesh died, quietly and peacefully. During her last days she would lift her head and look at me with compassionate eyes, as though her job was to hold my heart open during all the intensity and to hang around just long enough for me to know. "Sleep well, little soldier. I hold you in loving light," I whispered. That night I had a dream. My mother telephoned. "Please look after Kitesh for me," I said. "Of course," came the reply. And then I asked, "Is Dad with you?" The reply came again. "Of course." So my mind had that side of things nicely sorted.

It was a joyful moment when Pete showed me the Peace-tyre. It looked wonderful with smart yellow paint,purple climbing rope attachments and the sign rigidly fixed so anyone walking behind could read 'Pulling Together for Peace', all ready to dance up Kilimanjaro's ramparts, through dust, mud, snow or fire. We ceremoniously lit a World Peace Flame candle. Then rolled up the sheets of Nation Messages and General Messages into the two golden tubes.

Pete fixed them into the clamps inside the rim of the tyre.

So we were almost ready. Cards and emails came in wishing us well on our journey, many from local school children who had given us their Peace Messages. A few of them were specifically for Gaius. Now that's ridiculous!

I tore around in a panic trying to get the last things done. My printer went beserk trying to print off the speaking set of Messages. I sat down again and did it mindfully. All worked beautifully. Remember not to rush, I told myself.

Even so I raced down to Devon to say goodbye to Scott and family before leaving. My granddaughters Elsie and Bess picked two tiny stones from the beach to express their Peace Message love. At home, Bess decided she would sing her Message for me and gave an enchanting rendition of *Twinkle Twinkle, Little Star*. And she offered me Teddy, her most precious possession. With a lump in my throat I said, "No, Darling One, Teddy wouldn't be happy without you."

Elsie drew her Message. She lay on the floor and with great care crayoned an upward line on the paper and then, the second side of the triangle down again. "There," she said proudly, "Kilimanjaro!" Only her tongue became stuck in the middle of the long and difficult word. She looked up at me. "Can I come with you, Granny?"

"No, Darling One," I replied. "It's too big a mountain, but I promise I'll carry your Peace Message, which is like a little bit of you. And I'll carry it to the top of Kilimanjaro which is so high ... " I stretched my arms wide above my head, "that your Peace Message will touch the sky!"

I had promised. I didn't know what challenges lay ahead, but I had promised.

HAVE TYRE, WILL TRAVEL

31st August, 2011

"Boarding at 20.00 hours," said the lady at the Air Ethiopia check-in desk.

So this was it. Somehow I'd made it through the stressful weeks of preparation and packing. We'd nonchantly got our excessively heavy red kit bag through baggage control without having to explain why we were bringing a strange round thing with secret compartments. In my rucksack were paper sheets of 2,600 General Peace Messages and 220 Nation Messages, added to which was the UN Secretary General's Message, which had come in the day before. Thanks Universe. Pete and I grinned broadly and high-fived. Let the adventure begin.

Ann and Jackie caught up with us in the departure lounge. They appeared relaxed and happy, if somewhat unfit. "Here we go. We're ready to climb anything," said Ann enthusiastically, giving us a card from Ivy. It was a stunning picture of a six-pointed star. Inside was written:

" ... I shall be waiting for your call to fulfill the signal to activate the grid you place on Mount Kilimanjaro. Many of us will be gathered here .... Our minds can only touch the surface of what changes the star will bring ... May our souls fulfill the great purpose ... to benefit world consciousness."

"I see you've brought Gaius along," said Jackie with her

usual sweet smile, noting the rather large penguin that hung from my rucksack.

"Of course. He's the guardian of the crystals. That's his job on this journey." Hmm, I thought, that's news to me. Gaius is always full of surprises. I suppose it made sense though as in my rucksack alongside the Peace Messages was another valuable load. A few weeks ago Ivy had sent the all-important crystals which were to be placed at the top of Kilimanjaro. Not only had they, like those in our other five zones, been programmed to hold and amplify the energy of the Peace Messages, but also to manifest the grid in the African zone which would connect up to the other five grids across the Earth, creating the completed six-pointed star of Peace, which was to be the new portal of light.

On this occasion there were a lot of crystals, in fact quite a heavy weight to carry on the climb. Heavy at a physical level, but of course so precious that I was sure they would feel light. Individually wrapped in simple paper towel there was one golden pyrite, three blue lapis lazuli, six clear quartz, six fire tiger's eyes and a bunch of pretty picture jaspers. There were also six holding quartz crystals. I remembered what Master Advarr had said, "The placing will be timed by the power of the spirit," so I knew I didn't have to worry too much about how it would all happen. I just had to get them there and be in the right frame of mind, one of unconditional love. Does that work the same as one of service I wondered? At least on this venture we had Ann along who's not only psychic but clued up about the whole process.

Also in the rucksack was the summit-bag in which I'd made sure was a small object to represent each of our other five points of the star: an Inuit *inuksuk* from the North Pole zone; a Mount Kailas pebble from Tibet in the Himalayas; a picture of the goddess Pele on Mauna Kea from the Pacific – all carried in a llama-wool wallet from the Andes. Gaius insisted he was the one for the South Pole zone, though he was too big for the bag. I added a picture of the Dalai Lama, the embodiment of compassion; a picture that Beverley had sent of light shining from a six-pointed star around the Earth; my granddaughters' two little stones; and a little wooden bracelet representing the circle of life. Everything one could possibly need for an adventure.

"Did you bring any toothpaste?" Pete asked on the plane.

"No, sorry," I replied. Well, you can't think of everything.

I dozed fitfully through the hours of darkness. We weren't far from landing in Addis Ababa and dawn over Africa was painting an orange line across the sky when a picture of my mother came to mind. I remembered how worried she had been about me going on my journey to the South Pole. She had really struggled with that. Now I felt her say, "I shall be with you on this one, you know." That gave me deep contentment. It wasn't until a little later that Ann told me, "I had a spirit message from someone that must have been your mother. She looked very like you. I saw her tap you on the shoulder and say, 'I shall be with you on this one, you know'."

My brain could make no sense of this, but my heart understood.

If you've had no sleep and need to sit somewhere for three hours, then don't go to Addis Ababa airport. Even the earthy smell of the Ethiopian coffee doesn't make up for the far-from-comfortable chairs. But the great thing was that we were acclimatising. "Hey guys," I effused, "the altitude here's 2,400 metres. This is a wonderful start. Our bodies are already adapting by making more red-blood corpuscles to absorb more oxygen. Perfect! Wouldn't it be good if the plane was delayed." This idea wasn't well received by the tired-out team.

Back in the air, a beautiful Ethiopian air hostess served us a yummy meal. I passed the cake and custard to Pete. Would that I could pass it further. I knew that as we ate we were flying over the northeast border of Kenya. I'd seen it on the BBC News for weeks. Beneath the cloud, on the red dry land, this was where right now thousands of Somalian refugees were trying to escape from famine, walking for days on end having sold everything they possessed for food. Down there were people who hadn't eaten properly for weeks, people who have children, who look them in the eye wracked with hunger, and know that there is no food. Only dust and hope.

How can a parent live with that? I can think of nothing more heart rendering than not being able to feed my children. Suddenly tears came to my eyes. I resolved to work harder to raise more money for Tree Aid and its new project in Ethiopia on my return home. I'm sure they hold one of the major long term answers to famine. Surely the world must balance out. We must see the Earth in unity. To survive, each one of us must survive. We are all a bit of the whole.

Across the aisle an adorable little black girl with big round eyes and scraggly curly hair reached over for Gaius and gave him a cuddle. I watched her joy and my heart melted. I was looking into the happy face of Africa.

Somewhere we passed from the northern hemisphere to the southern. We descended into the old Kenyan port of Mombasa and then headed out northwest on the last short leg to our destination, Kilimanjaro International Airport. Wow, a mountain that's so important it has its own airport! As the plane lowered for landing we were level, almost eye to eye with Kilimanjaro itself. Oh help! What was it going to be like spending a night in the crater? I could see black rock on the eastern peak but the main summit remained hidden in mystery. Was it completely covered in snow? How far down do the glaciers fall? How steep would it be?

I craned my neck for the last glimpse as we droned past and barely breathed before another mountain shape came into view. Only on this one the cloud was breaking up and a long dark ridge to a summit was just discernable. Wow! This must be Meru. To me this one felt more feminine, like a matriarch who held the wisdom of the years. It wasn't only that it was smaller and lower, there was something about it that was softer.

I scarcely had time to sense it before the plane banked through the cloud, circled back on itself and we were coming in to land. An open dry brown scrubland came up to meet us. It was dancing with little dust-devils, dirt caught in vortexes by the wind and twirled up some fifty metres or so high.

They looked like pillars of exotic light that were welcoming us to Tanzania.

The guidebook said that the beautiful country of Tanzania has had an exceptionally long and volatile history, invaded by tribes from across Africa, then the Portuguese, Omani Arabs, the Germans and the British until modern- day independence in 1961. It has had to suffer the indignity of the slave trade and the ransacking of its gold and ivory.

Now it held wealth in the form of minerals and natural gas and in its agricultural based economy including cotton, maize, sugar, coconuts, tea and sisal. There were the typical African problems of poverty, aids and unclean water, which meant limited sanitation, healthcare and education. On top of that half its largely rural population was under fifteen years old. But it now has the saving grace of tourism, as over a quarter of the land is national parks or wildllife reserves. Of course tourism also adds to its problems, things like having to put up with a tyre being pulled up your highest mountain. At least this was to be a world first!

Unusually, so we were told, all the luggage arrived at the same time as its passengers, so we were delighted to see our red tyre kit-bag come through the system with no questions asked. It still looked like, well ... an interesting article to be carrying. But everyone knows that tourists are strange people. We soon mingled into the crowd and all was well.

We were warmly welcomed by a man with a mini-bus. The fact that we couldn't understand his version of English very well didn't seem to matter. No doubt we would get used to the lingo. I was too tired to think straight anyway and happily fell into the relaxed African manner. And then there was the heat. It was 36°C. No point stressing about things in the heat. I sat back and struggled to keep awake for the three-quarters of an hour bumpy drive and watched dreamily the jacaranda purples with hanging beans and beautiful black faces and dirt and poverty and gradually more and more lush green tropical vegetation. Until we arrived in the large and bustling town of Arusha and found ourselves at the Outpost Lodge, which was to be our base.

It was delightful. Strange and exotic bird calls resounded in a garden full of large-leaved plants with rooms rather like desert island huts for guests to stay in and an open central area for the no-walled restaurant and little pool. The staff were smiley and helpful. I sank back onto one of the beds in our room under a huge mosquito net which gave an air of a Bedouin tent. Ah paradise! By the time Nicholas arrived off his plane we were ready to enjoy a cool drink with him under a starlit sky to the singing call of cicadas. Then we slept, dreams interspersed with the night wind crashing dried equatorial leaves and pods onto the tin roof.

In the morning there was time to explore Arusha. A local guide was recommended to walk around with us. He was charming and presented Ann with a lovely flame-coloured African tulip flower. We were happy to enjoy his services, certain we'd then get to see the most culturally significant spots. The first place he took us to was an ice-cream parlour. Well, as I suppose the Dalai Lama would say, humans are human the world over.

We pushed through streets packed with vendors and would-be vendors selling from bikes, barrows, buckets and arms, everything from seven types of bananas, to long pieces of sugar cane to old shoes to squawking chickens. It was an explosion of sights, sounds and sensations. Especially at a wonderful produce market with basket loads of anchovies, beans, mangoes, papaws, avocados, melons, tomatoes, and all colours, shapes and sizes of other fruit and vegetables.

The most valuable thing we saw, to my mind, was a pole. It was by the clock-tower in the middle of town. A Peace pole. There are 200,000 of these scattered around the world, planted with the intentional focus for Peace. They have written on them the prayer 'May Peace Prevail on Earth' in different languages. I noted the Swahili on this one 'Amani na iwepo Duniani'. This point is said to be the dead centre of Africa, midway between Cairo and Cape Town. Whether it's true or not is immaterial compared to the wonderful idea of a Peace pole being central to Africa, a continent with more than its fair share of conflicts.

Heading back towards the Outpost, we passed large new hotel buildings going up. "Look, Chinese contractors," said Pete. "Ah, the Chinese get everywhere," giggled Ann.

I felt a pang of 'what about their oppression in Tibet', but said nothing. Prejudice and Peace don't work together.

We actually had to concentrate on where we were going to avoid large potholes in the pavements and the roads were jammed with traffic, but near a fine memorial to workers in the middle of a roundabout we were stopped in our tracks by a magnificent sight overlooking this great vibrant metropolis. Glimpses of it had been tantalising us through the streets as we walked. We were here in Arusha at 1,400 metres and there before us, outlined in dark rock rising more than 4,500 metres into a clear blue sky, was Mount Meru. There was one tiny cloud hovering like a smoke signal from a Peace-pipe above the summit. My pulse quickened. We would be there. After Oldonyo Lengai, we would be there. The mountain looked noble and beautiful and I felt welcomed by the sort of grandmother aura that I had sensed from the plane. Though certainly imposing, it looked possible to climb.

We returned to the cool shade of our little haven at the Outpost Lodge. Outside for me I had found a sense of the struggle of life and need for resources. Inside, apart from the request to use as little water as possible, we were in a set-aside space to rest and prepare with our lovely team support. How lucky I felt to have this space. I did know that with the right thoughts I can find that safe space within myself amidst life's struggles and it is always there in unexpected shelters. But for now I felt grateful for it to be physical.

Pete and I sorted the gear, strewn across our room. Yes, we were ready to tackle our three mountains. Oldonyo Lengai would be easy-peasy. It was only 2,900 metres. No worries there. Meru had looked benign enough today but I did feel a bit apprehensive. It was important for our acclimatisation programme to reach 4,500 metres, but I remembered the warning words: 'Never underestimate Meru. It is no pushover'. I would have to collect my thoughts for that one.

And Kilimanjaro ... well, that was the big one, the culmination of more than a decade's work. I looked longingly at the Peace-tyre in its red bag. It would be stored at the lodge until Kilimanjaro. I couldn't wait.

Before setting off to Oldonyo Lengai we wanted to connect up with our families. With the wonders of modern technology, Pete texted his children on his iPhone, whilst I emailed my three sons. Amazingly, within an hour I had replies from them all.

Mark said, "Take care of yourself, get back safe and thanks for being such a good Mum."

Scott offered, "Make sure that everything you do, you do happy."

And from Paul there was, "Go, expand beyond yourself into the unknown. There are no limits. Go into the mystery and wonder."

Yes, once your children have grown up and take responsibility for their own lives, then you can thank them for their wise advice and go out into the world to play.

I suppose it wouldn't hurt to do what I'm told. That is: to take care, be happy and head out into the mystery ...

MYSTERIOUS MERU

8th September, 2011

"One down. Two to go," Pete had said easily. Well, after the difficulties of climbing Oldonyo Lengai I was nervous about our second mountain.

At least now we had the Peace Lantern, sent to us at the Outpost Lodge from Peace Flame Paul in Kenya. It was a large Welsh miners' lantern, relied on for generations in the mines and so sturdy that they are also used to transport the Olympic flame. It stood 30cm high, wrought from brass with a copper plate showing the logo of the World Peace Flame. Ann struck the match to light the wick. Jackie placed the top back on carefully so that the light showed through the glass. We stared at it quietly for a while, mesmerised and mindful of the enormity of what it represented. We were undertaking to carry the light for Peace.

"Let there be light," said Ann.

"All the way to the top of Kilimanjaro," said Jackie. "Even if I don't make it, the lantern will."

"We can light it on Meru, too," said Pete.

I held out the palms of my hands to feel close and connect with it, like meeting up with an old friend. We had welcomed the flame. All was well.

"Now we have everything," smiled Nicholas.

We were complete – apart from the arrival of the rest of our team-mates.

Jacob and Gideon joined us for the evening meal. At the ages of 28 and 30 they, along with Jackie, were the youngsters of the team. No doubt that was why they didn't look tired after their long flight out. They were brothers, Rastafarians of Caribbean extract and were fit, strong and (I'm sure all the girls would agree) good-looking young men. If they'd lived in Africa they would be warriors, but as their home was in London Jacob worked with a youth incentive scheme and Gideon with a borough council. I suppose they were London warriors really. We greeted them in high spirits with stories of our Lengai climb and Maasai experiences.

"Have either of you ever killed a lion?" I asked, to give them a flavour of life in these parts.

"Eh ... I almost ran over a pigeon once," replied Gideon politely, as though it was a perfectly normal conversation in a pub after work.

Jacob appeared to be concentrating on ordering pizzas and had a worried look on his face. Perhaps he wasn't used to pensioners. Nicholas was trying to remember if he'd ordered or not and had lost his glasses, which were on his head. Pete had mislaid his wallet and having forgotten he'd already ordered two plates of vegetable skewers for himself, ordered two more. I was giggling uncontrollably and everyone at the table was bowing to me in mock reverence shouting, "Hail, Maasai Mama." The boys were no doubt regretting that they had joined up to this senior-moment club. Personally, I think this forgetfulness was all to do with the high altitude!

Two buses picked us up at 7.30am with a large group of porters, cooks and guides led by a serious young man with a shaved head called Jonas. He spoke quickly and I found it hard to catch what he was saying, which wasn't a good start. There were three fine-looking assistant guides. Raymond and Coolhand Luke, who didn't say much and Felix, who spoke most eloquently, so I could hear everything he said, but had no clear idea what he was actually talking about! C'mon girl, I told myself. Listen to people with your heart. You do that with mountains and have no problem communicating. That's how it had been with Sakimba, though there was no sign of him despite requesting that he be on our support team.

Perhaps I should be trying to speak a bit more in the local African Swahili.

"Jambo. Ninakupenda. Twendai! Asante," I tried out to the guides, putting together everything I knew. (For those who don't speak Swahili this means "Hello. I love you. Let's go! Thank you.") Oh, and of course a happy "hakuna matata". No doubt they were having the same problems communicating as I was, but it broke a bit of the ice.

We drove out of the traffic of Arusha, heading east through rich chocolate-coloured farmland. Then we briefly stopped at a little supermarket-type store for water in the village of Usa River and everyone clambered off and on again. There seemed to be a great many people squashed inside the bus just to look after our team of seven, plus the three more we would pick up. In spite of our happy Oldonyo Lengai team, I still found the idea of a large group plus support team really strange.

"I'd much rather just quietly set off by myself or with Pete or with only one or two others."

"Egbert, is that you speaking?" I asked inwardly. Egbert is my ego. I often have trouble with him. He thinks only of himself.

"I want to ignore everyone else and just pit myself against the challenge of this mountain," he replied.

"Egbert, go away! I'm trying to learn to work in a team. I keep hearing that we can't be in isolation in the world. That we are all interconnected as one. That we cannot leave anyone behind."

"Sounds like hard work to me. Much easier and more fun to go off and do your own thing."

"Hmm ... and how is that going to help the healing of the Earth?"

"Why worry?"

"Shut up, Egbert. You don't have a leg to stand on. I just know that helping the Earth is where I need to be. But I can't seem to find that same deep understanding about working within a team."

Egbert went silent.

Maybe Meru would be able to help? I peered out through the crowded bus but the day was cloudy and I couldn't see any sign of our mountain.

"I just hope we can all get up this one," said Ann wistfully from the little aisle seat beside me." My uphill skills haven't been too brilliant so far."

"You'll be fine," I reassured her. "There's a huge team to help."

"The Oldonyo Lengai journey was very much about tuning in with Africa wasn't it? What d'you think Meru is about?"

"Well, mostly it's about getting our bodies used to the altitude."

"And a trial run for Kili."

"For sure," I nodded. "Oldonyo Lengai ended up being a very personal journey for me. Like I was having to harmonise with myself. I felt very close and at one with the mountain. Now with Meru, I hardly feel I've connected up at all. I suppose every mountain has its own character. But it's as though there's something I need to do to open myself up. I don't know what it is. It kind of feels like it's the harmony of the team that's the important thing and I've got to find a place within myself to reach that harmony."

"Now that you've asked the question, the answer will come."

"Thanks," I smiled. "It's good to have you with us."

It wasn't long before we drew up at Ngongongare Gate, the main entrance to Arusha National Park, where Jonas organised the paperwork for our park fees. Here in a waiting pick-up vehicle we were excited to find Nick, Mary and her brother Philip who lived locally in the town of Moshi. Nick and Mary had flown in two days ago and had been staying at Philip's house. They had convinced him to join us for the Mount Meru climb. Wonderful. Happy greetings all round.

It was good to see them, particularly Mary, as a friend from my home area thousands of miles away. Already it felt like it had been months since we left England. She had a bandaged dodgy knee but was looking glamorous in pink flowery shorts, light pink shirt and yellow designer top as though out for a Saturday afternoon shopping spree. "Good to have the Vogue cover girl along with us," observed Pete with a hug. Nick, her boyfriend, didn't seem to be a hundred per cent well. As a banker his work had taken him on a busy tour of the East the previous week and had ended up in an Indian hospital due to a bad reaction to his inoculations. He was still recovering. Philip looked relaxed in sandals, with umbrella and beautiful carved stick.

Information boards explained that this area used to be occupied by Maasai pastoralists, forcibly evicted or not it didn't say, but was now strictly preserved for wildlife and well-behaved tourists. Ah, that sounded like us (as long as the pensioners did what they were told!). And we studied a 3D model of Mount Meru, which gave a stunning representation of what we were about to tackle. Wow, this could be awesome. Here was an only very gently active volcano with no tremors for half a century, though we could see that the enormous crater had had its entire east and southern rims blown away by some long-past eruption.

Our track in from the east at Momella Gate at 1,580 metres led across savannah grassland up through montane forestland to the Miriakamba Huts and then on up through a giant-heather zone to the Saddle Huts. From there we would climb steeply into the Afro-alpine zone and follow the knife-edge ridge of the crater rim around to the summit at 4,562 metres. It all looked so much larger and more frequently climbed than Oldonyo Lengai that I felt not even a twinge of fear, only excitement. And it was a very neat three-day journey up to gently cope with the altitude increasing by around 1,000 metres a day, plus an extra day to come down. Perfect.

We piled back into the buses in excitable mode and headed north at a fast rate on a bumpy and rough dirt track through green savannah. I spotting zebra, giraffe and baboons wandering along in their own peaceful timescale taking no notice of noisy smelly humans til there was a clang, bang, clang! Our bus came to a halt. It sounded like the exhaust had dropped off. On inspection it was only the engine protector. Ah! Hakuna matata. A large bit of metal was pulled off and thrown into the bushes and we continued on our way.

At Momella Gate we saw our night bags come off the roofs ready for the porters, so I gathered my rucksack, keen to set off on the four-hour walk to the first hut. But no, we had to wait for an hour or so for a lunch to be prepared. "You're in Africa now," said Mary laughing. "Chill out. Go with the flow!" Then when lunch came the carnivores ate the vegetarians' meals and it all became stressful. I was delighted when we actually got going.

Every group has to have an armed guard with them because of the possibility of aggressive buffalo or elephants. It used to be rhinos, too, but they had been poached out. We had as our guide a young park ranger called Bruno in army combat gear with a rifle slung over one shoulder which did seem rather incongruous. He led us off on a track across a little bridge over the Engarenanyuki River. Ah, how beautiful it was. I breathed in the warm clean air and relaxed. The sun was shining through high clouds, birds were darting around giving song and the open grassland was dotted with enticing-looking trees and shrubs such as wild olive and palm.

I was admiring a beautiful plant with pink-petalled flowers when a herd of school children came along in blue, green and striped yellow and black jumpers – the colours of the Tanzania flag. They stopped to chat, all smiling broadly, excited at having just seen some warthogs. Their teacher decided that he needed to take a picture of me, a lesser spotted granny, to add to their collection of animals observed, much to the merriment of the children. How nice to share their joy of the environment.

Waving goodbye and moving on a little I suddenly realised

that I was completely by myself. What had happened to my team? I looked around in every direction. No sign of them. I felt a bit uneasy and smiled to myself wryly remembering that I had asked to be without a team. Be careful what you think, I reminded mself. I went on a little further. How was it possible to lose an entire circus of guard, guides, cooks, porters carrying rucksacks and balancing large bags on their heads and multi-coloured Peace Climb tourists? I rushed on thinking they must be ahead, til I came to a spot which gave me a better view of the land and there in the distance across a vast swampy area to the north were little pinpoints of colour about to head uphill, people on the march. Oh my goodness, how did they manage to get that far away? I must have missed a turning in the track somewhere.

My first thought was to cut straight across the swamp so I wouldn't lose sight of them. But then I saw the heap of dark shapes between us, grazing. Definitely buffalo. I had laughed in the Ngorongaro crater when told that more people are killed by buffalo than any other animal. Perhaps I'd better listen now. It would be such a waste of all this Peace Climb effort if one of its pensioners ended up gored by a bad-tempered buffalo. Well-behaved tourist indeed! I turned and hurried back the way I'd come, annoyed with myself for getting lost so soon after we'd started.

I was almost back to where I thought I'd met the children when I saw two people. Phew, Jonas and Raymond. Was that a flicker of a smile behind Jonas' eyes? No, perhaps not. He just quietly sucked at his camelback water system, looking efficient and composed. Whatever the Swahili word for 'troublesome grannies' was, no doubt it was on his mind. They led me back onto a different track and followed a little stream around the swamp to a wide open grass area. There were quite a few buffalo around but one lone bull with huge horns in particular seemed to be causing Jonas concern. He turned to me and put his finger to his lips whispering, "Shhh," mouthing something else which was probably "they charge". We crept slowly by. I wondered if buffalo were selectively racist, like baboons are.

When we'd been with Marco, he'd told us that baboons would steal food from white people but not from black and we'd discussed an experiment to cover Jackie with mud and leave her with food to see if the baboons could tell the difference. Hmm, lots of interesting research to be done here.

There was no time to test the theory. We left the buffalo and the grassland behind and started a steady climb up a dusty well-worn track. Dense low vegetation closed in accompanied by crashing noises that might have been bushbuck but more likely baboons, no doubt looking for white people with food. Then we caught up with the others. And with Bruno and the gun. I'm reluctant to admit it as it goes against everything I believe, but there was a little bit of me that felt less vulnerable now that I was near Bruno and the gun. No, more likely it was being near my own personal knight in shining armour. Who didn't need a gun. Now I could understand animals who graze within sight of giraffes – because that's where they feel safest.

"Ah, there you are. You missed a giraffe and a pelican," said Pete enthusiastically. "There's loads of wildlife here."

"What I'd like to see more than anything is a leopard," I responded, feeling brave again. "I've especially worn my mock leopard-skin gaiters today so as to blend into the forest background. That sign back at Momellia said that tourists must wear appropriate clothes."

"Those granny gaiters have most likely scared them away," retorted Pete. "How can you possibly wear them?"

"Leopards are really elusive anyway," came in Bruno, looking doubtfully at my leg wear. He was the only one amongst us to blend into the forest colour scheme. "They hide in trees in the middle of the day, which is the only time we really want tourists to pass through. But I can show you some poo, for sure."

How thrilling. (I mean, how often in life is there an opportunity to be thrilled by poo?) and such a privilege to be walking through this abundant land. Our uphill progress was broken by a clamber steeply down into a little dell filled with large-leaved ferns to cross the Lenganassa River, hopping over wet boulders. As we walked further the forest became denser, revealing bright yellow orchids, red hot pokers and other plants that Philip was able to name with ace local knowledge. The trail then opened out to a lovely grassy bit with magnificent views east across distant lakes, with a large bird of prey circling overhead.

Here we stopped for a drink. Everyone happily flopped onto the ground enjoying the wilderness. It was too much for Nick, the hard-working banker, who decided that he just had to check into his office on his mobile phone, making the rest of us chuckle. Mary produced some wonderful flapjacks. Maybe the beauty all around was heightening my senses but I was sure they were the best I'd ever tasted. It was great to chat to everyone. Why had I been concerned about relating to a bigger team?

From here, Jonas and Raymond took Jackie and Ann's rucksacks so they carried two each; unobtrusively they were assessing where the needs were to keep the team happily together. We were going along steadily uphill but at a gentle pace which was wonderful to enjoy the trail which wound through increasingly thick forest accompanied by the rattling call of the colobus monkey. There were glimpses of the bright blue and crimson plumage of the punk-headed turaco bird through the trees dripping with lianas, lichens and mosses like in a fairy glen.

Then mist fell, reducing visibility but enhancing the feeling that we were in an all-enveloping magical story. By the time the afternoon grew old we were peered through thick grey cloud at a little clearing with half a dozen or so large brown and green tin-roofed huts, each with a hopeful solar panel waiting no doubt for that rare moment of sun peaking through the forest. We had arrived at Miriakamba at 2,514 metres.

There were beds for 40 tourists, but only a handful of others were around. I was happy to be assigned a small bunkroom with Jackie and Ann. Finding our porter-carried bags, I pulled out my sleeping bag and penguin pillow and settled in. It was warm and dry. I found us some bowls of water to wash in and there were even loos, of sorts. This was so civilized. It was good to chat with the girls – who were doing well – and took a variety of homeopathic remedies to cope with blisters, headaches and stings. Then we enjoyed tea and popcorn and afterwards a wonderful dinner of soup and spaghetti in the dining hut. It was by candlelight so it was difficult to tell what was in the assortment of jars presented as condiments, but all had been valiantly carried up by our support team, including everything needed for cooking, even the fuel. They had done us proud.

After a fantastic nine-hour sleep, breakfast was a similar gastronomic affair. Maybe I could get used to being looked after so well. We set off joking and laughing, into a now-rainy day. It wasn't really much different to walking through cloud, just generally damp but warm enough for shorts and waterproofs. And gaiters, of course, just in case leopards were out spotting. Pete and Philip smugly put up their umbrellas. Now that's going to scare every leopard for miles! The trail headed steeply up well-built steps like a ladder into an enchanted kingdom. We all slowly plodded upwards and waited when the porters powered by with apparent ease carrying their heavy loads mainly on their heads. "Jambo!" they shouted in greeting.

We discovered that the young man who carried both mine and Pete's bags was called Amani, which means 'Peace' in Swahili. Wow! How lovely that we had again attracted someone with a name that means Peace. What are the chances of that? Another porter carried our Peace Lantern safe and dry inside his jacket. There was something rather lovely about that too. Then splat! I trod in a large smelly cow-pat. Oh bother! It had to be buffalo poo. I didn't know they grazed this high, almost 3,000 metres. Couldn't possibly be elephant poo, could it? Certainly large enough. Perhaps poo isn't always so thrilling.

"Head in the clouds as always," laughed Pete. "I'm going to upgrade you from cloud nine to cloud twenty!" Of course he was watching where he was going!

We zigzagged on upwards very slowly, given time to see huge turquoise butterflies and to listen to the entire orchestra of birds screeching, tweeting and warbling. Little pink impatiens decorated the way along with red mountain gladioli and large-leaved lobelia shooting tall inflorescences into the canopy above. Most of all it was the fairy trees I loved, juniper, podo and hagenia with their hanging old-mans-beard offering curtains to push our way through in the mists. I was sorry to leave them behind when the steepness eased somewhat and the forest started thinning. But we emerged into sunshine. Wonderful!

Stopping to put on our hats we looked around and down at the clouds which were shifting in every direction and as we moved on, the verdant green of trees became smaller and was replaced by olive green shrubs dotted on grey and the distant purple of moorland with giant heathers. A sort of musky smell came with the more open country. The trail, now dusty, wound its way further upwards till the clouds moved away to reveal a peak above them. It wasn't the summit but a peak outside the crater rim known as Little Meru. Before long we could also see green tin roofs at its base. Nicholas, Pete and I arrived at the Saddle Huts, a similar set-up to the last camp, but of course higher at 3,566 metres.

"Aha! The old fogies get here first!" exclaimed Nicholas.

"Pensioners rule, okay!" said Pete, shaking hands with Felix to thank him.

"Karibu sana (You are warmly welcome)," he replied, smiling broadly. There was a nice feeling of affinity.

"Yeah!" I agreed. I felt great. It was good to be here with the drifting clouds now having closed us in again but with intermittent brightness giving a feel of an isolated eyrie in the sky. But there were no eagles. Just two large white-necked ravens preening themselves and dancing up and down on their spindly bird legs with heads on one side as if trying to hear what we were saying.

By the time the others arrived it was clear that those of us who had already had some acclimatisation were feeling better than those who hadn't. Both Jacob and Gideon collapsed with exhaustion headaches, feeling nauseous. Nick and Mary, dizzy and light-headed, were struggling to feel normal. Philip – who lived at 1,500 metres – had a head start, but wasn't used to physical exertion and was pleased to stop.

Ann and Jackie came in last with Jonas and Raymond, feeling okay and a little bit smug.

It was a dodgy business, this altitude sickness. Very nasty and to be taken seriously. It can lead to oedema of the lungs or brain and subsequent death. And no one ever knows who is going to suffer. It was just important to try and follow the rules to lessen it. Ascend in altitude gradually, take everything very slowly, drink lots of water, eat carbohydrates little and often, and take the pills that suit you. Pete was on Diamox, the standard doctor's prescription, which he had always found brilliant. It aids the uptake of more oxygen into the blood and helps both with preventative and treatment, particularly for those who need to nip up and down quickly. I had never liked the idea of its side effects – tingling extremities and weeing more – so had always worked with homeopathic coca.

We rested at the Saddle Huts with a huge and magnificent lunch. Everyone stuffed themselves, which was a good sign. And then felt well enough to take a short walk up Little Meru to 3,801 metres to gain useful acclimatisation. This would aid our bodies' adaption to the reduced pressure which meant less oxygen, by producing more red blood corpuscles. After some sleep then surely everyone would be okay for the climb itself.

It felt good to walk uphill without a rucksack. There was a certain freedom, accompanied by the soaring call of the white-necked ravens overhead. The trail zigzagged up through the heathers and shrubs leading us further and further into a bright windless sky of the clearest blue. The clouds billowed softly in a shiny whiteness that uplifted me and I found that my heart was singing. There was something about the light that was almost unreal, as though it had been cut with a knife and had sharp clean edges. What was this magic that filled the air? Was it to do with the ancient Maasai connection to the Earth?

I clutched my little talisman, feeling grateful to the tribes that had given this special land as a reserve for all people and smiled at my feeling of completeness. A peak of joy welled up on arriving at the top of Little Meru. I turned to face a shining hanging sun in the west and then was drawn to the southwest away and upwards where a covering of cloud rolled back to show for the fraction of a second a magnificent black knife-edged ridge leading around to a summit on fire with streaking clouds. The summit of Mount Meru.

It was a meeting.

I am with pillars of light held in a spiral energy. I touch the edge of something deep and powerful connecting to the Earth.

"Thank you, great Meru. Thank you for allowing us to be here in preparation."

" *Karibu sana,*" mellow liquid words respond. "This climb will centre your tribe. Be here in the spirit of service."

The spinning slowed. I blinked several times. The light was so bright. The ridge had gone. Just momentarily there was a summit touching the sky. And then swelling clouds, backdrop to the silhouettes of the team in front of me.

Suddenly I remembered ...

TESTING OF THE TRIBE

How could I have forgotten something so fundamental? I had been drawn to climbing this mountain initially because of the mystical name. Mount Meru. Mount Meru. It had an enigmatic air to it. In the far-back mythology of cultures and religions, both eastern and western, this was one of the names given to the symbolic meeting place of Heaven and Earth, sometimes called the Axis Mundi or the Tree of Life. There are long-held beliefs that stated that here was the home of the gods, so vital that around this point the sun was said to circumnavigate.

This was not just any old mountain name.

This was a sacred representation of consciousness itself.

Many physical places around the globe had intriguingly been attributed to this, in particular the North Pole and the South Pole. As such it was also the metaphysical name for Mount Kailas in Tibet around which we had circum-ambulated on our Himalayan Peace Climb. In the Andes the meeting place between Heaven and Earth was held by the Incas to be Mount Chimborazo, the location of our first Peace Climb. And the site of our Pacific Peace Climb, Mauna Kea, was believed by the ancient Hawaiians to be the meeting place of Mother Earth and Father Sky.

There were links with ancient mythology and our work today.

I could not ignore my exchange with Mount Meru.

If I'm to take for granted that all is interconnected

as one entity, one spirit, which I keep being reminded of, then humans are merely a little bit of a larger whole. So it should be possible, indeed easy with the right thinking, to open myself out to encompass the team. Okay, I would try.

I resolved to dedicate this climb to the service of the team. My tribe.

We left the Saddle Huts just after midnight under a bright full moon. I was sure I could hear my heart beating in excitement, but beyond this there was little sound apart from the crunching of boots. We were our tribe of ten, the four guides and a few porters, too. The night was so clear that we could see thousands of stars.

Thank goodness the weather's fine now, I thought. We had come down from Little Meru to sit in the dining hut and devour another huge meal to the sound of very heavy rain on the tin roof. There had been a discussion about the climb. Jonas had suggested we split into a fast and a slow group. After my talk with Meru I wanted us all to get there together. If it was going to work on Kilimanjaro we had to get it right here. Anyway, we all needed to go slow and above all we were the Peace Climb team. Together was important. I was delighted with the group decision to go as one party.

We walked in single file, Jonas leading the way. I fell in behind him. There was a string of little head-torch lights following up the sandy ash trail. Moon-shadows dancing gracefully with the movement. The cold air jumping with anticipation.

We plodded at an almost painfully slow pace, perfect for keeping everyone together, though so slow I worried that we wouldn't get warm and would run out of time, like on Lengai. But now at this altitude every problem could have serious consequences. I tried to hold in a positive light the doubts about the ability of the team. After only three hours sleep everyone had seemed groggy as we'd tried to shove down even more carbohydrates in the form of porridge before leaving. I felt sure each person felt nauseous as I did, but much of it was only nerves and would settle.

The main concern was the altitude sickness of Jacob, Gideon, Mary and Nick who'd all felt so bad yesterday. I'd offered around sickness pills and also some Diamox which a kind doctor friend had given me, but only Nicholas had decided to take it. At least the girls had opted to make tea out of some dried coca leaves that I had managed to smuggle out of the Andes where the locals chew them at altitude. And in addition they had taken homeopathic coca remedies.

Hold the team in light. Hold the team in light, was the mantra I fell into, enjoying the rare opportunity of some time in my own mind. And then I saw something interesting.

There was a gathering sense of our togetherness, overshadowed by Meru protecting us all with a wise elder energy, like a grandmother. Somehow it was being channelled through me. Wow! As a healer who works with energies this was not unnatural to me, but I'd never channelled a mountain before! I felt that to maintain the connection I had to concentrate on thinking of the bubble of strength for the team.

We climbed steadily into the night and its myriad of stars. The moon soon disappeared, leaving just us and the Universe. But concentration was hard due to frequent stops. First it was poor Nick, who vomited. Then there was water to be forced down and also wee stops. Then Nick was retching again and struggling with an erupting stomach. Could we actually go on like this and still keep together?

With relentless winding steepness and a sense of the rock dropping away on either side, a sign loomed at us out of the dark inscribed 'Rhino Point 3,800 metres'. On top of a rock plinth was a heap of old bones. What's this all about, I wondered. The remains of some flying rhinosaur? Some pensioner who couldn't make it?

We had almost joined the crater rim, from where we could follow more or less the horseshoe ridge itself. First though, to my surprise, we had to go down across a steeply sloping rock-wall.

The team slowed down further and spread out. There was a sense of unease. It involved a lot of balance and trust without being able to see how far was the fall should there be a slip. Perhaps this was a good thing.

I knew only too well how fear could take hold. This was all a mind game, convincing those that hadn't done this sort of thing before, which was most of the team, that all was well. Look, everyone's doing it. We do this all the time. Just keep on going. I felt sure that Jackie and Ann were okay, that they were being helped. That everyone was okay. Half way across Jonas waited for me and we turned and watched the little line of lights making it across the face. "This is the most dangerous bit," he said, his words escaping onto the night breeze without anyone else hearing. The strength held us all safe and secure. We had passed what's known as Helichrysum Depression.

After that it was a steep climb to the lip of the crater. Here we were in the teeth of the wind. It brought the smell of the vastness of the night. It played on our cheeks and flapped loose clothing, but thank goodness not too violently. I now knew we were crossing the jagged edge of the ridge. That to our left there was a drop of nearly 2,000 metres, plummeting straight down into the forest on the floor of the crater. To our right, well, I wasn't sure. It wasn't another cliff face, but it was steep enough so that the angle didn't really matter: You were going to kill yourself anyway if you took that route. But we were fine. Grandmother Meru held us close in her embrace through the dark. Sometimes we scrambled over giant boulders using our hands and I enjoyed the hard touch of the mountain against my cold gloveless fingers; sometimes we followed across scree slopes, the way trodden into an ash path; often it was just a mix of rock, stones and dust, the true mantle of a volcano.

On and on through the night we journeyed, each in our own thoughts, each glued together by the bond of shared endeavour and by something too intangible to comprehend. Then, it must have been around six hours after leaving the hut, Jonas halted. This was Cobra Point at 4,350 metres. No self-respecting cobra would come near this altitude, so perhaps it had been named out of respect for the fear which serpent and mountain alike command. Certainly the guidebook had said: 'This place is not for those with vertigo'.

There was a change in the sky around us. The moon was visible again, but a dying red moon hugging the darkness of a horizon which was becoming delineated by a blue wash to the east which pulled up a swathe of other colour: charcoal brown, then fiery orange and finally yellow, across a mass of warm grey.

Dominating it all was one huge, unmistakable shape which reached into a sky now empty of all but light becoming brighter by the second. Rays of fire were displaying out behind the shape bringing it alive, now casting golden light on the surging cloud between us, as though stilled in a moment of time that calmed and locked its Peace and beauty forever. We witnessed a mighty orb, firing gold. Never had I looked into the eyes of a dawn so majestic, so full of wonder. The sun in its daily cycle had rebirthed Mount Kilimanjaro.

Jambo, Kilimanjaro. We honour you.

We are one spirit.

Nicholas was right behind me. I turned and beamed, "This is one of life's greatest moments."

"Never to be forgotten," he replied quietly. It was special to share it.

There was movement behind him. I looked down to a pillar of rock we'd just gone past. Hugging close to it, coming up the trail, there, alongside the steep drop straight down into the oblivion of the cloud, was Ann with a big smile on her face being led by the hand of the man named 'Peace' who carried her rucksack. Following not far behind was Jackie, holding hands with another young porter in a broad-brimmed hat who had her rucksack.

Wow! So that's how to do it. Ask for help. Attach yourself to a guardian angel, or porter as the case may be, give him your burden, know that with help all is possible and off you go. Seeing them here so close to Meru's summit touched me. I found myself crying, and smiled through my tears. Yeah, this time they were going to make it.

Then followed Nick, watched over by Raymond, his head bent under his windproof hood, panting in agony. How had Nick fought through?

Philip was waiting for Mary, who was struggling with a blinding headache. Her look was one of grim determination. She would do this. She would.

Also now coming up to our waiting gathering in the soft dawn light I could see another porter with the London warriors. Neither of them said anything. They didn't have to. It was written all over their faces. This was hell. Why hadn't they stayed in London?

Our shared experience was being felt in many different ways.

Where was Pete? He's missing all the magic, I thought. He must have had to stop for some reason and is taking it carefully to catch up. Ah, I spotted his golden windproof in front of the yellow trousers of Coolhand Luke and red jacket of Felix, bringing up the rear of the party. They were coming over a crest of the ridge, which swept dramatically away in the curve towards the east, dropping into the bubbling sea of foaming cloud, only to surface briefly to show the peak of Little Meru, like an island in the ocean.

This was the entire team accounted for. I felt so proud of everyone, so utterly proud. And we weren't even there yet.

Sometimes when you feel completely filled up with emotion and you think there's no room for anything else something beautiful will ease in through a crack in the side showing that there are no limits, showing that joy is the inbreath and the outbreath, the fabric of life itself.

There was a sweet sound beside me. And then its echo responded from my other side. And then further up the mountain came the refrain and its echo further down. Voices were creating flowing melodious music like I'd never heard before. Back and forth it grew til every African with us was singing his heart out in a prayer song that I felt through the very cells of my body. It was as though they were simply keeping time to the rhythm of the mountain, expressing the sound of the Earth.

I wiped more tears from my cheeks. How privileged we were to be part of this wonder.

"Twendai!" called Jonas and we all moved slowly on. Now my gaze turned to the west. Like on the other side we were looking down on an ocean of cloud tinged pink in the low light and the horizon here swept gently with the curve of the Earth. But reaching towards it, we could see the massive shadow that Meru had thrown across the sky. And around the shadow summit itself, reflecting the point that we now stood hung a complete circular rainbow.

"Wow, look! How amazingly beautiful!" I declared, but no one else seemed to see it, perhaps lost in their own struggle. It was that point on the mountain when we were so close yet so far. When time stretched and the summit had to be there any moment but just never seem to appear. We skirted around the western face, clambering over a jumble of rocks with no sign of a path, just occasional green markings along the way to say that someone had been here before us. The air was thinner now. We had all slowed down even more.

"Take ten steps and then stop for a breather," said Jonas. I rather liked that rhythm. It suited me. I was careful to keep my head still and do no sudden movements which I knew had helped me previously at altitude. But I felt great. I knew that I was held in the bubble of the strength of the mountain. And I knew it was coming through for the others. And then we were climbing nearly vertically using hands too and looking up I saw a little marker in the sky. Coming closer it became a metal flag painted in the Tanzania colours.

And then I was hugging Ann on the summit. It was she who got there first. Alongside us was the sign 'Socialist Peak 4,562 metres'. Jackie and Nicholas arrived soon afterwards. The others staggered up to join us on the jumbled rock pile, mostly head down, doubled over with gasping and retching sounds. I took it on myself to greet each one with a hug and a "well done," especially for Mary who was in floods of tears. Then Nick was crying on my shoulder, too. Pete dawdled in with "Well, that was not a piece of cake!" Was he being serious? He seemed in high spirits though as we high-fived. Then finally up came the London warriors looking ghastly and all-but passing out. Our whole tribe was there.

Somehow we really had all made it.

Looking around there was still cloud in all directions; it felt like we should be able to see the rest of Africa. But there was only Kilimanjaro, standing alone above the clouds. Waiting for us, waiting for our Messages of Peace. Like the rest of the world, waiting for Messages of Peace.

This was actually a very poignant day. It was the 11th of September, the tenth anniversary of New York's terrorist disaster of man attacking man. Kilimanjaro was playing its part in helping bring Peace, we knew. Right at this moment there was a Peace pole being established on its slopes. We would soon be there to spread the Peace energy.

But time to focus our Peace thoughts here. Ann helped me spread out the UN flag and the prayer flags and Pete took the Peace Lantern from the porter and organised it with Jackie. It lit with our last match. We chanted 'Om' and six 'Amani's, whilst Ann chanted:

"May Peace prevail on Earth!"

"To Kilimanjaro and beyond!"

Philip looked puzzled. "Tell me," he asked. "What is 'Om'?"

"It's the sound of the Universe," I replied. "So we're connecting up to all that is. Kind of like everyone singing the same song."

Due to our wrecked state, I felt all our hearts had simply resonated together. Ah, I thought, perhaps that's where the meeting place of Heaven and Earth really is. In our hearts.

The light of Peace shone from Mount Meru.

I smiled, feeling deep contentment. I had managed to hold the intent of service. Maybe this had made it easier for me because I had been focusing on the team and not myself. I had been stepping back from self. Come to think of it, perhaps it was a way to express unconditional love. And perhaps that was why I'd had no fear. That pleased Mum, I was sure. She'd been with me, helping me. I just knew that. All had been harmonious. And surprisingly I'd not felt the altitude at all. No doubt taking the homeopathic coca pills had helped and also the swimming preparation building up my lungs. Mostly I was just happy that all our team had reached the summit, though not without a severe struggle for those less acclimatised. Thank you, Grandmother Meru.

Buffalo willing, the big one was yet to come.

AT SCHOOL

Jackie twisted her ankle. Oh, no! It happened on the descent from Mount Meru; her foot stumbled in a particularly squelchy bit of mud. Something as simple as that and yet as serious as that. Just when we thought we'd prepared well and were becoming excited at the time drawing near for our most important work. Would she still be able to do Kilimanjaro? And if she attempted it with a dodgy leg, would it slow us down so much that it threatened the team's chances of success?

Jackie's ankle swelled up to twice its size, and we all felt for her. She bravely limped onwards down the mountain, helped by Jonas who carried her across the river on his back. This made her giggle. But would she be alright?

Once we were all safely at Momella Gate, where we had started our ascent seemingly a lifetime ago, Philip thanked everyone in Swahili on our behalf and we gave the ranger, the porters and the guides what we hoped was more than the right amount of tips. Most had a wife and small children at home and had had to push to find employment on the mountain in the first place. The tips added around fifteen per cent to their wages, and although awkward for us as we had to find the right amount of cash to give to each individual, it was crucial for them.

We were given certificates for having climbed Mount Meru and everyone was all smiles. Even Jonas. We were grateful for the professional way he and his team had made sure that we all had a successful and safe journey. Not to mention carrying Jackie.

I was sorry to say goodbye to Bruno. I felt I'd learnt a lot from him. He was a young man totally dedicated to his ranger work. Not only was he so very knowledgeable about the fauna and flora, but he was also sensitive to the welfare of the environment. He declared, "I'm concerned about the changes happening at the moment. The rains don't usually come this early. Something is affecting the environment here. Something is upsetting the Earth."

"This is the sort of imbalance we're trying to address at a wider level with our Peace work on Kili," I replied. "Would you like to write us a Peace Message?"

"I'd be delighted. It'll be from my tribe, the Pare."

He thought for a minute and then presented his Message: "I want to advance people all over the world to conserve wildlife resources and nature, and to ask developed countries to give funds for this."

"Thank you. So tell us, what is the biggest need here?" I asked.

"Education," he replied without hesitation. "In fact, it's only thanks to a kind Spanish lady that I myself am able to take my environmental diploma." He added, "There's not one African family unaffected by poverty. That's what's behind all the cases of aids. You know there are five million orphans in Tanzania because of aids."

"We're helping by raising funds for your local Ngongongare School," came in Mary. "It's really important to us." More important it seemed than climbing another mountain. Even though she looked better today, she was still saying, "I swear I won't do Kili. People at home won't be impressed, but I really don't care." Would she come round? How quickly could she forget just how bad she'd felt?

Nick was somewhat better. "I wanted to test how I would feel not taking any pills," he confided. "Well, now I know ... horrendous!"

This altitude game certainly wasn't much fun.

Now at only 1,500 metres, the air felt liquid again and we could all breathe. Our bodies would have acquired valuable acclimatisation, which would stand us in good stead on Kilimanjaro. But what about the last two members of our team who had only just arrived?

Rima and Jess were waiting for us as we left the park. They had been hanging about for hours and managed very little sleep since flying in from London yesterday. Even so, they were in high spirits and greeted us with exuberant tales of friends they'd already made in Africa, or rather, would-be friends who banged on their door in the middle of the night. It seemed that our level of go-for-it fun would now increase. There were hugs all round. It was great to have them with us at last and they fell into the unity of the team without a second thought. Our tribe was complete.

Ngongongare Secondary School was only five minutes' drive away, a handful of low half-built tin-roofed buildings surrounded by dust, dried grass and a few sparse trees. A sign said 'Education for the future betterment'. We were greeted by a group of youngsters in olive green jumpers, white shirts and loose ties. One of the girls sidled up to me. "Karibu Mama. My name is Joyce." Her beautiful smile was marred, like all the other children, by the brown marks all over her teeth, caused by the fluoride from bore water.

"Hi, Joyce! I'm Tess. Nice to meet you. How old are you?"

"I'm sixteen. How old are you?"

"I'm sixty-three."

At this, the schoolgirl went into an uncontrollable fit of giggles, as if it was inconceivable that anyone could actually be so old. That, it seemed, was the end of my conversation with Joyce.

We were ushered into a sparse teachers' room where we were welcomed by six teachers and the deputy head, Mr Elioha Miley, who spoke to us about the school. "We are happy that you have come to visit our school for older children. Four years ago there was only a primary school in this area, but the local community has been working hard to build this one. We have nine partly finished rooms, a football pitch and a tree nursery for the garden project. There are ten teachers, half of them part-time and some non-teaching staff. And 508 students of which 266 are boys and 272 girls. The subjects we teach are Swahili, English, biology, chemistry, physics, maths, geography, history and civics." He spoke with pride at this accomplishment.

"What are your biggest needs, Mr Miley?"

"There are many. Most of the money has to be found by the parents so we are in considerable difficulties. Apart from finishing the existing construction we need a hostel for both students and staff to stay in. Many have to walk ten kilometres to come here every day. We would love to have a playground, admin block, science labs and proper toilets. There is a big shortage of books, currently only one for every ten students from a mobile library. But the most urgent need is for water. Not having water affects everything. After that, it's the installation of electricity and then computers. How wonderful it would be for the students to be able to work with computers."

Oh, so basically there was the need for everything that we take for granted in our western schools.

To our embarrassment, three cooking pots were brought in and we were fed a delicious meal of spaghetti, vegetables and stew. Of course we couldn't refuse this hospitality, but couldn't help wondering whether the children had eaten anything themselves.

Afterwards we were taken outside where the entire school was lined up in front of us, a sea of eager, curious black faces. Putting their hands on their hearts, they sang the Tanzania national anthem with such dedication and affection that we were all deeply moved. How, I thought, have I lived my whole life and not seen how utterly beautiful African people are?

The prefects then sang a sweet welcome song to the 'guestees'.

We were up next. We each introduced ourselves and thanked the children and Rima caused great laughter by demonstrating a miming sequence that everyone followed. With this she broke down every barrier of language, age, culture and country. She's a natural teacher. We then presented the prefects with six footballs, six netballs and some pens and paper pads. It seemed a meagre gift compared to their needs and we all wished we'd brought more.

Finally we milled around with the children, chatting. Though all their classes were taught in English, their ability in our language wasn't that good. Often I found it was the universal language of a smile and our couple of words of Swahili that won through a conversation. Basically they were just kids, like kids the world over. Some confident, several unsure of themselves, many sticking close to friends, some being teased and many fooling about with banter. But most were giggling and having fun, revelling in life's experiences and all deserving the chance to respond positively by being cherished and given opportunities.

It was important not to forget them. To remember our responsibility in sharing our wealth. But also to accept the lesson they gave us ... that it's not always physical stuff that makes us happy, but our attitude to what we do have.

Back at the Outpost Lodge, we shamelessly savoured the physical stuff: comfortable beds, the swimming pool, showers and all the food and drink we could take on board. The team came together at dinner and sat round the table discussing how things had gone on Meru. Though elated at having achieved it, there was a general feeling of shock that the mountain had been much tougher than many people expected. This gave an undercurrent of mostly unspoken doubts about Kilimanjaro, particularly with Jackie sitting there, foot on cushion. Pete reassured everyone that we had an excellent acclimatisation plan with a nice slow ascent ahead of us and "It'll be a piece of cake". If he'd known then what type of cake, he might not have been so relaxed.

I discovered that the internet was on, so grabbed the opportunity to check my emails from friends who were proposing to climb their own mountains and speak out Messages on 21st September. There were also Peace Messages themselves still coming in. I scribbled these down to add to the pile of Messages to take to be read out on Kilimanjaro, though they were too late to be in the tyre.

Ah, the Peace-tyre!

We brought it out and Pete proudly showed everyone how he had fitted the two golden tubes containing General and Nation Messages. The sign, looking clean and sparkling new, reading 'Pulling Together for Peace'. Its time had come. Our time had come.

"We will pull the tyre to the very top of Kilimanjaro, the highest mountain in Africa in the name of Peace!"

"To 6,000 metres!"

"All of us together!"

"The Kilimanjaro Peace Climb team!"

"Plus one," a voice said from behind.

I turned.

There stood a Maasai warrior in his white beaded jewellery and red cloak of courage.

"Sakimba!" I threw my arms around him. "You made it. Are you coming with us?"

"Yes. I've signed up as a porter, just so I can join you," he beamed.

"Fantastic. Our own Peace Climb Maasai warrior. Look, here's our Peace-tyre. I suppose it's natural for you to connect up to the Earth with rubber as your people wear shoes made of car tyres ..."

I stopped, suddenly realising how incongruous it was to have a Maasai warrior in this enclave tourist stronghold. Did I need to be more sensitive to the inter-mixing of the cultures of the world? Was I wrong to encourage him to come with us?

"This is Rima," I continued. "We've presented her with some Maasai car tyre shoes. She's a tyre-girl. She runs marathons pulling tyres before breakfast."

I introduced Sakimba to the rest of the team and he joined us for the meal. I gave him a copy of my *Cold Hands Warm Heart* book as I had promised on our donkey trek. I wrote in it, "Thank you for your strength of heart for us and for the world". He said that he would pass this on to the new little baby Sakimba in the mud hut.

Behind us, the Outpost's tourist entertainment was taking place. There was a team of young local acrobats, dressed in mock traditional gear, doing amazing stunts on the concrete by the pool. They threw each other in the air, held extraordinary off balance poses and danced with fire to the accompaniment of exciting African shouts. We were mesmerised. Afterwards, they passed round the hat so that they could feed their families. It seemed that it was possible for our different cultures in our differing worlds to happily collide.

The following evening, after a day of repacking our kit, we assembled at the tables by the pool for the team briefing with our new head guide for Kilimanjaro, Freddie Achedo.

"Call me Mountain Madness," he said flamboyantly, with the cheekiest grin ever. I couldn't help but smile with him. He had been voted the top mountain guide of the year. Well, if personality was anything to go by we could see exactly why. He was certainly a live wire. How could anyone not love Freddie?

"I've climbed Kilimanjaro 481 times," he said, not boastfully, but more as though he thought it was an amusing fact. It could just explain why he was so confident that he knew what he was doing. "We'll leave at 7.30 tomorrow morning. On the mountain you'll have a 5.45am wake-up call with tea in your tents. Then you'll be brought washing water at 6.00. Breakfast will be at 6.15 and we'll start walking at 7.15."

"That all sounds very well organised," said Pete, obviously impressed.

"Make sure you get lots of rest, eat all you can and drink three to four litres of water a day," continued Freddie. "And your most important instructions are – don't do too much thinking. Think with your heart!"

Thank you, Universe. Wherever you found this guy, thank you.

Felix was to be assistant head guide again. Some of the team had reservations about him; for me, though, there was one important question he asked that outweighed any other considerations: "Please can we, the guides and porters, be part of the Peace Message reading? We want to help Peace."

Even though I knew the rules were that the porters were not allowed to fraternise in any way with the clients I replied enthusiastically, "Yes, a thousand times, yes!"

The conversation took a different turn. "We hear that a hundred people die every year on the mountain," said Nick, deeply concerned. "And that most deaths are altitude related."

Ann was shaken by the idea of people dying on Kilimanjaro and had became anxious. "My aunt died recently from oedema."

"Nothing to worry about," said Freddie reassuringly. "We carry emergency oxygen and if anything did happen, we could get you down and in a hospital within twelve hours."

Oh, so that was alright then.

"I can't wait," said Mary, totally unenthusiastically. But at least she had decided to come with us. Yeah! She confided in me, "I had a text from my fifteen-year-old daughter saying 'Remember in your world there's no such word as can't.' I didn't have any choice, did I?" Then she continued, "And there was a text from Maureen reminding us to keep asking for help. I do know that. I'd forgotten on Meru. Keep asking for help and help will come."

It seemed that Jackie was good at that principle.

Freddie was staring intently at her. "How's your ankle?" he asked. She couldn't fudge this answer; she had to get it right.

"It's fine," she said convincingly.

"Show me."

She managed to somehow courageously show him a normal walk, complete with a big smile on her face. Freddie hadn't seen her, as we had, limping around and using ice-packs. Also, Ann had been working on it with all her different remedies. It needed a miracle I thought, but then Ann is good with miracles. Nicholas was in need of his own miracle to make the internet connect, frustrated by all the work he wanted to do before we left.

"This is Africa, mate," said Nick.

"Maybe I'll just have to forget business."

"Good idea. I think I'll do the same."

"Jessica, how're you feeling about the climb?" asked Freddie.

"Well, the longer we talk about it, the more nervous I get. Especially after hearing about people dying. I just want to get going."

"How about you, Rima?"

"I'll be fine if I can get some sleep," she replied. "I don't seem to have connected with sleep since leaving home."

"Yeah, it certainly helps," said Jacob. "Gideon and I slept twelve hours last night and feel normal again."

There was definitely a sense of unity through the team. I hoped it would last.

Anyway I felt sure that the reading of the Peace Messages would above all bind everybody together. There's nothing like the glue of common purpose.

"Guess what," I said excitedly. "Between us we represent the whole world. Pete and Nicholas are European ..."

"We're British, if you don't mind," interrupted Pete in his best posh accent.

I glared at him and continued, "Rima, Ann and Jackie are Asian. Then Jess is North American. Jacob and Gideon represent Central and South America. Mary and Nick are from South Africa so African. I can represent the Australian continent as I have an Australian passport and we've even got the Antarctic covered with Gaius." I felt smug that this had happened apparently by chance. "This is so brilliant. We're setting out to show a focus of all nations coming together in Peace and we represent all the continents."

Afterwards we sat down to eat. "Where're Ann and Jackie?" I asked.

"Gone out."

"They can't do that! We were told it wasn't safe to go out by ourselves."

"They're scared camping in the bush or climbing on a mountain, but the fears of the nightlife of Arusha town are nothing to them."

"But why ...?"

"They couldn't bear to take on another mountain without first going out for a Chinese meal!"

Sometimes our cultural heritage is strong. And blood, as they say, or in this case sweet and sour egg foo yung, is thicker than water.

I had much to learn. School was obviously not just for youngsters.

FINAL PIECE OF THE JIGSAW

14th September, 2011 – Day One

"C'mon, beautiful," Pete urged, as always in 'go' mode from the moment he awoke. "It's climbing Kilimanjaro day! I'm taking our stay-here bags to the storeroom, so see you at breakfast."

I blinked open my eyes and stared at the soft light coming through the white mosquito netting. An early morning chorus of birds was busy trying to bring my senses into the day.

I groaned, wanting to stay in the stillness, to drift gently and to savour the enormity of what we were doing. This is it. After all the hard work to collect the Peace Messages, the trials of the Nation Messages. The preparation for the climb and the gathering of the team. The focus of the two acclimatisation mountains. Now, today, we would be on Kilimanjaro. The culmination ... No, it was more than that, far more than that. This was the final piece of our jigsaw, over a decade of work towards our six-pointed star of Peace.

I'd better get out of bed.

Excitement was in the air. It was catching, as though something was winding up our energy, stirring us into action. Everyone rushed around with bags and gathered at the Outpost entrance. Here we all posed in bright yellow T-shirts that Nick had had made for us, sporting the logo 'Kilimanjaro. Climbing Together for Peace.' Gaius posed, too. He didn't want to be left out. It's not often a penguin gets the chance to be guardian of special crystals ... crystals with the important job of holding and amplifying the energy from Peace Messages that was to close a deal with a cosmic star! I had them packed safely, wrapped in a little bag and a sparkly maroon silk scarf at the bottom of my large day rucksack, on the back of which Gaius would travel, hopefully without being too battered by rain and snow.

"Not that penguin wrecking all the photos again," said Pete with a wry smile.

"Top priority," I replied.

He shook his head and rolled his eyes, checking that he had the multi-tool in his pocket. I had the feeling he thought some things were more important to bring than penguins.

We waited while Ann sorted out the morning's special treatment for Jackie's swollen ankle, that of rolling a hot hardboiled egg over it, which is the old Chinese remedy for a bruise. At least from a vegetarian's point of view it looked better than the British equivalent of using beefsteak.

Our support team arrived. We faced them gathered in a semi-circle to greet us with a magnificent East African welcome. Freddie took the centre. He was wearing long shorts and gaiters, so Nicholas' gear was obviously the height of fashion. He was the showman through and through. Arms out high, fingers pointing he shouted, "I'm Kichawa Mlima! Mountain Madness! Karibu to Kilimanjaro!"

He then started dancing outrageously, hips swinging wildly and conducting the entire African team as they sang a repertoire of back and forth songs. These were called by a handsome young man Andrew, whose job was food server in the mess tent. Everyone clapped rhythmically, including Felix and Raymond who we knew from Meru and three other assistant guides, two young men James and Calvin and an older kindly soul named Anthony. And there were porters too numerous to count among whom I spotted Sakimba joining in the fun.

We all clapped and cheered. "Well done, guys! Magic!"

shouted Pete. Was there a better way to head out to climb a mountain? Was this how it was to be?

With the dancing hakuna matata ringing in our ears we set off in two large jeeps with our personal kit bags on the roofs tied down with tarpaulins. Even the vehicles seemed to be swaying and bouncing to the wonderful rhythms of Africa. I turned to the smiling Freddie in the seat behind me. "We would like to do a little starting ceremony to light the Peace Flame. Will this be possible?"

"Yes, of course," he replied and then suddenly looking very serious said, "On the mountain, you know ... we won't let you down."

"Asante sana, thank you," I replied warmly, knowing that he meant it whole heartedly.

And he repeated, "We won't let you down."

I had a sense then that at some greater level all was being organised, that everything had fallen perfectly into place, that the Universe was totally supporting us. I could scarcely believe how good it felt, as though all my life had been in preparation for this time.

Even when I started to feel car-sick that sense didn't leave me. I had to close my eyes and breathe deeply. I understood what the nausea meant in the way of my own inner journey. I'd experienced it before. It was a breaking down of the lower self to generate vulnerability, which encourages feelings of unconditional love. I would come to Kilimanjaro in a humble way.

I took a sickness pill when we stopped at a shop. A man approached me outside selling bracelets, so I bought a very smart brown-and-gold collar for Gaius with the word 'Kilimanjaro' embroidered into it. As we continued I still felt horribly sick. I closed my eyes and tried to hold the stillness, that healing place within and quietly asked for help in my mind. A gentle sensation of energy responded, like a guardian angel. I felt its loving presence enfolding me like the cloak of courage. I knew it was affirming that it was always there for me.

Maybe, I thought, this focus will help me on the mountain.

I opened the window and was aware of the smell of the fresh rain on the dust as we went into open savannah land travelling towards the morning sun. I moved into a deeper relaxed state.

I'm holding the team in the light. I'm here for service. See, it's like unconditional love. And Mum's here, too. She's telling me to keep in mind that Peace Message that I like so much: "Remember to keep your heart open".

Feeling better I opened my eyes to see that we had passed the airport area and were heading north, closer and closer to Kilimanjaro. It wasn't possible to see the mountain, though there was considerable cloud amassing ahead, however there was a strong sense of presence. After all we were drawing near something gigantic, something sixty kilometres wide, eighty kilometres long and six kilometres high.

Our approach in the vehicle was from the west, so we could take a variation of what's known as the Lemosho Route. This was the one, we were told, out of the handful of popular routes, that should have fewer people on it and a good chance of success due to it taking seven or eight days to reach the summit and therefore more time to acclimatise. The other routes generally lasted four or five days. This was important. A lot of people don't make it and have to turn back suffering with the effects of altitude sickness in the form of headaches, breathing difficulties, nausea and other low-oxygen states. I had read various statistics on this. The internet encyclopaedia states that sixty per cent of climbers don't make it to the summit. Out of the 30,000 or so who attempt the summit each year, that's a lot of disappointment.

The beginning of the route is rather remote to reach. After travelling around extensive rolling foothills decorated with tropical farmland, we eventually arrived at forest plantations and our vehicle stopped at a small hut to pay a forest tax. There seemed to be a problem with the porters' bus, so whilst that was being sorted out Pete and I wandered around, between piles of dried soya bean straw. We were on chocolate coloured soil, fertile due to its volcanic origins, all the nutrients and minerals brought up from below the surface, a gift from Kilimanjaro.

We chatted with a young woman radiating the joy of expectant new life. I was intrigued to hear that she had had forestry training, like me. "My African name is Aikase which means 'thank you again'."

"How lovely. What trees do you work with?"

"We manage pine and cypress. And also grevillea and acacia. It'll all be chipped and used for paper. We need more timber though. Most of our country's fuel needs come from wood, from charcoal. Oh and we have some eucalypt." She pointed to a five metre high stand behind us. "These are only one year old and will be used for poles."

"Wow. What richness here. When is your baby due?"

Her hands held her tummy and she smiled proudly, "Very soon. Very soon. She is to be called Lollan, which means 'beautiful woman'."

We left her delighted with a little gift of money for the new baby. She left us delighted with a Peace Message from the Chagga people of Kilimanjaro: "Plant more trees for the new generation." Happy at the exchange between our two cultures we climbed aboard our vehicle again and headed off through large plantations of pine. Here we spotted a ten-strong troop of colobus monkeys, little black gentlemen with shaggy white ruffs, cloaks and large bushy tails, feeding and swinging in the trees, screeching as they went. There were meant to be blue monkeys, bushbuck and even buffalo and elephant around but the only other mammal we saw was a tiny mouse scurrying across the track.

We finally arrived at Londrossi Gate, poised at 2,360 metres. This was the western gate of Kilimanjaro National Park, a UNESCO World Heritage Site since 1987 and a hive of activity. There were porters and would-be porters everywhere. The dodgy bus carrying our team of porters limped in. Out poured the 41 Africans who were to support the 11 Peace Climb Team members. What a circus. As on Meru, part of me longed to just be a small team carrying all our own needs. But then this was the local way and it meant we would be involved with the Africans themselves and importantly, giving employment.

This was their land. They were allowing us to be here.

Whilst we signed the Park entrance papers, the porters were lining up for kit inspection. They each had to carry a small personal rucksack, with an allowance of 5 kilograms in addition to 20 kilograms of the group equipment. That was a lot of paraphernalia, including our personal bags, the tents and mattresses, the cooking stuff and food. The group loads were stuffed into white canvas bags to be carried on their heads, but they looked huge and unwieldy and awkward with bits of things jutting out that would seemingly throw the carrier off balance on flat ground, never mind the steep and rough ground we expected to pass over.

But everyone seemed happy and there was an air of relaxed anticipation. I watched Sakimba chatting to some of the other porters whilst chewing a large piece of sugar cane. He smiled at me and it was at that moment that I thought I detected a sense of unease in his eyes, though I couldn't place what it was about.

The young assistant guide Calvin was brimming over with enthusiasm. He bounced up to me. "Great to have you with us, Mama. I love you." That was obviously the standard sort of greeting around these parts. Yes, I liked it. I wondered how it would go down at business meetings in the City of London.

Our Peace Climb members were pacing around, excited that finally we were about to start the main adventure. Only Ann and Jackie were peaceful, focussing quietly on healing the swollen ankle using a pendulum. The rest of us studied the huge wooden billboards with lines of rules. They kindly requested that all esteemed visitors, 'refuse and expose corruptive practices, advances and or gestures.' Ah, thank goodness we were esteemed! There was multiple advice about altitude sickness, such as if you have a sore throat or a cold do not go beyond 3,000 metres. No mention of twisted ankles, so that was alright.

Eventually it was time to leave. The strongest jeep ferried us all in turn along what might have been termed a track but more exactly was a series of rutted terracotta mud puddles through a swathe of rainforest and spewed us out into a little clearing. I looked around. Oh how lovely! We were surrounded by an abundance of large leaved equatorial foliage, dancing in a profusion of differing shades of green. Interspersed were the wide trunks of forest giants reaching to the sunlit promise of an open sky. At our feet was a carpet of soil, muddy leaves and droppings, some of which I recognised as giraffe. Tiny flowers and grasses poked up between. With a deep breath I relaxed as my nostrils took in the welcome smell of damp earth.

This was Heaven, here on the lower reaches of Kilimanjaro. Could this be one of those meeting points of Heaven and Earth? I stooped to pick up a black feather. Maybe this was a gift from the white-necked raven who squawed at our presence overhead loud above other calls and tweets and the rustly sounds of movement and life. Perhaps it held good wishes for our journey. Either that or he was thinking easy pickings of food. I placed it in my hair anyway, acknowledging our connection.

Freddie looked at home here. He told me that he'd been a guide for thirteen years and was aged thirty-six. His face lit up as he talked about his two daughters, aged eleven and five. Then he spotted something. His expression changed.

"What's *that*?" he exclaimed, pointing at the large item that Pete was preparing for the climb.

"Ah. We were going to tell you about that," I muttered. "That's our Peace-tyre. It holds all the Peace Messages. We need to pull it up the mountain."

I held my breath. Dread crept into my mind.

No doubt over the years he had had to put up with all sorts of weird and wacky stunts from his clients. Westerners are a funny lot and often attempt strange things on climbs with complete disregard for the problems that altitude has on the body, and their knock-on effects for the support team. Plus, we had no permission from the Tanzania Parks Authority. There was a lot riding on our head guide's attitude.

What would his reaction be?

KILIMANJARO
HERE WE COME

"Well," Freddie said finally, a bemused glint in his eye. "I have to say, it shows class to want to pull a tyre all the way up to the top of Africa's highest mountain."

I breathed out. I shouldn't have doubted the Universe.

Egbert, my ego, puffed out his chest with pride. "We'll be the first people to pull a tyre up Kilimanjaro."

"Go away, Egbert," I responded inwardly. "It's all about the intention we do this in. A symbolic action. A focus for the world. That we can all pull together for Peace, regardless of race, religion or status in life." It seemed to put him in his place for the moment. I would have to be more mindful of Egbert. He has a nasty habit of cropping up unexpectedly. One never can tell with egos.

By the time all the Peace Climb team and support team had gathered the little clearing sang with human activity. The head cook, dressed in an apron and red woollen cap, established a kitchen in one corner. He sat on a bucket surrounded by two camping-style gas stoves, various pots and baskets of colourful vegetables and fruit strewn over the dirt.

Quite suddenly it started to rain and there was huge clap of thunder.

"Ah, the Gods are with us!"

But it was a serious tropical downpour and in no time at all, even though the westerners rushed for their waterproofs, everyone was soaked. Apart from Pete, who wandered around smugly under his umbrella.

"It's not called a rainforest for nothing," said Mary squeezing the water out of her yellow jumper.

The blue mess tent was erected with a table and chairs and soon Andrew brought in a pot of mushroom soup, plates of vegetables and pineapple pieces, bread and thermos flasks of hot water for drinks.

"How impressive is this! On jungle facilities!"

Everyone agreed. It looked like our bodies were going to be really well fed.

I looked across the table at Rima and we exchanged glances. I knew she was feeling the same as I was. Awkward. Here were we sitting inside with a lovely lunch being well looked after, whilst everyone outside was wet and hungry. It didn't seem right. Even though we were the clients and had paid for this service, in human terms it didn't seem right. Was this how it was going to be again? Would we just have to get used to this inequality? Was this how the world was?

The rain stopped as suddenly as it had started. The tent was dismantled and we prepared to set off. But first there was something important to do. Our starting ceremony. I felt that it was important to ask for a blessing and a harmonising from the mountain itself for our journey. We all gathered round the Peace Lantern in the middle of the clearing. Pete placed the tyre there, too. The Africans looked on, intrigued. Whatever were these westerners up to now?

"We're climbing for Peace," I announced to the throng in a loud voice.

Felix asked if he should translate so I nodded. He then proceeded to raise his arms and gesticulate wildly, speaking to everyone in Swahili for the next five minutes. Wow! I knew his language in English was often elaborate and politician-like without understandings that were easy to spot, but even so he spoke for so long and with such animation that I wondered how Peace could be such a complicated concept here in Africa.

I continued, "Thank you, great Kilimanjaro for welcoming us." Then I looked round at all the different faces and raised my arms, too, caught up in excitement and the stirring of the energy at the start of this our adventure, shouting, "We are all one human family! We are one blood! We are one mind! We are one spirit!" I sensed an uplifting. "We are each one of us on this journey for Peace!" As Felix translated at length and the Africans all laughed and clapped, I wondered again what he had actually said.

Then silence. Everyone watched Ann strike a lighter and whilst Nicholas held the lantern, light the wick. I knew that both of them believed fervently in our mission for Peace, so it was lit in a loving intent of purpose. It took a little while to light. The flame burned. Nicholas carefully screwed the lantern lid over it. The flickering image shone through the glass. African and westerner, porter and client alike all stared intently for a moment at the light. There was a sense of something powerful, a light that reached far beyond just our little group.

Ann prayed, "Dear Lord, please guide us on our journey for peace up Kili. Thank you. Amen."

All the porters responded, "Amen."

Surprised at this, I looked up at all the black smiley faces. So everyone understands English fine anyway. And they appeared to be of a predominantly Christian-based faith. But more than that I had the feeling that they were with us at a heart level. We really were all in this together. We couldn't have planned their involvement this way but it was exactly what was wanted.

Freddie waved his arms at us, keen to get going as the afternoon was running out. Though he couldn't resist a merry song and dance, it appeared, out of sheer exuberance for the occasion.

Then the assistant guide Anthony, small and wiry and steady as a rock, led off with a characteristic side to side gait at a slow pace to make sure no one went too fast. Pete in his usual efficient and practical manner fixed together the long pole he'd devised on which to hang the Peace Lantern and gave one end each to Nicholas and Nick to proudly be the first guardians of the flame. The lantern swung between them as they went off, tentatively eyeing it at first and then striding along confidently. The light was small and not easy to see in the daylight, but the symbolism of what it represented was enormous as it shone out leading the way.

Jacob grabbed the tyre. "Gideon and I would like to have a go first," he said. "And this way we won't have to do it later, we'll have done our bit." He laughed flippantly, but then admitted, "You know we were kind of thrust into this Peace Climb because we wanted to do the mountain with our cousin Mary. It represents Africa and our family's always had a deep connection with Africa. And I thought the tyre was just some sort of a silly stunt. Now I'm surprised at the sincerity you guys have. And actually we're honoured to be part of this."

I watched as they took one of the rope handles each and side by side strode off. Something within my heart lurched. We're meant to be pulling the tyre. Its sign says 'Pulling Together for Peace', not 'Carrying Together for Peace'. It's really important that we pull it. And I longed to show them how to attach the front rope to their rucksacks so it could be pulled the entire way. I was stopped by Rima's laugh. She has a catchy, raucous, unmistakably Rima laugh. I looked over at her as she was setting off to lollop ahead and film everyone passing by. She could see my reaction and was watching my back as soul sisters do. And I knew what she was telling me: "Team work. You have to let go of how you've done it before and how you think it should be. To work in a team you have to let others do it their way." She was right. I smiled and relaxed. She, like me and possibly Pete, were the only ones who would really like to pull the tyre the whole way, for the mere challenge of it. The sharing was in itself a challenge for us. But we had to work together.

I watched Ann and Jackie pick up their rucksacks and set off wondering how they would manage carrying them, having needed so much help on Oldonyo Lengai and Meru. Jackie seemed to be limping only a little bit, which was encouraging. Mary went next, looking dapper in her pink flowery shorts.

And then Jess, in her fit, easy style. I shouldered my battered purple and pink rucksack, Gaius riding high in his characteristic side to side gait, grabbed my sticks and followed on behind. We had begun.

The path led us like a doorway through a dense wall of rainforest. We were heading east but the trail meandered steeply up and down and up, crossing watercourses dense with large-leaved vegetation and round trees and over logs and before long the jungle closed in, covering any sense of the sun setting behind us. Soon we could barely see the hazards that the Africans were pointing out to us – stinging plants, columns of ants and tree roots which littered the track, threatening to fell any unaware passersby.

Dusk fell quickly, understandably as we were only three degrees (around 330 kilometres), south of the equator. The dark shadow of a bat fluttered close by and somehow I felt welcomed and this helped me open my senses to the forest. I could feel aliveness. Like little lights of life all around, mirrored by the night stars above, which momentarily appeared when gaps in the tree canopy allowed. It was as though a new shift had arrived. The nocturnal shift. My untrained ear listened to the sounds and I longed to know what they were all about. What noise does leopard make? And his prey? He was meant to be around here, but we knew how elusive he was. And through the twilight and descending darkness our little Peace light seemed to burn more and more brightly.

Then: disaster.

The flame went out. Oh no! It was our symbol. Our one constant. As long as we kept the flame burning, all would be well. It was for the world. We carried the Peace light for the world. The lantern had been swaying back and forth on its journey up and over steep inclines with rough jarring movements. It couldn't have been caused by the wind could it? It must have had a blockage or lacked oxygen somehow, but then Pete had cleaned it to perfection at the start. Could it be that the altitude change in atmospheric pressure was beginning to have effect as we climbed higher? But it had been okay on the top of Meru. We waited for Ann to catch up with the lighter and it relit instantly.

Calvin took over the carrying of one end of the pole from Nick and then I took over from Nicholas. It felt so precious to carry the light, such a wonderful symbol of our journey. I loved it. Also I loved the fact that everyone was sharing the load of carrying it. Next, Sakimba took over on the other end as we climbed steeply up a muddy rooted bit where I had to hold the bar high with one hand whilst negotiating pulling on tree roots with the other to keep the lantern from swinging wildly out of control. Sakimba turned to wait for me.

That was when I was hit by the strangest feeling. I had done this before with Sakimba. Somewhere, somehow he and I had carried a light together before. Crazy as it sounds, could it have been in another lifetime? When? Why was this to be important now? Sometimes these feelings come not with any answers, but just with a strong sense of knowing. Okay, I would accept its mystery and the beauty of its mystery. I said nothing, but just enjoyed the connection of purpose it gave me. How good it was to have him with us.

After that the light went out a couple of more times. But with many hands rushing to help, between us we managed to keep it burning though this slowed down our progress. By the time we heard a gathering of human noises and the path came steeply up to a flattish spot perched amongst tall trees there was a full moon shining. It gave enough light to see a collection of tents closely together and dark human shapes moving around. We were at the ingeniously named Forest Camp, at an altitude of 2,821 metres. There was another team squashed into the site too. Every available piece of ground seemed to be taken up by tents or trunks or ropes attaching one to the other. This was Camp City.

I felt really confused. Where was our team? What were all these tents? Whose was what? Eventually, by clambering over multiple guy ropes Pete and I found the tent designated for us with our personal bags in the porch. By the light of our head-torches we could see two big mattresses in an inner little 'room' that zipped up against the insects (and I supposed anything larger that might venture our way, such as snakes, though any self-respecting snake would I'm sure have already slithered off to some quieter evening's entertainment.) It all felt damp and rather strange, but it was home. Pete and I high-fived. We had survived Day One.

The cook and porters must have travelled a lot faster than us, as we enjoyed a wonderful dinner of soup and fish and vegetables to the light of the Peace Lantern and two candles speared into potatoes. Everyone seemed tired and in a rush to get to bed, but there was important work to do.

The first of the Peace Messages had to be read. I handed round the papers to all of the client team plus Felix, Calvin and Sakimba and one by one in a circle we spoke out around 400 Messages.

We included the Silent Minute Prayer: "Source of my being, help me to live in Peace and save my home, the planet Earth." It was good to know that we were joining the millions around the world who focus in at 9pm to help Peace with this collective power of positive thinking and prayer.

It took us around an hour. Ah, wonderful. Mission for Day One accomplished. Now we could retire to our tents and relax.

Or so I thought. Leaving our daysacks in the end part of our tent's porch, we unpacked the sleeping bags and night-kit from our personal bags. This was when we discovered what we had actually packed. Things like the house keys from home and the cat's hairbrush! Pete stuffed his duvet jacket into a pillowcase for his head. I just arranged Gaius comfortably. The list of essentials to bring had not included penguins, but sometimes one must show initiative in life.

Even with such luxury, sleep eluded me, thanks to an upset stomach that churned all night. My body must have been letting go of something. Timing could have been better. It was not the easiest thing to crawl out of my sleeping bag, noisily unzip and zip up the two tent doors, climb through the cats cradles of guy ropes, twanging them as I went and search for the bucket-sized tent with bucket inside which worked as the loo. Thank goodness for the full moon.

I was exhausted and shaky by the time morning came and barely had the energy to appreciate that every day we were to be woken with a bowl of washing water and mugs of tea. Or in my case a mug of hot water. But today, there was a different sort of wake up call.

Nick poked his head into the doorway of our tent, looking concerned. "Tess, come quick. They're sending Sakimba home."

FACING THE LION

15th September, 2011 – Day Two

Oh no! Not again! Sakimba couldn't be denied climbing with us again. What was going on?

I remembered how desperately upset he'd been last time this had happened at the foot of Oldonyo Lengai. After that it can't have been easy for him to have found a way to actually travel across to Arusha and wangle his way into the porters' team for Kilimanjaro. And then to work with those in an already close-knit team from different tribes as an outsider. I knew of a couple of other Maasai on the support team, but they were local and had been living in a town lifestyle. Sakimba was still very much part of his village, part of the land, part of the old way of being in harmony with the Earth.

I felt Sakimba's pain. It was as though he had to continue to face his lion.

Mary and I went to find Felix to ask him about the situation. He was his usual polite self but explained, "Sakimba hasn't been following the procedures for the porters."

I smiled to myself. I could see that he would follow the laws of the Earth above all other procedures.

"We have to have a team that works," Felix insisted.

"Of course we understand, but we feel in part he's here because of us," said Mary. "We feel responsible."

"He has to go home," Felix replied firmly.

"Isn't there anything you can do?" I pleaded.

"No. The decision has been made. He has to go home."

"But ..."

At this point I spotted Sakimba, his wool hat pulled down over his hanging head. Wretchedness spilling over.

"What is going on?" I asked him gently.

"I just want to carry the light for Peace," he said.

A lump became stuck in my throat, "We know the situation. It feels just like before doesn't it?"

He nodded dejectedly.

One of the porters went by and shouted "Peace and Love!" Everyone, it seemed, was embracing the spirit of the climb, but just at the moment it was too ironic.

Felix spoke to Sakimba, "You'll have to walk back down to the road-head and make arrangements to find your way home from there."

I took a moment to ask inwardly what's the highest thing we can do here, helping me stand back to see the bigger picture. My answer was simple and clear. Just hold the situation in the light. Okay, then. I pictured a loving thought bubble around us all.

Just then Freddie appeared and took Felix aside to find out what was happening. He must have seen the concerned look on our faces.

Felix stated, "Okay Sakimba, you can come if you do what you're told."

Thank goodness. Hugs and smiles and sighs of relief. I wondered if it was tribal politics again. At least this time we didn't have a repeat situation and things had moved forward. Sakimba smiled; I could see the spark in his good eye. Ah, the lion lived on in him.

I rushed to pack my sleeping bag and personal kit ready for the waiting porters to carry, along with the tents. Also I threw down some breakfast of ginger tea and toast and honey, hoping that hot food would settle my griping tummy. The problem with Sakimba had been resolved. At least for the moment.

The support team started their joyful singing. My spirits again lifted.

Anthony once again led off. "Polé, polé!" he told everyone. "Even slower today and you'll adapt to the increasing altitude. Make your foot hover before you put it down." Rima wanted to take the tyre but Jess, looking striking in a blue sunhat and pigtails decided that she was going to be the first today and actually carry it over one shoulder. This would need a certain amount of strength, but she seemed to manage it impressively with no problem and a big smile. She was, after all, trained by the US air-force.

Rima took Jess's rucksack for her and wore it on her front, as well as her own on her back. I already knew that Rima's strength of mind would enable her to carry as many rucksacks as she decided to. She and Mary took one end each of the pole with the lit-up Peace light swaying between them. Nicholas, Nick and the London warriors set off chatting away happily, looking well rested from the night's sleep. Although I couldn't understand quite why Jacob had a gangster-like scarf over his mouth. It appeared to be since Nick had complained that he never stopped talking politics. Ann followed serenely, tuning in with gentle prayer. And then Jackie.

"How's your ankle today?" Pete asked, keeping an eye on the weaknesses and strengths of our team.

"Yeah, it's great now," she replied confidently, shouldering her daysack with its yellow waterproof covering. A white bandage over the swelling told a different story, but the important thing was that she was positive. She was showing courage. She had Ann's constant support. And I'd seen Raymond carrying that sack on his front yesterday, so she was being helped by the guides. It wasn't long today before I saw James carrying it on his front. Ah, I thought, her sweet smile will get her anywhere. I just hope that anywhere includes the summit of Kilimanjaro.

The forest welcomed us with its morning beauty as we took the trail up. Bird music accompanied us and it was possible to pick up the high pitched calls of the blue monkey, common here. Mostly the gradient was steadily upwards but at times we were clambering steeply out of little watercourse ravines heading east towards a high ridge.

Porters soon began passing us carrying impossible looking loads, some on their necks and some on their heads. Mostly they travelled fluidly as though it was all fun and easy. No doubt happy that whatever else they would be able to feed their young families. We realised that the first group must be with the other team that had been at the Forest Camp with us. They greeted us with "Jambo" and passed without a trace into the forest from whence they'd come. When greetings became "Peace and Love" or "Mambo Jambo" we knew they had to be from our team. Many stopped to give us a three staged handshake that said "Cool, Man!"

Sakimba carried Jackie's big rucksack as his porter's load with his own small allocated sleeping bag tied on behind. That appeared to be all the personal gear he brought. Happily he didn't have to stay with the other porters but managed to walk with our Peace Climb team and the guides.

I would have felt good, except for one small problem. Well, it may have been a small problem as far as I could see for everyone else. But it gnawed away at me. It was actually a huge problem. The light in the Peace Lantern wouldn't stay lit.

There was plenty of fuel. We weren't much higher than 3,000 metres so there had to be loads of oxygen in the air. I remembered we had lit a lantern on the Millennium Climb at 6,176 metres, the point nearest the sun at the turn of the Millennium in the Andes, when we had been given the honour of being the first to take the World Peace Flame to South America. At that altitude, as it would be on the summit of Kilimanjaro, there is only half the amount of oxygen that there is at sea level. Surely now at half this altitude there shouldn't be a problem. But it wouldn't stay lit. Everyone had turns at relighting it. It would last for a little bit and then blow away like a dandylion wisp in the wind.

"I can see no technical reason why it won't stay alight. It must be the movement," Pete said as Nicholas and Sakimba took over the pole. "But all this stopping is too much delay for our schedule. Freddie's team won't like it. We'll just have to carry it without the flame." He saw the look of anguish on my face. "Anyway that's how the World Peace Flame generally travels and is relit at its destination. We can light it every evening at dinner." There were resigned comments of agreement.

I was heartbroken. I had always envisaged us on Kilimanjaro with the flame lit the entire way. It was so symbolic. The light for Peace leading the way; the beacon of hope. I felt like crying and turned away, overwhelmed by the consensus of the team. But I could do nothing to change it.

I walked along a little way behind the others, head hanging low, feeling heavy. Surely this couldn't be happening? I had experienced disappointment before, but this was not a personal thing. It was not disappointment for me. This was for the world. So why did it feel like my failure and that I had let Kilimanjaro down? I held the talisman on my necklace between my fingers and connected up with the mountain, speaking softly, "I'm sorry Great Kilimanjaro," and brushed a tear from my cheek. In response I received a mind picture of a lion. Oh, was I facing a lion too?

And then I thought of Sakimba and his resolution to be with us and climb for Peace. And the Maasai spirit. Remembering my cloak of courage, I visualised it enfolding me. I am a warrior too. A Peace warrior. I lifted my head and relaxed my shoulders, brushing past overgrown lianas dangling across the path. That's when it came to me. I smiled to myself. I'd never actually promised Kilimanjaro that we would be carrying the light for Peace physically lit. Just that we would be carrying the light for Peace. Yes, Pete was right. The World Peace Flame energy was carried by candles and lanterns and it didn't actually matter whether they were lit or not. The energy was just as powerful either way and could be physically lit at any time. In the same way that my senses had been open to the lights of life in the forest last night, now I would be open to holding the flame lit by the light in my heart, the light in all our hearts.

"Of course," agreed Mary as I explained the turmoil in my mind. "We can hold it lit from our hearts."

What a wonderful lesson I felt I had learnt. I had to remember. It would mean a connection with the flame that I didn't have before. This was a time of growth. Thanks, Universe. It would be nice to have some warning when these lessons are coming along. But thanks anyway.

There was something else to think about. My turn came to have the tyre. I jumped at it. At last! I attached the end of the lead rope to the cord loop on the back of my rucksack via the karabiner. "Come along Peace-tyre," I said affectionately, and was off. Yeah! It felt so right. My shoulders and hips took the strain, my leopard skin gaitered legs strode along contentedly, arms swinging backwards and forwards with the sticks. My heart sang.

Why, you well may ask, does pulling a tyre along the ground make one happy? Very good question. Maybe the short answer is that it's fun. And if something amuses you in life then it's going to work more easily. The long answer of course was the expression of the symbolism for what we were doing. Pulling together for Peace. Like the Peace light, it was the focus for our mission. It gave great purpose to the moment. Sometimes it's easy to drift along without any great purpose. How good it feels to have a dynamic reason for existing.

As we came to a steep pitch strewn with heavy roots Calvin, undertaking his job of assisting the clients wherever possible, picked up the tyre behind me. My ego immediately jumped up and down, annoyed. "Oy! I want to do this all by myself."

"Egbert, go away," I sighed and cast a grateful glance at Calvin.

By the time both Calvin and James had picked up the tyre behind me he was mad with rage. "I'm perfectly capable of pulling a tyre up a hill!"

Rima, who was photographing me, laughed. "You're going to have to let people help, you know. Everyone wants to help."

"I know. I know," I replied. "But it's not easy is it?"

"It's a very good lesson."

Oh no. Not more lessons! They're like busses. I'm aware of none for ages and then suddenly they all come along at once.

But by the time Calvin took over carrying the light and Sakimba came to help me, guiding the tyre from behind with the tail rope, Egbert was firmly put in his place and I was concentrating on working within the team. I would get there. Everybody has to be part of working together. And wasn't it lovely that everyone wanted to help. Wasn't it?

We all paused to study a large bees' nest at the side of the trail, precariously perched in the dead branches of a bush. Vulnerable as it looked the old bees know a thing or two. They know that by all working together they can create something greater than the sum of the parts. Service for the hive. Maybe I could learn from them.

The track became steep as we climbed steadily and gradually a change became apparent. The forest around us was less thick. We were open to more sky. And the vegetation was different. Gone were the large trees. They had been replaced by impenetrable people-high heathers. We were heading into expansive moorland, a different geographic zone entirely. Kilimanjaro holds representations of all the lands on Earth. We had come through equatorial grasslands and forest and were heading into moorland. After that we would be in volcanic desert and then polar icecap. In some ways it was a bit like walking from the equator to the Antarctic or the Arctic. So here was a nice comfy well-rounded sort of thought that the final mountain of our six-pointed star pulled together all the eco-regions of our planet.

And also a nice comfy sort of thought that it was time to stop for lunch. Not just a sandwich sitting on a rock by the side of the track. Oh no. All set for the Kili-cuisine, the tables were out, gaily decorated by checked green cloths and chairs with armrests to collapse into. The tables were loaded with china plates and bowls, there was a large pan of hot soup, noodles, bread and sauces and peanut butter and flasks of hot water for a variety of drinks. What more could a worn-out Peace Climb team ask for?

A large familiar black bird standing alongside looked as though he had one or two ideas.

"Hello, white-necked raven," I said.

He put his head on one side as though listening.

"You again."

He stared impassively at me.

"Anyone would think you're following us. So what's your part in all this? Are you acting as some sort of guide?"

He began to strut up and down, pontificating.

"So you are, eh? Tell me how do you white-necked ravens communicate between each other? Do you send out 'Peace Climb alerts' from one of you to the next?"

I could've sworn he puffed out his chest and folded his wings neatly behind his back.

"Are all the individuals of your species working together as one? Do you have a joint shared mind? Could it be that humans have a joint shared mind? Maybe even with all beings?"

He paused and looked at me out of the corner of his eye, a piercing, beady eye. There was no question it was intelligent. Maybe even wise.

I laughed. "Well, thanks for watching over us, anyway. We're going to make it to the top of the mountain, you know. And I guess it's good that the natural systems appear to be on our side, too."

With this he flew off with one easy flapping of wings and soared high into a wide sky full of hazy clouds.

He may not have had the lunch he was after, but we stuffed so much food into ourselves that it was difficult to sleepily gather, ready for the afternoon's struggle.

"Looks tricky from here on up," said Gideon. "And we're getting into the altitude that caused us so much trouble on Meru."

"It'll be a piece of cake," said Pete.

He and I took the lantern. Nicholas started off taking the tyre. The terrain was steeply undulating, thickly carpeted with a now dryer-type vegetation. From time to time between descending mists we had a birds-eye view of the folds of these, the lower slopes of Kilimanjaro which were now all too obviously chaotic. There didn't seem to be an easy route

139

to follow. The trail zigzagged in a generally eastern direction and then to the southeast as we started to climb the Shira Ridge. It stretched steeply upwards with a drop on either side. Its surface consisted of scattered boulders.

This was not good tyre-pulling country, even for expert tyre-pullers like us … well, some of us, that is. Anyway no one had the choice. Sakimba decided that this was a job for an experienced warrior. He grabbed the tyre tightly, holding its considerable weight in one hand and carried it boldly onwards. From then on it involved negotiations to prise it off him.

As it happened this was quite a good thing. The weather started to roar at us. The sky darkened. Wind arose. Thunder clapped and stalked around threateningly. We all rushed to put on waterproofs, except for Nick who couldn't find his and Pete who already had his on as he knows about these things. Then the rain came. First it just poured down. Then it came in torrents. By the time the hail came we were all soaked through anyway, so this was the icing on the cake to make us really cold. The gradient of the ridge eased somewhat and from the top of the ridge there was meant to be a great view across the plateau. Ah well. In heavy cloud we followed the path down the other side into camp. It was named Shira 1. The altitude was 3,505 metres. Today, after around eight hours we had travelled almost eight kilometres and climbed about 800 vertical metres.

The camp felt forlorn. There was one dilapidated little ranger hut and loads of muddy flat exposed space in between rocks for our team's tents. There were no other teams around. The porters' tent, the cook tent and the mess tent was not yet up, so no hot drinks. Our six client tents were. Thank you porters, I thought, at this moment it was lovely not to have to put our own tents up. Though thoughts of drying out were dashed on seeing puddles inside them. Cold and tired and shivery I curled up out of the wind clutching my still nauseous stomach, feeling only dampness and chaos and misery.

Eventually the rain stopped. At dusk the guides wanted to take everyone up on a little climb to the top of Shira Ridge to an altitude of 3,959 metres to gain some acclimatisation.

This was utilising the old successful technique of 'climb high, sleep low', to prepare the bodies for less oxygen. Rima, Jess, Mary, Nick and the London warriors were developing altitude headaches, so it was important for them to do this. Nicholas, knight in training, as always with an accepting smile on his face, and Pete, no doubt in need of some knightly exercise, joined them too.

Ann and Jackie were too tired to go. I decided to huddle round a candle in the mess tent with them to try and dry out. Ann confided, "There's a good possibility that Jackie and I won't make it. We'll go as far as we can. The important thing is that someone carries the crystals and places them on the summit. Some of us may have to go down, but at least somebody has to make it."

"Yeah, don't worry Ann," I replied trying to put her at ease. "I know there's going to be six people. I've always seen six people there." Anyway, however bad I felt, it just wasn't in my thought pattern to not make it.

Although feeling low we could do the important job of reading out the day's Peace Messages. As always some of the ones from young children really touched and lifted us; "I wish that my sister was not disabled, but I pledge to help make all disabled have a good life."

Andrew and his assistant kept the flasks filled up with ginger tea. Ah, how that brought warmth and comfort to my stomach. I vowed never to go anywhere without ginger tea again.

Later, warm at last in sleeping bags, Pete and I phoned my son Scott to wish him happy birthday on the satellite phone. We had brought it with us to phone Ivy when the crystals were placed on the summit and also to let everyone keep in touch with their families when mobiles weren't working, but most of all from my personal point of view to be connected to Scott and Nella for news of the birth of my grandson. How wonderful it was to speak from a tent on a faraway mountain. No news yet. Officially two days to go til the birth. If he hasn't arrived in four days time Nella would be induced. They were on tenterhooks, but all was well.

I said, "Sending loads of love from here, though it's been a bit cold and damp and miserable. I so wish I could be with you."

"Mum," Scott replied, "there's always problems, but remember you are on an adventure!"

He was right. I'd almost lost the joy of the adventure that each moment holds. Yes, I must remember how good it is to really live in the present moment with the excitement of not knowing what is around the next corner.

We should always listen to our children.

To my great delight I was then able to speak with my granddaughters Elsie and Bess. They sang me their favourite song, *Twinkle Twinkle, Little Star*.

"Thank you, Darling One," I said to Elsie then asked, "What's Daddy having for his birthday?"

"We're getting him a baby," was the reply.

WOUNDED KNIGHT

16th September, 2011 – Day Three

I was concerned at being so far away for the impending birth of my grandson, though I knew that somehow it was connected to our mission, our 'new birth of Peace' mission.

"You can't change things. All is as it is," Pete said reassuringly with a long overdue cuddle. It's not always easy keeping a relationship going happily, even when you are on the same adventure. And with a large team to relate to, the 'couple' bit can get taken for granted. Then at last we connected with a good sleep.

I wasn't sure if it was the familiar call of the white-necked raven that woke me or the guys shouting "Tea", but I opened my eyes feeling different. Everything felt clearer. Great what sleep can do. It was cold. There must have been a good frost. I went through the interesting process of washing and getting dressed inside my sleeping bag to keep warm, and made sure I took my pills. Whilst Pete was taking his twice daily half a Diamox, the standard altitude sickness prescription like the other men on our team, I took my glyco-nutrient supplements. I was also trying ginkgo biloba which I'd read was meant to be good and added both ginger and ginseng tablets to see if they helped the altitude effect. They felt useful to me. And most importantly the homeopathic remedy coca which I already knew helped me, being careful to suck a pill mindfully and gratefully. There was surely no need at this altitude to take the malaria remedy I'd been taking lower down.

Pulling on my duvet jacket and flip-flops, I headed out of the tent. The heavy cloud and dampness of yesterday had gone. The sky was clear blue with just wispy bits of white. And today for the first time there was wind, but it wasn't this that grabbed my attention. Looking east into the dazzling morning sun, around fifteen kilometres away and magnificent in its presence, stood the higher slopes of Kilimanjaro, known as Kibo. For the first time we were close enough to see the huge outer crater rim along the skyline. I was mesmerised. "Hello brother Kilimanjaro," I spoke. "Thank you for playing your part in our Peace Climb. I stand with you." And smiled to myself at what we were undertaking.

Then it struck me. I was staring at a mountain mostly the colour of deep indigo blue. From this view there was only a small amount of white. This consisted of heavy ice along the top, tongues of glacier reaching down and patches of snow clinging a bit further down. Even though it was the end of the dry season and I'd read that the icecap has shrunk by eighty per cent in the last century, still I was surprised by the lack of snow. I had always envisaged a solid snow-capped peak. Maybe as we ventured further we would see more.

My preconceived picture was partly due to the different meanings of the name Kilimanjaro that I'd read about. 'Shining' ... yes indeed something so immense surely had to be shining. 'Mountain of greatness' ... There was no doubt about that. 'White mountain' ... well, something had changed there. It was no longer physically white, but there certainly was a sense of light emanating from it. Perhaps all of these names mean the same anyway. Though I particularly liked 'white mountain' as it was the same as that of our Pacific Climb on the world's tallest mountain, Mauna Kea in Hawai'i on the opposite side of the globe. There was something nice and happy and balanced about that.

Certainly my stomach was a little more balanced today and tackled excellent porridge at breakfast. I grabbed some dry bread and honey to take with me. It seemed that the rest of the team was not eating all it could and was slightly subdued. Except for Rima who was also struggling with her stomach and lack of sleep but was outwardly upbeat as always. "It's only the altitude sickness. I even get that on Snowdon at 1,000 metres!" she said. "My strategy is to take things slow and easy." There's a first for everything.

I reluctantly forced my feet into boots still wet from yesterday, Yuk! Ann had tried wearing plastic bags on top to try and keep hers dry, but I don't think it had made much difference, except to her fashion credentials. Added to which she now had nicely burnt boots trying to dry them on the cooking fire. Apparently, she and Jackie had a Chinese laundry set up in their tent, so the morning tea porter had to face the hazard of smelly socks in his face on entering. At least the weather today seemed better for drying out our gear as we went along.

Freddie gathered everyone for the morning song and dance. This time he grabbed Mary who was wearing charming pink trousers. "Ah, good to see Miss Vogue is up for it," said Pete. Interesting how new names are born and can change how you feel about yourself and how other people feel about you. She was pulled into the limelight and forced to dance outrageously too. She rose to the occasion beautifully. Ah those teenage years at night clubs had not been wasted. Before long everyone was clapping and smiling too. Could this ritual be useful at the beginning of tense sessions at London's Houses of Parliament, aiding positive top-government decisions? Could it similarly be useful around the world?

Or perhaps all that was needed was for government members to hold the Peace Flame in their hearts like we remembered to do now adding to our feeling of being in good spirits as we shouldered our rucksacks and set off on Day Three. Sakimba had the Peace Lantern, which meant that he wasn't fighting for his self-imposed responsibility to take the tyre. This left it available, much to Rima's delight. It was her turn to pull. "We need to call our tyre 'Amani' since that means 'Peace'," she said.

"Excellent idea." How could anyone argue with that.

Amani bumped and tumbled happily along behind Rima, over flattish but rocky ground weaving between the stunted heathers. Until a shout came from Pete, "Oy! Not so much pulling the tyre upside down. Watch out for the bolts holding on the screws. We don't want to lose the Peace Message tubes." At least he hadn't seen Jess and Jackie actually claiming rides sitting in the tyre. That had tested the precious bolts!

Calvin came to help and he and Rima carried Amani between them. "I know we're not all pulling the tyre together as we had imagined," she said to me. "But this is a good solution. We'll carry together. It's about us. We are one family. Let's go. Twendai. Polé, polé." It wasn't til she disappeared behind a large rock for the third time that it became obvious she was being frequently sick. She waved everybody onwards with, "Don't worry. I'm just giving myself to the mountain. It's an important ritual."

Ah, the natural elements will love that. It's the African way. I will give a little of me and you will give a little of you ...

Nick came and took the tyre from her. He carried it on his back. "Well, this is a new method. Humping together for Peace!"

By now all the porters, similarly heavily loaded up, were overtaking us. African and client exchanged "Poa!", "Jambo!", "Peace and Love", "Yeah!" and the special handshake. Team spirit and comradeship were building up.

"We have to get the porters involved with the Peace Message readings," Rima said.

"I agree. We cannot leave anyone out. I'm sure they'll get brave soon."

A new porter came by carrying a basket on his head. Oh, it was Pete. He was trying out the head method. I couldn't see us using it though on English trips to the supermarket. Better to stick to pulling groceries in a tyre! In spite of his fooling about I sensed he was a bit dodgy. Was the altitude sickness attacking him?

"Are you okay?"

"Yeah, but I'm actually having more difficulty breathing here than at sea level."

"Bad?"

He nodded.

Hmm. Didn't sound like my knight in shining armour, but then he had had altitude problems in the Antarctic.

Ann, as always looking out for others, offered him some special water that she called holy water which had been blessed by Ivy with prayer and positive light for the journey. "I'm feeling good," she said, "Every step a prayer for the light. It seems to work."

That reminded me how much I missed time to myself and some meditation time to be with the mountain. It was hard to find it with a big team to chat to, lovely as that was. I hung back a little and tuned in to my own stillness. I looked at the mountain, held myself in the light and relaxed.

I know that when I hold this high inner state I don't need Diamox. Hmm. Interesting.

I see the spirit of Kilimanjaro as pillars of light, just like the experience of the spirit of Antarctica as pillars of light two years ago on our last Peace Climb. The vision brings tears to my eyes.

Then I see shining spirit clouds dance on Kilimanjaro and I know the wonderful circle of support of gathering energies. My eyes well up again. This has been planned forever. Everything needed is here.

The voice of Calvin brought me back with a start. "Mama, tell me. What is your star of Peace?"

"Ah, well ... it's a six-pointed star depicting perfect harmony which we're kind of painting across the Earth, by sending off Peace Messages from six far points. We've already done North Pole and South Pole, Himalayas and Andes, and Pacific. That leaves only Africa to complete. This is it. This is Africa."

"Wow! And I'm part of it ..."

"Yes you are, an important part. The place of harmony, the star, is made up of two triangles coming together. I suppose it's like physical and spiritual forces coming together. Kind of like the meeting place of Heaven and Earth. One triangle is the physical Earth reaching up to the Heavens. The other is the Divine reaching down to Earth. They interlock, creating the six-pointed star. Whichever way up it's always a six-pointed star. Always a state of balance and harmony.

"My family name is Hermany."

"Nice synchronicity." I smiled and continued, "The six-pointed star is a very ancient sacred symbol used by many peoples over the ages. The healing group I work with, the White Eagle Lodge, they use it."

"This gives you strength?"

"Yes, and my belief in the work that we're doing. And you can see why it's so exciting now. Why our Kilimanjaro Peace Climb is so important. It's the final point of the Earth which brings all the other ones together.

"You are Maasai Mama," he stated.

I didn't quite understand what he meant, unless he was referring to the Maasai sensitivity of working in balance with the Earth. But Sakimba, who had been listening alongside us, seemed to understand perfectly. "Yes, she is a Peace warrior. It is for Earth healing."

I smiled and kept walking, negotiating tricky boulders littered across the path. I felt slightly overwhelmed by the power and responsibility of what we were doing. So to change the subject I asked Sakimba, "What do you believe happens when a Maasai dies?"

He replied, "All Maasai spirits go to Oldonyo Lengai, mountain of God, for healing. Then they come back to the same family for more lives. This happens again and again. So you see we are one family."

This gave me a wonderful thought. What if my new little grandson-to-be is the reincarnation, say, of my father who passed on quite a few years ago now? I laughed at the silliness of it, but the idea brought a lump to my throat.

I looked towards our mountain top shrouded in white cloud and over the plateau below it saw the reds, yellows and multi-colours of our team snaking its way across the sparse olive green heathers.

"We are one family!" I shouted.

"One family!" echoed Felix up ahead.

"Hakuna matata!"

"For Peace!"

Freddie was bringing up the rear. "Don't do too much thinking!" he shouted.

"Yeah! Think with your heart!" I shouted back.

Further sounds of our human group communicating wafted over the vast open moorland, carried with the wind. I loved the feeling. It was almost as though this journey was the gestation period for the coming together of the entire team. We were bonding stronger every day. There was a lovely sense that everyone was looking out for everyone else.

I was particularly worried about Pete. He looked decidedly wobbly. I waited for him whilst he went behind a boulder. Ann came by.

"I keep seeing light floating around the mountain," she confided.

"Yes, me too," I replied. It was good to have a connection with her about the sensitivity which we both had but which others might think weird. No, which others definitely did think weird! Apart from Jackie who heeded Ann. I told her about my vision.

"Yes," she confirmed. "Master Advarr has told me too that if I hold myself in a higher vibrational state, then I don't need Diamox and I won't get altitude sickness." She plodded steadily on.

I knew it was no good saying anything like that to Pete. It didn't make sense at a practical and sensible level. But his face was now looking drawn and grey around the edges.

"How are you, my dear brother?" Calvin came up and asked him compassionately. Well, that sort of comment has to make one feel better whatever one's belief, doesn't it?

"Not too brilliant. Low energy. But nobody said it was going to be easy, did they?" he replied and smiled.

"Drink lots of water. Polé, polé."

We continued on a flattish though rock-strewn track with expansive views across the wild plateau. We were on one of Kibo's lava flows. Calvin was pulling the tyre. I directed from behind with the tail rope. As we walked he asked me, "Do you have many tribes in England?"

"Well, sort of, but things are different ..."

"I'd like to visit one day."

"You will. You will if you want to enough."

Then he told me, "I'm from the Chagga tribe. Traditionally we revere Kilimanjaro in many ways, such as burying our dead facing the summit; or the side of a village nearest the mountain being the honourable side where important meetings take place. And in return the snows have always been there for us, to support life. The old tribal ways are still significant, especially the names. You can call me by my real name – Monisi – if you like."

"Sure, Monisi."

He continued, "I'm already 24 years old and very keen to go to college, but as I have no parents I'm earning some money with this guiding job so that my younger sister can go through college first."

His love and sacrifice for his sister was humbling.

He continued, "I'd like to leave my coming-of-age bracelet at the summit as part of your ceremony. I wear it continuously. It's special to me. It'd be as a gift from my tribe for Peace. Would you mind?" He showed me the shiny solid chain on his wrist.

"We'd be honoured," I smiled.

Amani, like Peace, jumped around and settled every now and again. I tried to keep it in balance. It was a nice job, and better than trying to carry one side of the tyre which I found too heavy. My problem was that whilst actually pulling the tyre or the beautiful job of carrying the Peace Lantern it was impossible to also scribble in my diary. I was actually becoming quite adept at doing that whilst just walking along. Though I was sure there was a good chance of not being able to read my writing later. But we all changed jobs frequently and tyre and lantern passed from person to person in a sort of natural flowing motion. There was always someone keen to take the next stint.

I think everyone was glad that the blue mess tent had been put up for the lunch stop. The wind was quite severe and we all collapsed gratefully at the respite. Those of us not feeling nauseous tucked into yummy soup and rice and beans.

Even Rima tried to force some food down, doubtful though that it would stay there. It was stifling hot. But Mary said, "It'll cool down. Sakimba says that the mountain has told him it'll rain later."

"Hmm, a pretty handy sort of weather forecasting service."

We had a short Peace Message session. The sentiments helped keep our thoughts on the bigger picture: "May the winds blow love, Peace and harmony to all the corners of the world." And as it was taking over an hour to speak the daily allocations, doing some now relieved the evening session when everyone was tired after a long day on the trail.

After lunch Pete was struggling with a severe headache and not good at all. We were now approaching 4,000 metres, the zone within which it was possible to contract cerebral oedema. This can be life-threatening. I knew all about that from my experience on Chimborazo in the Andes when I was certain that I was going to die. I wouldn't wish that on anyone. Altitude sickness was not something to be taken lightly. From our previous expeditions we knew too that it was something that often afflicts the strongest and fittest. We tended to forget this, perhaps because there seems to be no rhyme or reason to it.

Certainly, people die every year from it on Kilimanjaro. I'd read in the British newspapers discussions on why so many people are taking such great health risks by being on this mountain. I think it's because that without the altitude it would be the easiest of the world's high mountains to climb. Without the altitude ... The statistics were that above 3,000 metres as we had been for 24 hours, 75 per cent of people have symptoms of some sort, ranging from vomiting, headaches, difficulty sleeping or problems with coordination.

Thankfully I felt good at the moment and my thought processes seemed about as chaotic as normal. Sakimba carried Pete's sack for him and made sure he stopped frequently for water. I thought of the times Pete had carried my sack for me like this on top of his own.

Our trail took us past a tiny stream with frogs croaking and small fish sploshing. Then up and down jagged volcanic ravines and up across rugged open country. Sometimes we were using hands to guide us alongside rocks. I loved the hard rough feel of them. Even though the sun had now disappeared behind threatening cloud it was beautiful. The way was decorated with little tussocky clumps of dry white flowers known as everlastings and heavy leaved whorled plants like groundsel and the giant lobelia that somehow found ways to colonise this harsh landscape.

The best thing was the cave. We came across it suddenly at the side of the track. A huge long overhanging roof enticing us in. It looked as though it had been formed by molten lava that had unexpectedly solidified, leaving large gaseous holes. The ground and some of the ledges were carpeted by rare grass. It was the sort of place that said to me, "Now let's wait here a couple of months and see what we can think and discover." I had been talking to Raymond when we found it. He was proudly carrying a Peace sign on the back of his rucksack. I discovered that his real tribal name was Lema, so was reminded again of the two worlds the Africans seemed to live in. We entered into the shelter of the cave. There was a feeling of direct contact with the Earth. Almost a tangible loving energy. "Wow," I said, "How beautiful. This is magic."

"What's magic?"

"It's the meeting point of visible and invisible."

"No, I think maybe this is God."

"Yes, God is magic."

"So, same thing."

"Yes, same thing." It was as though this exchange of our deepest thought processes, happening between us all, was an opening to the brother energy that was needed for the work ahead.

I took some pictures of others in the cave. It was whilst taking one of Sakimba with his arm round Jess that I noticed how affectionately he looked at her. Ah, I thought, how lovely. That's more than brother energy. Had he lost his heart to her? I didn't think then how many problems that could create. But I knew Jess to be at a turning point in her life and that she was relishing the opportunity that a major adventure was giving her to stand back from life to see things from a different perspective. Anyway her middle name was Love, so she was bound to be okay!

As we left I was aware of being followed by swathes of bright mist that Ann and I called 'spirit cloud'. She had been singing as she walked and I heard the words of her sweet voice over and over again in my brain, "Healing, healing for Peace". I was reminded that we were on a sacred journey.

The welcoming sight of our tents came just as the rain started. The only other dwelling, was an old pyramidal hut in a state of collapse up against a sheer rock face behind. The camp seemed a perfect site set apart for us and made me feel that precious thought. I'm home. We found the right tent and I unpacked our sleeping bags so Pete could collapse into his whilst I arranged some ginger tea for him. This was Moir Hut, meaning 'heart' in Swahili. At this, the end of Day Three, we had ascended 650 metres, travelled 9.5 kilometres and were now at an altitude of 4,166 metres.

However it wasn't the end of the day for poor Rima and Jess. They had a compulsory acclimatisation walk to do as they were behind with this important process. The rest of us ate popcorn and read out Peace Messages.

Rima and Jess came back for supper in good spirits, bringing a red curly wig with them. They had obviously been supplied with a different kit list from the rest of us. That was enough to set the entire tired team into ridiculous fits of giggles. Particularly when Pete actually fell asleep at the table wearing it. An interesting type of senior moment! After our nightly feast came the nightly ritual – the filling up of our water bottles with precious hot water.

It took a long time for the support team to heat enough water for us all. At least at this camp there was a stream close by. We all knew that this was the way to have a warm sleeping bag and hold some warmth for the night. It made all the difference for a good night's sleep and everyone became quite anxious to make sure they had a hot water bottle. Tonight, Nick made a big sacrifice. He gave his water bottle to Pete. "I shall donate mine to Dr Death here," he said. Pete would not forget that kindness in his hour of need, though he wasn't so sure about the new name. Certainly, that sort of deed doesn't go unnoticed at the gates of Heaven!

I lingered before going into our tent, looking up at the vast night sky. The only sound was the friendly chatter of the crew in their tent. Would my little one be born tonight? Which star-beam would he come in on? There were a million stars. It was so beautiful. The Milky Way was clear. Here on this part of the Earth there is no light pollution and we were above the clouds and close to the snows on Kilimanjaro's glacier. I felt I could almost reach out and touch it. I fingered the talisman around my neck. I am with Kilimanjaro. We are one spirit. This place is magic. This place is Peace.

Inside I listened to Pete's sleep breathing. Yes it seemed to be rhythmical. I had known times at altitude when his breathing had severe gaps, which was scary. But he seemed to be okay. Ah, my wounded knight ... Could it be that our Earth is like a wounded knight? Outwardly strong, giving help where needed, quietly fixing everything that needs fixing, making sure that all is safe and well. But inwardly hurting, struggling with systems, not able to breath, disorientated, not able to adapt well to the physiological changes needed under environmental pressures. Do we heed the silent cries for help?

Beyond Time and Space

17th September, 2011 – Day Four

Day Four dawned less cold but with more grey. We were to have an acclimatisation morning, climb up to above 4,500 metres and back down to Moir Hut for a gentle afternoon and a second night here. Great. I liked this plan. It would give the porters an important day off and give Pete and Rima a chance to recover. Pete, thankfully, was a lot better. Almost back to his old self, throwing his weight around. Personally I think it was the thought of his new name, Dr Death, which speeded his recovery. However, Rima was still at death's door. She'd basically sicked up everything she had. Nothing was left. She'd been up half the night due to all the water drunk and couldn't sleep anyway and had the worst headache of her life, along with nosebleeds. Altitude can do that. I took some sickness pills into her tent. She could barely lift her head.

"Everyone keeps giving me so many instructions and different remedies that I can't find any time to sleep," she groaned. Obviously, apart from altitude sickness, she was suffering from overcare, a very nasty disease.

The rest of us left her and set off behind the camp up a short steep scrambly climb, avoiding the sheer rock face. It was good to travel light without heavy sacks. Even Gaius stayed in the tent. The guides conscientiously helped Jackie up.

Her ankle appeared to be recovering well, but she has such a gentle appealing quality to her, almost childlike, that there never seemed to be a moment without a guide holding her hand. Then we crossed a gently sloping bit and clambered steeply up the side of a ravine heading for a ridge top. There was barely any vegetation apart from little circles of everlasting flowers. Mostly we tramped across rock, a red brown volcanic rock that I liked. But we were in heavy cloud, so there was little else to see, except ...

"Ah, some poo!" exclaimed Sakimba. "It's jackal, see there's some mouse bones in it." I looked. It was just like, well ... poo. Sakimba looked cold. Somewhere he had acquired a red warrior cloak which he had tightly wrapped around him against the cold and damp. And he had told us, "I don't wear gloves. I just put grease on my hands." Well, the Tibetans use yak butter, so it must be okay, but I guiltily thought of the pile of gloves I had at home from which I'd chosen a pair to bring. The rest of us appreciated all the heavy waterproofs that we wore as it started to hail.

"I only asked the mountain for no rain," I giggled. "I forgot about hail or snow." My weather forecasting methods weren't up to those of Sakimba's.

"I remember the mountain covered in snow twenty years ago," he said wistfully, "when my father was chief and my mother's eyesight was still good and they'd point out the white-haired old man of Kilimanjaro and his snow beard."

My eyes took in the rock all around us. There were little piles of stones built as markers for this high point. They reminded me of the inuksuks in the Arctic, the signposts of the Inuit people which point out the safe and fruitful directions to go. There was certainly no snow lying at the moment. I thought of all the debate on global warming. Were the people of the world today heading in a safe and fruitful direction? Would we leave a beautiful world for our grandchildren?

We sat on the ridge-top until it became too cold, knowing that it was helping our bodies adapt to the lack of oxygen. Then we headed back to camp, where the rain fell heavily.

"We'll be so acclimatised by the time we get to the top of Kili," said Mary, "that by then it'll be like Pete's piece of cake." I nodded encouragingly. But I knew only too well that we couldn't take anything at altitude for granted, that there would be tough times ahead and that there was a good chance that not everyone would make it.

I bumped into Freddie on the way to check on Rima.

"That grandson of yours arrived yet?" he asked.

"No, not yet. Could be any minute."

"Make sure they give him a good name. Go for 'Freddie' after me."

"Ah ..."

"Or 'Mountain Madness'. There's a good name."

"Well ..."

"Or 'Shaking'. Here, I'll write down the African for it. It's one of my names too." I passed him my diary and he wrote 'Akatingisha'. It looked a good name, yes, but I just couldn't imagine my grandson's future schoolmates pronouncing it, let alone spelling it.

The afternoon was quietly restful apart from the arrival of another small team, similarly mixing together African and western culture. They set up camp alongside us. But there was plenty of space and it was good to chat to an American granny who was one of the clients. She'd been told that most people underestimate the difficulty of doing Kilimanjaro, but still went ahead. It seemed that this journey was a granny sort of a thing to do!

By the evening the weather had cleared and we could see the beard of the old man again shining high on the slopes above us. The temperature dropped and appetites returned to enjoy the excellent supper of soup and spaghetti. Many of the Peace Messages in the reading session afterwards were poignant: "Peace starts with everyone having enough food and clean water."

In the middle of the night I dragged myself away from my warm sleeping bag to pay a visit to the tiny bucket loo tent. I sleepily came out, pulled my duvet jacket tightly around me and stared upwards. There was a bright moon, not quite full. I was enveloped by the power and beauty of the star-spangled sky. It spoke to me.

In these Millennia of time there is no time. There is insignificance of one little being, but as separate yet part of all that is, then there is greatness. Millennia of time and continuity of flow go beyond time and space.

I know this to be true and that Kilimanjaro watches and waits with me and that we are on the same mission and that all is well. All is written in golden threads and we must follow the path and exchange some of ourselves for some of others. That is the African way. Great Kilimanjaro, help me to see the way. Help us all to see the way and help us to hold sanity in the altitude that threatens our thought processes. I know that all is well but I have to confess I'm worried. I'm worried how we'll all cope in the crater, even though we'll be staying there as a vigil for Peace. It's not sensible. It's bonkers. Okay, yes, as Freddie says, I will try to think less and make sure I feel with my heart ... Great Kilimanjaro, it is an honour and privilege to walk your slopes, to come close for Peace. We will not let you down. Beauty. Love. Boldness. Ah stars, you speak such language and each of us holds a star, a star of Peace, in our hearts. What magic, what treasure, what joy. To ride on a starbeam of life and love and infinite wisdom. No beginning, no end. Here is the journey. Here I am. I serve.

I glanced at my watch. The time was 2.31am.

NEW BIRTH

18th September, 2011 – Day Five

"Tess! Wake up! There's a message from Scottie."

My eyes flipped open. It was light. Dawn had broken.

Pete listened on the satellite phone and relayed: "Baby born 12.31am English time. That's 2.31am our time. His name is Bodhi." He then let out a 'Yeeha!' Not any sort of a 'yeeha,' but a full decibel Pete 'yeeha' that nearly burst my eardrums and that informed the camp and the mountain that yes indeed my little grandson had arrived.

So he's to be called Bodhi. I knew it was one of the possible names, picked up from a hero in a film. It was the name I loved the best. Whilst it's popularly translated from Sanskrit as 'enlightenment' or 'supreme knowledge', it literally means 'awakened'. It is the name of the Bodhi tree, the large old sacred fig tree with heart-shaped leaves which Gautama Buddha was said to have sat under in the sixth century BC before reaching enlightenment. It is revered as a cosmic tree, joining Heaven and Earth. Ah, here we go again ... Could it be that this new generation carries power which will help our world to find its way with harmony and beauty? Certainly those born now are arriving onto a different Earth than when I was born. This is a higher vibrational Earth.

As we phoned Scott back I was shaking with emotion.

Perhaps Freddie's right about this African shaking name! I pressed the phone hard against my ear to hear above the wind. "Yes," I heard Scott on the end of the line sounding more together than I did and thrilled to bits in spite of the absence of sleep, "We had the natural birth we wanted and all went so well we're already allowed to take Bodhi home from the hospital."

I rushed to find Sakimba. As I was pouring out the wonderful news I realised I was jumping up and down in excitement just like the Maasai warriors do in their ritual life-expressing dance. Breathlessly I asked, "Please can you do the ceremony? You know, give him a traditional welcome to the world like you did with the newborn baby in your village?"

"Of course. I'd be honoured. And I'll sing the blessing song," he replied looking around. "It'll have to be from the highest place. Ah ..." He pointed to the east. There beyond the high point we had reached yesterday was a distinctive cake-shaped little mountain silhouetted along the horizon. It didn't look as though it would be easy to reach, particularly at this altitude, in fact quite a rock climb, but such are the duties of a Maasai warrior.

"Do you think it has a name?"

"Unlikely."

"Well, let's call it Mount Bodhi for him."

"I'll start out right away."

I swept into the breakfast tent to the hugs, congratulations and cheers of everyone. Ah, the onerous duties of being a granny! There were smiles all round the table. Joy is contagious. "It's just so fantastically exciting," I effused amongst everyday breakfast conversation.

"Have some fruit and porridge."

"D'you mind if an American dips her bread in the marmalade?" Jess asked Pete.

"Only on a special day when there's been a new birth," Mary interjected.

"He's a Peace baby!" I declared.

"Yeah!" said Rima who appeared to have recovered somewhat from death's door. "I'm lighting the Peace Flame for him."

Training – Granny style

Training – Knight style

"Climb Oldonyo Lengai?" said Jackie. "You must be joking!"

"Try Mount Meru, then!"

Standing: Jacob, Gideon, Pete, Nick, Nicholas   Sitting: Ann, Jess, Mary, Rima, Jackie, Tess, Gaius Penguin

Kilimanjaro's main summit, Kibo crater
Mount Meru in background

Jess 'out on the pull'!

"Thank goodness I don't have a porter's load ..."

The Peace Lantern held by warrior Sakimba leads the way
Followed by Tess, Pete, Nicholas, Anthony, Felix and Ann

Gaius Penguin on guard duty at the crystal site

Freddie takes a bow, Rima and the porters sing

Ann tackles the Maasai dance with warrior Sakimba
(with sunglasses)

Warrior Bodhi, training in Maasai cloak of courage

Kilimanjaro births the light

"To welcome him," said Gideon.

"Who wanted the marmalade?"

"You did! You're having another senior moment!"

"To shine like a light in the world, with the new generation," said Jacob.

"It feels like I'm floating on air. I suddenly feel amazing. I'm jumping all over the place, like I could do anything ..."

"We need a marmalade committee meeting!"

"It just shows. Don't get stuck in the physical. It's all to do with the mind."

"I like being stuck in the physical," said Pete.

"Typical!"

Merriment is contagious, too.

A tiny seed-eater bird with white stripes on his wings fluttered into the tent and sat exactly above my head. What's that all about? No doubt he was sheltering from the harsh wind blowing outside, but just then I felt a strong sense of my mother and laughed at the thought that she'd hitched a ride on this tiny bird. Surely she was sharing in the family happiness.

"That bird's a good sign," said Jackie.

"Very high altitude for such a little chap," said Nicholas.

My mother would have said that she liked the fact that her great grandson was born on the 18th. She always related to numbers like that.

"The 18th is a good date to be born," came in Ann as though she had read my thoughts. "One and eight make nine which indicates completion. Bodhi's work will be to do with completion."

"Well, we need to get going to complete this climb," said Nick, trying to stir us. "Let's go. The guys are waiting for us."

Outside I wandered a little way amongst the rocks and stretched my arms to the forever expanse of sky above me. "Thank you Ngai for the birth of my little one. Thank you." The sun was shining fiercely. And there was Kilimanjaro with all his attendant snows greeting me clear as a bell against the azure blue. It felt like a welcome to Bodhi. "And thank you, Great Kilimanjaro," I whispered, my eyes overflowing, leaving a coolness on my cheeks as the tears were carried away by the icy north wind. I was too filled up with emotion to notice the low temperature. I'd actually been really cold in the night, but realised I hadn't kept with my cardinal rule of tying my sleeping bag tight at the neck to make my own sleeping micro-climate. Not much point having hard-won polar experience and then taking no notice of it!

We set off, one behind the other up the tricky steep scramble near the camp. Nicholas carried the Peace Lantern, having ditched the long pole. I carried the Peace penguin enjoying Gaius' gentle movement as he bobbed up and down on the side of my rucksack, delighted to be on the go again after his enforced rest day. Except he was indignant that I'd tied my underwear to dry on the straps of my rucksack and they'd already become wrapped around him. I fancied I could hear him saying, "I am the crystal guardian. I can put up with being a pillow, but a washing line is just too much!"

As the going became easier across the barren valley conversation picked up. "I'm feeling on top of the world," said Nick as though reflecting the general mood. "I've had my shave this morning, and a wash ..."

"What a fantastic new day for a symbolic new birth," said Ann, standing aside to let the porters overtake us carrying their heavy white loads on their heads.

We slowed down for the steep bit, and conversation eased as drawing breath became priority. Energy was used sparingly. About half way up the side of the ravine we were able to look back across the desolate grey-brownness of the volcanic desert, across where we knew our campsite had been and further out over a sea of bubbling white cloud to a distant pinnacle on the horizon. It was Mount Meru, proud and beautiful and somehow with us. "Thank you, Mount Meru, for our preparation and for standing with us," I smiled.

But it was about three-quarters of the way up with Anthony leading slowly, accompanied by much puffing and panting from the team that another sight in front of us greeted our searching eyes. Up ahead the little cake-shaped mountain was now closer. Behind it there was a rainbow circle surrounding a blazing sun, like a guardian holding protection. The north wind swirled and brought shouts.

Screwing up my eyes I could see a silhouette on its summit – stark against the skyline. Sakimba was waving his warrior cloak. I knew his shouts wafting down to us were the same as those of the welcome to the Maasai baby in the mud hut: "Thank you, Ngai, Great Sky, for this new day and for all the miracles, and also for delivering this beautiful baby." With the lenses of the video cameras we could make out the sun picking up the red of the cloak and I was reminded of my experience overcoming fear with the warrior cloak on the sacred mountain of Oldonyo Lengai, of finding inner strength. Ah. I know my Bodhi has been given the gift of courage. I know him to be a little Peace warrior.

Taking a deep breath I shouted up the mountain, "For Bodhi! For new birth!"And the echo was carried off by the wind.

Pushing ourselves up the last of the steepness we reached the inuksuk stones where we had sat yesterday. There we collapsed onto suitable sitting rocks and drank some water from our bottles. Gideon and Jacob sucked lollipops to keep their blood sugar levels topped up whilst we waited for Sakimba. He disappeared over the far side of Mount Bodhi and surprisingly quickly was back with us, grinning from ear to ear.

"Thank you so much," I greeted him. "It means a lot to me and my family."

"It had to be done for sure. It was a harmonising with the Earth for Bodhi," he said. "You know, I woke up at 2.30 this morning and prayed."

"The time he was born!"

"Ah ..."

Surely Sakimba is an old soul, I thought, marvelling that I also had been awake then. And again I had that feeling that we had worked together before somewhere.

"Now I know why I had to come on this climb," he said. "I knew I really had to come but didn't know why." He grabbed the tyre as we continued.

"You okay taking that?" I asked.

"Yes," he beamed, looking intensely happy. "Peace is really light."

The trail now led a little downwards away from Mount Bodhi and we headed north, boots crunching on a gravelly path twisting its way between the heavy grey rocks and jumble of stones. I knew that Rima would be thinking the same as I was. Conditions were perfect for tyre pulling. "Please can I pull Amani now?" she pleaded with Sakimba. It was relinquished reluctantly and she happily jogged off with the tyre bouncing along behind shouting, "For Peace!" It was good to see she had her old energy back.

"Shaking!" Freddie shouted after her and started throwing his hips around. She laughed and seeing me looking longingly at the tyre generously said, "Here, have a go for a bit. I need to do some filming."

She filmed Freddie doing his song and dance routine. He didn't need any encouragement.

Delighted to be able to take over the tyre, I brushed some of the dust from the rope and attached it to my rucksack karabiner. Just then Sakimba spotted something on the ground a little way off the track. "Hey look," he said pointing at what seemed to be a scattering of coal black glass as though someone in a drunken fervour had smashed a bottle over the head of an overzealous lead guide. "It's obsidian, see ..." He handed us lumps of flint-like angular rock. "We Maasai use it for healing, especially for heart problems. It's been forged in the fires of the Earth and then cooled."

I turned a piece over in my hand. It was cold and sharp, "So it's lava. Like part of an exploded volcanic bomb ... "

"Feels very grounding to me," said Ann.

"I can see flashes of green and pink in this bit," I said.

"That's rainbow obsidian ... very rare. It's a gift from Kilimanjaro," replied Sakimba.

I slipped the piece into my pocket to one day give to Bodhi. It was his heritage. Then I set off with the tyre. I went fast out of sheer exuberance. Felix picked up the end rope to guide it.

As I glanced behind me I saw that we were accompanied by a low flying friend, white-necked raven. "One spirit!" I shouted.

"One family!" called Felix.

"One blood!" I shouted.

"One blood!" echoed Felix.

"One mind!" I shouted.

"One mind!" came back.

"For Peace!" I heard across the windswept mountain from other members of our team, the same purpose joining us all.

We were catching up James in front. He was plodding gently with Jackie's rucksack on his front as well as his own on his back. "Ishingaling!" he shouted. I searched in my brain for the meaning of ishingaling and remembered it's the Maasai word for thank you. Ah, James must be Maasai too. Yes he seemed to have the same sort of gentle strength as Sakimba, though perhaps he'd had more western life opportunity.

All was well with my world.

I resolved to write down this adventure, to share it with those who didn't have wonderful opportunities like us. And I would dedicate my Africa book – the story of the final point of our six-pointed star of Peace – to my grandson.

Our clockwise path around Kili reminded me of walking around Mount Kailas in Tibet, known as doing the kora, where it is said that to complete this circuit 144 times is to reach enlightenment. I remembered the harsh windswept feeling of the landscape which resembled so much the moonscape we were on here. And the warmth and hope of the Himalayan Peace Messages we had spoken out then.

In my experience, when you feel good you draw further good things.

"Mama Tess," Felix said, "I have talked to the porters. They like what your Peace Climb team are doing. They will partake in the Peace Message ceremony reading today."

"Oh wonderful! Thanks so much, Felix. That means a huge amount to us. It's the coming together. The working together."

"One family."

"Exactly. Never mind the rules about porters and clients ..."

All my initial doubts of Felix had gone. I could understand him now, he appeared to really believe in our cause and was supporting us all he could.

As was the incorrigible Freddie. We came down into a dry creek-bed, parched and dusty with just a few stunted heathers and beige tufts of grass. Here and there where moisture had gathered were whorls of the brave everlasting flowers looking like large white scrubbing brushes on the march. Beyond to the north we looked down on a stunning cloud ocean voluminous and bubbling to the distant horizon. The curve of the Earth was apparent. From this perspective we were the sky. We were the sky!

"Your goal is the summit," said Freddie, " but it is also to enjoy the beauty of your journey along the way."

"Yeah, for sure," and indeed what a privilege it was to view the world from this high place.

"See here," he continued, "we can read the tracks. This is where buffalo and eland cross the trail. They come to lick the soda salt here." He saw me scribbling notes in my diary, so added, "And of course you'll put a photo of me in your book."

"Of course!"

"We have many clients, but we will remember the Peace Climb team. We have similar goals. You know I've been on the trail for the last twenty-six days. I miss my family, but I love this work. And next year I'm going to climb Mont Blanc and after that Aconcagua and Everest. I'm ready for the world!"

Well, if to sing and dance your way through life with a devastating smile is the answer to everything, he would have no problem. But was the world ready for Freddie?

I heard the characteristic rush of beating wings and looked up. The white-necked raven with a smile on his beak flew overhead. "Hey brother!" I shouted and imagined he tilted his wings on the flypast. He seemed to forever accompany us. He certainly wasn't going to leave us in Peace.

We headed up out of the empty water course towards the next ridge on the skyline as high Kilimanjaro disappeared from view behind dancing cloud. Rima and I had taken it in turns to pull the tyre but now we gave in to Sakimba's insistence. Monisi gave Freddie the lantern and walked with me. "Hey Mama, look. Everlasting flowers. Always shining, just like you." I marvelled that he could say things like that and it seemed to come genuinely from the heart.

His words gave me a needed boost. I had gone suddenly into a low blood sugar level state and developed a migraine; I have them very occasionally. When this happens I get flashing lights in my eyes so that I can barely see for half an hour or so. I didn't want to tell anybody, not even Pete, so I gobbled some emergency chocolate and walked close behind Sakimba til it had gone. I remembered I had also had a migraine the day my son Scott was born. Some things never change.

My eyes were just clearing when we reached our goal for Day Five and came into Pofu Camp at 4,027 metres, a little lower than last night. There were varying thoughts on what its meaning is, such as 'place of eland' or 'further', both quite descriptive, but I felt it was more likely 'thank goodness we've made it.' It was at the top of a ridge. There was little flat ground, but some lovely rocky outcrops and quite a bit of the giant heather vegetation. Over six hours walking we'd covered a distance of 10.5 kilometres. Rima and I were happy to have been pulling the tyre for much of that.

Everyone was exhausted. Jackie, looking younger than ever with her hair in plaits, was particularly tired and had been carried piggy-back and helped diligently by James and Raymond for much of the way. What a welcome sight it was to see our tents all up and most importantly the blue mess tent with lunch. We all collapsed gratefully at the table, Nick and Mary fell instantly asleep, but woke up to devour the meal with the rest of us.

It wasn't til quite a while later that we realised that there was no water at this camp. The porters had had to travel long distances, far longer than us, on top of their regular carry to find a stream and bring back what we all needed for the entire camp for afternoon, evening and morning in the way of drinks, cooking and washing. Things were easier in the

Antarctic when you just had to melt the snow. Bring back the snow cover!

With tired grumbling bodies we grabbed jackets and dragged ourselves out of the tent for the Peace Message reading. Rima had insisted that it would be easier for the porters to join us if we all gathered outside. She was right. They were all waiting for us. Heavy mists had come in. It wasn't possible to see up to the crater rim or down across the clouds above the plains of Kenya. It was as though we were in our own little cocoon. The tyre was placed in the dirt in the middle, giving some shelter inside to the lantern which lit up, but needed to be relit every few minutes. I had torn in half the pages of the day's allocation of 400 or so Peace Message so there were enough to go round for our entire gathering of all the porters, all the guides and all the clients. I felt quite emotional that at last we had everyone involved. No one should be left out of Peace.

Rima and Mary started things off by singing the prayer of St Francis of Assisi which had been sent as a Peace Message, which set the tone that this was a sacred ceremony. Then in our usual way we took it in turns round and round the circle to speak out a Message each. Most of the porters struggled to read and were helped by others, but bravely all tackled their challenge before them. There was more of a feeling of oneness of the team than any other moment since we had begun. Barriers had broken down. It seemed that everyone realised that what we were doing was not to do with any particular group or religion, but on behalf of all people.

My individual allocation came to an end with "Thank you for all your loving hearts". The porters smiled at this as it related particularly to them. Also the one I added: "May we all shine a light from the summit of Kilimanjaro." At this moment the mists cleared and the summit snows shone in a fierce light which reflected back from the white clouds beneath us. It was a breathtakingly beautiful sight. I was filled with the joy and wonder of nature.

Everyone seemed re-energised as we dispersed from the gathering. At last there was time to contact Scott and find out how Bodhi and Nella were. Pete was already bringing out the satellite phone.

"All's well, Mum," Scott said, "and Bodhi weighed in at 9lbs 1oz. He looks sturdy and incredibly contented."

"So he should be," I replied. "Within a few hours of being born he's had a welcome to the world from a Maasai warrior, a mountain named after him and a book dedicated to him. Not a bad start in life."

From what I had been told about my own birth, my main start in life consisted of being smacked on the bottom to confirm I was breathing. Now as I snuggled into my sleeping bag on a far away African mountain I thought, well, 63 years later I'm still concerned about breathing. Doubts whirled round in my mind. With only two more days to go before summit day, would we all find enough oxygen in this rarefied air to not only breathe but to have the energy to climb two thousand more metres successfully?

Everything depends on whether the team is acclimatised or not ...

ONE DREAM AWAY

19th September, 2011 – Day Six

I couldn't sleep. The worries spun round and round in my head mingling with the bubbling joy of the day. In spite of the huge physical demands of the trek I couldn't let my body relax. I was sure that my breathing wasn't suffering to any large extent from lack of oxygen, but it was no surprise to not sleep at altitude. Eventually, sometime in the early hours I realised I was too cold. Perhaps this was to do with losing weight, which was inevitable with our continuous walking, despite the good food. But no doubt I wasn't taking enough in. I'm not very good at stuffing in large amounts. And don't much like butter so probably was low on necessary fats needed.

But I was really lucky to have a decent sleeping bag; I was sure most of the support team had very flimsy ones. Mine was marked as being suitable down to minus 20°C and tonight it can't have been much below freezing. We had been told to expect conditions down to minus 20°C, but that surely was in the summit crater higher up. The bag worked on the principle that it held in warmth, but if the body itself wasn't warm enough then there was nothing to hold in. From my Antarctic training I knew that a good option was to go outside and run round the tent to raise the body temperature. Hmm, that might be interesting here, not only tripping over guy ropes and rocks, but certainly waking up the entire camp. So, no, it had to be the eating-chocolate technique. I rustled around and found my emergency supplies and then snuggled up close to Pete. He can sleep through earthquakes.

There's something about being at altitude that haunts the mind with intense dreams and visions.

I am a warrior. I proudly walk the plains, young, strong, invincible. My bare male chest the colour of ebony, the grasslands dry and tawny. I approach a small rocky outcrop. I am hit by a feeling of dread. My easy pace quickens. On the far side I see my brother, the one I run with. He lies face down in the dirt. There is blood. I kneel to touch death. Around his body are the prints of a lioness. I raise my face to the sky and let out a howl of pain and twisted anger.

He stands, alert and calm, beside me saying, "Come brother ..."

I woke to another stunning day of total beauty. White-necked raven was standing guard outside on a lichen-strewn outcrop overlooking dazzling white clouds below. "Morning, brother!" I said. He acknowledged me with a stare from a beady eye and a slight tilt of the head. He obviously was taking his guiding duties seriously.

Our route today took us further east along the Northern Circuit at a similar altitude to yesterday. We started off, one behind the other, up one of the tentacles of Kilimanjaro which looked like a deep grey mud-flow that had suddenly been stopped in its tracks and solidified. It was quite a steep scramble hanging onto knobbly volcanic holds which rasped at the hands and I wondered how the porters could possibly manage this with their heavy awkward loads, though Sakimba flowed up carrying the tyre in his usual effortless way.

Mary was okay carrying the lantern with free hands as Nick had fixed it onto the back of her sack alongside the useful notice 'Keep calm and carry on.' Jackie had presumably read this and had accepted a lift on James' back, fireman style. Good thing he was beefy. I didn't need to worry about her. Nor Rima who was happily singing a song she had just composed which kept all our spirits up.

Suddenly I noticed that my hand was covered in blood from a cut finger. I had no idea that had happened. As I stared at it a drop collected, fell to the ground and disappeared into the parched desert dust. Strangely that pleased me, as though I was giving a little of myself to the mountain. Though Egbert piped up, "If this is the only sacrifice the mountain demands of me then I don't mind at all. I'll be getting away lightly."

"Who're you kidding, Egbert?! The crux is yet to come."

To appease the mountain for my triviality I thought I'd better take the blood seriously. And I knew what I had to do. "Hey! See here," I called to those around me. Rima, Raymond and Sakimba stopped. And then James came up too. "Hold up your hands. Would you like to be blood brothers?" It appeared the most natural thing in the world for us to hold forearms vertical, elbow to elbow and to clasp hand to hand. The others it seemed had cuts too. The blood mingled and we laughed, but some sort of bond was created. It was as though this ancient tradition carried something stronger than I was prepared for. We were now brothers at a deeper level. It was similar to the feeling I'd had in my dream. I told Sakimba about it. He nodded and smiled as though of course this was how it was. Do we too often lose this feeling in our modern world? Of brothers we run with? Later, I found the remains of the biscuits that had been to the top of Oldonyo Lengai in my rucksack and shared them round. That made me feel good, too, as though it was connecting my brothers up with that first part of our Peace Climb.

As the trail started turning southeast, passing tracks of eland and water buffalo, a mountain was appearing on the horizon. It was shrouded in shifting cloud, but then suddenly cleared to show a huge jagged peak. This was Mawenzi, Kilimanjaro's second-highest peak at 5,149 metres. I remembered having seen it from the plane and from Meru as part of the silhouette of Kilimanjaro flanking the main rounded crater of Kibo. It looked a serious climb. I called to Sakimba, "You're so lucky the baby didn't come today or you'd have had to climb that one!" He laughed and kept walking. We both knew that a warrior with a lion in his heart doesn't shirk his duties. We didn't know then how severely this would be tested.

After the morning on the move we came down into Third Caves camp at 3,971 metres. We had only covered a distance of 6.7 kilometres, but there was still a similar distance down and back up the mountain for the support team to collect water for this camp. The only cave I could see was behind the tents in a ridge of volcanic jumble. It was brown, cool and inviting inside, but looked only just big enough to sleep one person comfortably. Sakimba claimed it quickly, placing down his sleeping bag and taking his boots off. Home! I felt jealous. I'd far rather sleep in a cave than a snug dry tent with big mattresses! Jess and Rima thought the same. Ah well, we have to behave like clients, I suppose. We were just heading to lunch when we saw his feet. "Sakimba! You've got huge nasty blisters. They must be incredibly painful."

"Oh, it's nothing," he said, "just the old boots I borrowed from a friend in Arusha."

"You must drain the fluid out of them and put plasters on. Have you got any?"

"They'll be fine," he said. "Look, we've got company." Four white-necked raven brothers circled overhead, croaking loudly.

"Wow! A squadron of them. What are they telling us?"

"They represent peace and love," he said.

"I think you think everything is peace and love," I laughed.

Jess and Rima tended to his feet with Ann's plasters.

Over lunch we did a Peace Message that said: "Life begins at the end of your comfort zone."

Hmm, I thought. Maybe it does. Certainly everyone seemed eager now to get going and actually climb to the summit. That was a good sign. And most importantly, everyone seemed able to breathe easily. Of course we'd had only a half day walking and we'd come down in altitude, but it was still a good sign that we were acclimatising well. So the entire team was keen to do an excursion up towards the edge of the lava flow between Mawenzi and Kibo, known as the Saddle.

We plodded slowly up the dry water course for an hour

or so in heavy grey cloud and sat on some knobbly rocks at around 4,200 metres. Within five minutes we were really cold. Rima had the solution. To run back down. Yeah! wonderful. She and Jess ran down fast, Pete and I jogged and everyone else walked fast. The potential for more people with twisted ankles in such an isolated and desolate spot was thrown to the wind. In no time at all we were warm and felt great. As we flew down the sky split open over Kenya, as though someone had taken a brush and painted a blue stripe across it. Ann called it a stairway to Heaven.

That night after we had eaten well on fish, rice and vegetables, some of the porters joined us in the mess tent and brought their own Messages of Peace and Love. One read: "Even as porters we don't like the world to be a battle field, we like the world to be a peaceful place in order for tourism to continue."

In high spirits we sang all the western songs we knew. And then slept well in our tents above the clouds under a waiting starlit sky.

We were ready for whatever high Kilimanjaro was going to throw at us.

Bring it on!

Gaining Altitude

20th September, 2011 – Day Seven

"Ten minutes til we leave!" called Pete in his ordering-me-about voice. He was understandably trying to encourage everyone to be on time but the way he did it annoyed me. If someone else had said it I wouldn't have been cross, but it was one of those silly issues that relations bring up. I bit my lip and rushed to gobble the eggs and porridge that my body didn't want. Then struggled as usual to tame my sleeping bag into its stuff-sack and pack my personal bag so that the porters wouldn't have to wait to collapse the tents. But I was still fuming.

C'mon girl, I said to myself. We had far worse things to worry about in the Antarctic where we lived right on the edge of sanity most of the time. And how did I cope then? It was with unconditional love. Of course. So now I shot him a thought bubble of unconditional love, and almost immediately felt better. Thank goodness. See, it wasn't about the relationship. It was about me. Even though I knew that being at altitude stresses not only the body but also the emotions and the mind, once again I was being reminded to hang onto life's hard-won lessons on how to cope. As always, it was to do with how to change my attitude towards what life was throwing at me; that was the only bit I was in control of.

Today, at last, we would be turning from the circuit path and going uphill towards the summit. Ready to go, I was adjusting Gaius' travelling position on the back of my sack when Sakimba came up and gave me a gift. He had given Rima a bracelet and had something for Jess, too. Mine was a beautiful little Maasai necklace. The chain was slithers of porcupine quills between bright Africa-coloured beads. From it hung a tiny shell. "This is from the lake in Embakai crater near my village," he said securing it around my neck. "It will give you extra power."

"Wow, thank you so much, Sakimba," I beamed. "It's lovely." I fingered it along with my talisman. They sat well together. *"We are one spirit"* coursed through me and I felt again that connection with the Maasai lands and their sacred mountain. The connection came not only with Oldonyo Lengai but also with Meru and Kilimanjaro as parts of one whole. This necklace would hold that sense of oneness.

There was only one uneasy question in my mind: what does Sakimba know about the need for extra power on the climb ahead? But the thought went off happily along its journey.

Our cavalcade set off into yet another beautiful morning. A blue limitless sky enticed us on our way heading south up the wide desert track we'd taken yesterday evening. Today we could see seemingly forever. High to our right the Kibo crater ridge was clear on the horizon, graced from this angle by one small patch of snow. Far to the left, mighty Mawenzi stood like a lost dragon, too jagged to fit in with the roundness of the lava deposits we walked through.

Rocks and dust, more rocks and more dust. Although I could even taste dust in my mouth, I was intensely happy. I was pulling the tyre with Pete. He had attached his rucksack rope and karabiner to a loop half way down the pulling rope, the end of which I had attached to mine, so we were able to travel along almost side by side, sharing the load. We had to watch in order not to trip the other one up with our sticks, but otherwise it worked brilliantly. Step by step, perfectly synchronised. This was how I had always envisioned it. This was how it was meant to be. Pulling together. Yeah!

The movement reminded me of the lovely feeling of harmony Pete and I got when we did synchronised skiing. We'd pick a nice wide snow slope, align ourselves level and ski down, turning at exactly the same time, one of us shouting, "turn! turn!" to keep us together. It's the ultimate of being in tune with each other and something we love. Now pulling the tyre felt the same, side by side we could chat easily. It was satisfying to look back on all the months of work to achieve this Peace Climb, and also the thirteen years of the previous Peace Climbs. We had done this together. It had been hard work, but a long and happy road. I had felt supported all the way, particularly with his practical ability to make my ideas happen. At first he had thought that because I liked to look at things in the non-physical, I must be a witch (I've been called worse things!). Gradually he had changed to just thinking of me as being weird. And eventually he accepted that I simply saw things differently from the way he did.

It was a good, balanced partnership. And along the way we had raised over a hundred and twenty thousand pounds for charity, inspired over twenty-two thousand individuals to do Peace Messages to make a difference and created unique expeditions to carry these messages to the ends of the Earth. All for Peace. All to create a six-pointed star of Peace to shine across the Earth. Now we were so close to completion. As we slowed for a rock I turned and gave Pete a big hug. I loved him and I loved the work we were doing. I felt incredibly lucky.

Pulling the tyre uphill at the altitude of more than 4,000 metres quickly took its toll, even sharing the load. It was completely different from pulling earlier across the Shira plateau and along the traverse of the Northern Circuit. Now, there was less atmospheric pressure so the air was thinner and so less oxygen available. The sheer physical effort of not only walking uphill but heaving from our shoulders and hips put extra stresses on our bodies. Every little movement became tiring (even before someone asked, "Aren't you tyred out yet?").

I could hear Pete puffing and panting beside me and I knew the film footage that Rima and Nick were shooting would have their own gasping sound effects. I started feeling dizzy and my head was spinning. Luckily my pockets held a few emergency supplies of dried mango and nuts which I now shared with Pete. This helped. Also Nicholas picked up the guiding rope behind the tyre which meant there was less sudden jarring. He looked like he was doing well in spite of our worries about his age and inexperience. His quiet gentle strength had been steadying for the group, though now I did notice an unusual grim, determined look that accompanied the heavy breathing.

I was grateful when we stopped for our first break and could take off a layer of clothes and drink some water. It looked like everyone else was glad, too. James had been carrying Jackie's pack and Anthony and Raymond were sharing Ann's, so happily everyone had been keeping up the pace and we had arrived together. We sat getting our breath as the first lot of porters walked by. No one except for Rima seemed to have the energy to shout and exchange handshakes today, so there was mostly just a soft exchange of "Jambo" in between Jacob expounding on African music.

Ann and I handed out homeopathic coca. Interestingly it was the girls who were taking these for altitude whilst the guys were taking the standard Diamox. I think this scientific study indicates that girls are more daring! Though Pete reckons girls acclimatise better than guys. Could be to do with the distance the blood has to travel to reach and indeed, in the case of pensioners, find the brain, or maybe the number of brain cells itself!

Clouds were sweeping high across the crater rim as we stood up trying to convince our sluggish bodies to start again. "I'll take the tyre from here," said Sakimba.

"No you won't. Don't touch that tyre!" said Pete in his sternest ordering-about voice, indicating for me to clip in again so we could continue pulling together. Was there to be a fight? Sakimba accepted it for the moment, but took up the lantern. He walked just in front of us, holding it up as though lighting the way. Lovely. We were reminded to hold the light for Peace in our hearts.

The gradient became steeper. There was less conversation now. Just boots plodding step by step, kicking up the volcanic dirt. Pete and I set a steady rhythm which made things easier as the body goes onto automatic pilot and doesn't have to think what it's doing. My thoughts turned to the Antarctic where we did the same and where little tricks of the mind like that made all the difference to beat the cold, the vast distances and the isolation. There we had pulled our own sledges.

Now, pulling together, I realised that this is how it must have felt for Captain Scott and his team a hundred years ago, hauling together their one large sledge as they trekked to the South Pole and sadly, their eventual deaths. And I felt the added camaraderie and closeness that pulling together brought. I knew without a shadow of doubt that this principle would also work on the world stage, all nations pulling together for Peace. I knew because our Nation Messages reflected this. I prayed that our Peace Climb would help raise awareness for this.

Due to enjoying being in my mind it seemed no time at all before we stopped for our second break and could sit on some rocks and chat. "Has anyone seen the raven today?" I asked looking up the mountain into fast descending cloud. I realised I hadn't seen him lately and wondered if we were reaching the limits of his ability. We were now at around 4,600 metres, higher than Mount Meru, higher than all of our team, except Pete and me, had ever been before. How high could the raven fly? Would he give up on us now? I had the feeling he was too tough to do that but perhaps the limiting factor would be that there wasn't enough for him to eat here.

"I saw him before breakfast," said Jacob, "when I was washing my face, but not up here."

"Pleased to hear you've been washing!" said Mary, somehow still managing to keep up with her Miss Vogue image in a fetching bright pink top and sun visor.

When we stood up after the second break, Sakimba picked up the tyre. Felix grabbed the lantern. Pete said nothing.

But I wanted to continue pulling. "You okay taking that?" I asked Sakimba as we moved on.

"Fine. For a warrior it's nothing. It's like my spear."

I rose to my full warrior height, though still only up to his chest, "I could take it here."

"No. You have to save your energy."

Hmm. I didn't want to save my energy. But then I realised that that same instruction had been given me in the Antarctic. I hadn't wanted it then either, but looking back it had meant my energy was there for the right time when needed. So maybe I should heed it now. And it did mean that I could continue writing as I walked. I knew I had to make sure I'd let go of the idea of pulling it all the way myself. There was no sign of Egbert within me. I really am trying hard to accept this and yes am able to do it. My understanding has grown. I feel good that I'm happy to let Sakimba and the team help. But then he said, "I'll take it tomorrow too on the summit climb." My heart lurched. I knew what his promises meant to him; he would take it. Let go, I reminded myself again. Let go! Let go of what Egbert wants to do, of all sense of the importance of self. We're working for the team. We're working for humanity.

This time I knew I really had let go. I felt the lightness. I looked at Ann who had a sense of luminescence. She smiled, "Every step for the light."

"I can see spirit cloud everywhere."

"I can feel the energy too. It's incredible."

"It's the gathering of light-beings."

"How fantastic!"

Mawenzi had disappeared from view as had the summit crater ridge. Heavy mists were swirling around the nearby rocks which had taken on a reddish hue with olive green lichen. One tiny little white flower clung to the edge of a piece of lava. Visibility was down to a few metres, but we seemed to somehow be in our own shining world. I felt amazing. I felt as though uplifted on wings of light.

I hung back to wait for Pete. He'd slowed right down, his head was low and he didn't look good at all. "Headache?" I asked. He nodded as I gave him my water bottle and helped him find a muesli bar. Then Ann came to see how she could help.

So I hung back to wait for Rima. She also was suffering but didn't like to admit it. Though she did say, "I'm sorry I'm not going any faster." Could this really be Rima talking? She explained, "I don't want to revisit how I was on Day Three. I'm allowing my body to adjust at each level. Pressure and chaos need to level out. I'm trying to keep my breathing even."

"If you can talk easily while going along you're going the right speed."

"Yup, no it's okay. I want to make sure I don't let you down. My goal for this trip is to support you guys."

I shot her a grateful soul-sister look and then caught sight of Freddie bringing up the rear. Even he looked tired, well, a little tired. He had been working for many days on end, but even so the sparkle in his eye still said a song and dance was about to burst forth. He pointed to the side of the track where an arrow and some words had been written in stones. "Not far now to the campsite," he nodded.

"Any water there?" I asked.

"No, but we've already done the carry. After this we can use snow from the glaciers."

My pulse quickened. We really were getting closer to the snow, closer to the summit. Upwards and upwards we climbed, steeply now through shining mist which billowed up behind us too. It was not possible here to see more than a couple of metres in any direction. The lone figure of a porter struggling to adjust his load came and went in the mist. It was a lot colder. The wind was rising. The clouds we were in were wet; I felt drips liquefying on my hat. The campsite must be close. I can hear others ahead, but see no one. I love the beauty of it and the sense of the teams of light-beings surrounding us. I clasp my talisman and power shell ...

I know one spirit.

Kilimanjaro, Great brother, I stand with you. Blessings and thank you. And also to Ngai and to all light-beings. I will undergo my allotted task and pray for the openness to know. We hold the world in light and far far beyond. I am surrounded by the beauty and light of angelic wings and the sounds of cymbals and tingshaws. I know joy at the closeness. All is in preparation for what will soon take place.

From the shining mists I heard a cry of, "Campsite," though saw little through the swirls of cloud. Then I caught a glimpse of the faded green side of an old tin hut. The porters who carried bags for Pete and me were alongside it and greeted me with a big smile. I felt welcomed. Peering around I could just see more of our wonderful support team putting up tents closely squashed together at varying interesting looking angles and surrounded by a multitude of loose rocks.

This, at 4,722 metres, was School Hut. How exciting to be so close to our goal. Only one day and 1,173 metres in altitude to go. We had left this morning's camp in brilliant sunshine and after four hours climbing had travelled more than 5 kilometres and gained over 750 metres. Just like Pete always said, I had floated in on a cloud! Even the camp name sounded portentous. School, eh? How much more learning would have to take place here?

I was ushered into the hut. There was a table and benches and sardine bunk beds. Our team was strewn around the table passing round the camp registry book. Nick was filming. "How're you doing?" I asked him.

"Terrific!" he said energetically. He never did seem to quite relax, but then he was an international banker.

Everyone else apart from Ann was slumped at the table looking really tired. She beamed happily, "I found my legs were carried up by spirit."

Jackie was too exhausted to talk but managed a giggle.

Pete, in a senior moment daze said, "I've been carried up by angelic help today!"(Later he was to deny all knowledge of having said this, but it's on film!).

"What!" I exclaimed completely stunned. Was this my Pete talking? "What's Ann been doing to you?"

"She gave me holy water to drink," he said.

"Can't say I found any angels to carry me," said Nicholas, "but it feels high enough for them."

"No, I didn't have any angels either," said Jacob blinking

hard from tiredness. "My legs did all the work and don't I know it! It's feels like it's been a long long journey. I've been anticipating the top for so long. I've had a headache for days, since around 4,000 metres. I just want to get there and get off the mountain."

"Hang in there," said Gideon. "The time's 12.19pm. If we make it, 24 hours from now we'll be men. Bring on tomorrow!"

At that moment there were loud crashings all around us and the hut vibrated as though we were being shaken in a tin can. Staring through the open door we could see hailstones bucketing down. Then the hail turned to snow. In two minutes the misty grey was transformed to white. Thank you Kilimanjaro, I quietly intoned, thank you for waiting til at least some of us were sheltered.

Sakimba chose this moment to present Jess with a necklace and took an inordinately long time to place it tenderly around her neck. She looked up at him and smiled and then gave him a big hug. Did he really have a chance with Jess?

Energy was drifting back to the team.

Pete looked up at the beam crossing the roof of the hut, "Ah, something to play on." So Rima obliged by jumping up and doing a few pull-ups. Then just to truly show off she and Jess lay back on the beds and did rapid succession sit-ups. The men looked on in amazement. I blame the homeopathic coca.

By now the snow storm was abating a little and the porters had valiantly managed to put the tents up. Pete and I found ours set at an awkward angle on a slope with snow pouring in one end. We collected rocks and devised a channel for the melt water to go through the tent and out the other side. This was small beer compared to the problems of the main mess tent. It had a big rip in its roof and snow was mounting. Nick tried putting Pete's umbrella through the rip and then opening it up, but the brolley wasn't hefty enough and collapsed under the weight of the snow, pulling the roof down further. Everything was too wet for tape, so finally Monisi came up with the idea of laying a sleeping bag over the top. This reduced the problem to only a slow drip. The lunchtime stew pot was placed under this as a collecting pot and seemed to improve the potatoes and vegetables; the stew was voted the best ever. I did wonder, though, whose sleeping bag it was.

Mary was already in bed. We asked Nick, "Is she okay?" and Gideon enquired in a cousinly sort of way, "Has she had a wardrobe malfunction?" Nick just shrugged his shoulders and took her a plate of food. It seemed that, in addition to a tough day, it was more of a relationship sickness problem than one of altitude sickness. Hopefully a good night's sleep would restore harmony and we would have our glamorous Miss Vogue back, her relationship with Nick intact.

Actually we all had to think a bit about clothes for tomorrow. Up to now we had mostly been coping with heat in the day and cold at night, but nothing too extreme. Today's weather conditions showed us that from now on we could expect anything and even though we were so close to the equator, at this altitude it was possible to have polar temperatures. Tomorrow was going to be steep, much steeper than anything we'd experienced so far. The main enemy here would be sweat. "You sweat, you die!" Pete nonchalantly explained, passing on some polar training to Jacob and Gideon who looked aghast.

"But we can't stop sweating ..."

"It's important to wear your wicking thermals. These allow any sweat to go through them away from your skin. It's wet skin which causes a dangerous drop in body temperature. Don't wear too many clothes when climbing, but carry something warm and windproof for when we stop."

On hearing this Nicholas rushed off all the way to his tent muttering something about rescuing his trousers, only to come back saying that apparently he had already rescued them and it was only a senior moment. Does being at altitude bring on more or bigger senior moments? There could be some interesting research to do here. I didn't like to ask what he had actually rescued his trousers from.

The team seemed a bit calmer after lunch and welcomed all the porters and guides into the mess tent for the Peace Message reading. It was a bit of a squash but all the bodies together warmed the place up. And there's nothing like having someone's elbow in your earhole to add to the relaxed feeling of a sacred ceremony. Certainly everyone – client and support team, westerner and African, them and us – seemed to accept that we were now just one team working for Peace in the world. That in itself was quite an achievement which had originally seemed impossible, but now was able to come and gently sit on our shoulders (the only place there was any room.)

I made sure I included the Peace Message sent from a young friend of Peace Flame Sheila. I'd promised to read it on the summit, but something in me was niggling to do it now: "Merry meet, Great Spirit. Please teach me how to be a stronger version of myself, so that I can overcome my fears and always do my best."

After we had expressed joy and love and warmth of heart for all peoples with our Tanzanian brothers we sang and danced (well, wiggled anyway!).

Then Freddie spoke to us, expounding in his endearing African drawl, "It may be seven or eight hours to the summit tomorrow. But make sure on the way, if you find other groups, tell them about the Peace. Tell them that Team Kilimanjaro is bringing clients that want to make Peace in Africa and in the world. We are in different colours but together. Hakuna matata."

He leaned forward to add emphasis, "And tell others that the Kilimanjaro glacier is melting due to global warming and may be gone completely within fifteen years. Say that together we can do something about reducing the petrol and the industry, so that the snows can build up again."

I nodded and thought of all the Peace Messages that children had written promising to do something different in their lives to reduce carbon dioxide emissions and show respect for the Earth. Would it mean that far away on an African mountain the snows could return? Okay there are many weather cycles and other factors involved and many different opinions, but the children had believed these things possible ...

I asked, "What about after the summit, Freddie?

When we go down to our camp on the crater floor, will we feel the warmth of the Earth in the crater?"

"I may say that ... or not," he replied confusingly. "But I'm sure it's going to be warm cos I'm going to pray for you, cos you are truth people."

"Thank you, Freddie."

If by 'truth people' he meant genuine, authentic and from the heart then that was good. That was the way that Peace worked to my mind. But to open your heart you have to become vulnerable. There can be risks involved in expressing your truth. Sakimba was about to be reminded of this. I felt that he already knew it, but he was still about to be reminded ...

We wanted to film him singing the Maasai blessing song which he had sung out from the top of Mount Bodhi to welcome my little grandson. Rima prepared the video camera whilst Sakimba wrapped his red warrior cloak around him and settled himself in a chair, making sure that Jess sat close beside him and was warmed by the cloak too. She watched him with fascination. He lit the lantern and placed it in the Peace-tyre on the other side and put on his sunglasses. Of course, all film stars have to wear sunglasses.

"Thank you very much," he began speaking particularly slowly and deliberately, "for all the work for Peace and the coming together, the pulling together. It is so important for all nations. And as a Maasai I relate to Peace. I am very proud to be part of this. I will tell my people and it will help open the minds of the new generation." He clicked his fingers purposefully.

"There are problems. Much of our Maasai land has been stolen and even now is being taken from us, some by westerners who for sport and greed want to shoot our wild animals, who are our brothers, and with whom we have always lived in harmony. Particularly the lion with whom you know we have a special understanding. But we want to continue with our culture and shine a light for all people. I would be happy if our Maasai spirit is known around the world."

Then he stood and with many hand gesticulations sang the blessing song. Except it wasn't a song. It was more like a mesmerising sound of the wind blowing timelessly through dried grasslands or a strange beast yowling in tune with an endless starry sky, strung together with words of passion and meaning. The sound circled round and round with an aura all of its own.

"Ngai bless you," he finished, then said with a look of deep hurt. "I'm sorry I don't sing well, but this is very sacred to our culture." He blew out the flame which had somehow stayed lit, grabbed the tyre and rushed from the tent. Rima followed him. Why was Sakimba so upset?

I found Rima in tears, sitting on her sleeping bag. "It was Jacob and Gideon," she sobbed. "They were laughing at him. He was bravely pouring his heart out in the way of his tradition and they were sniggering."

I hadn't seen or heard them; I'd been totally engrossed in the song. But Sakimba obviously had. Again, along with Rima, I felt his pain. He was still being tested and having to find courage to face his lion. I also felt pain for humanity. How can we find a way to respect and be open to different cultures? To be sensitive to those of others? It was all about the one-family principle which we were trying to uphold.

"It was understandable," she said blowing her nose. "If you weren't tuned in, it could sound like a screeching cat having its throat cut. But that's not the point. And I'm sure it was the sunglasses that did it." She giggled and sighed.

"It's the living in two worlds isn't it? The old in harmony with the land and the new in harmony with commercialism," I said. "But it's always been so lovely that Sakimba has been proud to share his customs with us."

"Mmm, bit like stone-age people living in the modern era," she agreed and went off to find him.

Dusk was beginning to swallow the day. Mawenzi, Kilimanjaro's dragon, could just be seen, barely higher than us rising above purple clouds which billowed like smoke out into a pale lilac sky.

When she returned she confided in me, "He was okay but acting a bit strangely. He just wanted to talk to Jess."

At dinner the mood started off tense. Everyone was particularly hungry for the fresh oranges and water melon that had been laboriously carried up the mountain. The light of the Peace Flame and the two candles cast uneasy shadows on the sides of the tent. We were all focussed on what tomorrow might bring and that unspoken question, would we actually make it to the summit? At times like these a life distraction can be useful. Pete was pleased he'd managed to say happy birthday to his daughter Anna on the satellite phone. Here he'd found a really exciting message for Nicholas who, not wanting to be outdone by a granny, had previously declared that he was about to have a grandchild, too.

Today Nicholas's daughter had produced a beautiful little girl named Isla! That made him now a grand knight of the realm, which went well with the fine new beard he was sporting. Isla had arrived a week early. Wow! Talk about confirmation of new birth. What are the chances of two babies arriving during a Kilimanjaro climb? Perhaps this little being had contracted to be part of the new Peace energy too! It seemed perfect that Sakimba had just done the blessing song so we could attribute this to welcome her into the school of life. After all it had been sung high from 4,700 metres at School Hut. The news lifted us all.

"I believe everything is falling into place," said Ann. "This climb is a powerful event. And remember Ivy and her Wattle group in London, around 24 dedicated Earth healers, have now already started the 24-hour vigil for us."

After we had eaten Freddie came with all the guides and spoke to us. "Tomorrow we could do a fast and a slow group. Anyone want to be in a slow group?" Everyone in the tent put up their hand. "Oh, well, that's easy then. We go as one group." There was no way anyone wanted to split up anyhow. That would have defeated the whole purpose. Hmm I thought, the guides know this, but they're preparing for the possibility of some of us feeling really lousy. Felix explained at length that we would indeed feel lousy, but then he pointed at the lantern with its flame burning brightly and said, "But we shall be following the light for Peace." Ah, I thought, everything's worth it for that one comment.

The next decision was what time to leave. Generally, climbers set off before midnight to try and reach the summit for the sunrise, then head quickly back down to a lower camp a few hours away. Because we were unusually booked in to camp only three quarters of an hour away from the summit in the crater, we had the option of leaving at dawn. It was strange but everyone unanimously decided that dawn at School Hut would be wonderful. It can't possibly have had anything to do with remembering how awful it felt getting up for a midnight departure on Meru and the fact that the leaving-at-dawn plan included a night's sleep.

Around this time there was a kerfuffle at the door. Sakimba entered, swaying all over the place like a fish out of water. He tried to hold on to the side of the tent and collapsed noisily to the ground. Freddie and Felix glared at him. It seemed he was intoxicated by something stronger than homeopathic coca. Altitude, ridicule and love perhaps. It was a heady mix.

When everyone left for their tents, Sakimba pulled Rima to one side, entreating, "Please, I must tell Jess I love her."

Rima responded in the gentlest manner possible. "Jess has told me so I know. Listen, Sakimba. I'm sorry, but there can never be anything between you and Jess," she explained giving him a hug. He turned away. Totally dejected. Altitude, ridicule and a broken heart was an even more potent mix.

I could only focus on what had to be done. I repacked my gear, pulling out the flags and thermal tops, ski trousers and neck gaiter I'd brought for the summit bid and the crater when it would be colder and reminded myself to put my duvet jacket in my rucksack tomorrow, too. Because of this I would be carrying more just when I could've done with it being lighter, but at least my bag for the porters would be less heavy for them. The things that I considered vital I had carried in my rucksack with me every day anyway. There were the paper copies of the Peace Messages which were a few originals from children including my granddaughters, Nation, General and extra ones gleaned along the way; the bag of crystals wrapped not only in a maroon scarf but also somehow in their own sense of six; and the little summit-bag, containing the items from the other five points of the star; a picture of the Dalai Lama; the two little stones from my granddaughters; the wooden bracelet; the messages from my sons; the picture of a shining six-pointed star; and a diagram of the required configuration for the crystals. All items came in service for Peace.

Snuggled in my sleeping bag and by the light of my head torch I wrote up my diary. Then I lay listening. I could hear heated exchanges from the porters' tent. Was it about Jess? Pete had said that Monisi had already asked her to marry him. And another of the porters seemed to have fallen at her feet too, except Nick said he was going to be sent down due to having malaria. How many more men were sweet on Jess?! Sakimba's behaviour wouldn't have helped things. And he was no doubt in trouble with the guides, too.

Beside me Pete's slightly strained and erratic breathing was a comforting sound. He seemed to be okay, so that was good. Well, I thought, this is it. The last day has finally come. There seems to be a lot of challenges around already for the team. I've scarcely had a moment to think of myself, but I feel fine. So what do I want from tomorrow? Well ... for the entire team to be okay and to get there. But, actually, I'd love to be able to pull the tyre. This is the way I want to arrive, in the energy of our symbol, the whole purpose of the climb. But I wouldn't ask Sakimba to relinquish the tyre. I couldn't do it, not after what he's been through today. It means so much to him. He'd promised he would carry it.

I found stillness and opened myself consciously to the Divine flow of life. I remembered that Sakimba had given me the gift of an open heart for the climb of Oldonyo Lengai from which I had learnt about holding myself together. On Meru I had learnt about holding a team together in the way of service. Now, I wondered, what would Kilimanjaro have to teach me?

SUMMIT BOUND

21st September, 2011 – Day Eight
United Nations Peace Day

Mawenzi the dragon was breathing fire. He painted swathes of gold and burnt orange across the eastern sky, bringing to life his dark outline above a sea of amethyst cloud. It was as though a legend long foretold was taking place and on this extraordinary morning it was Kilimanjaro that birthed the light.

"Thank you for this beauty," I whispered, feeling small and humbled before such grandeur.

A blazing expanse of radiance burst through the fierce display of colour in the heavens. This was the sunrise of the September equinox, when day precisely equals night. From ancient times it has always been a time of power and balance and an expression of the peaceful rhythm of our Earth. Never was it to hold such significance.

The light diminished the blackness, revealing tents interspersed with patches of snow on volcanic gravel and the activities of a human lair. The movement of bodies was portraying long dancing shadows that pointed towards a steep slope to the west – the challenge ahead. There was a different feel to the camp today. A sense of purpose was over-riding last night's nervous tension.

"Thank God for Sakimba," said Nicholas looking up anxiously

at this shadowy rise and breathing hard after the exertions of his preparations to leave. "I certainly couldn't manage the tyre." But he did happily strap the Peace Lantern onto the back of his pack. What greater incentive could he have to keep going when things become tough? It seemed suitable that as our grand knight of the realm, he was to be the carrier of the flame on this important day.

Whilst we waited for the others I mentally checked that I'd done everything. The night had seemed very black and cold when we were awakened at 5am but I'd gone through the routine of washing, dressing, taking pills and forcing down breakfast to the light of the Peace Flame. I'd made some sandwiches of dried bread and honey, filled up my water bottles to two and a half litres, one containing Empact, packed my personal bag for the porters and visited the loo tent three times. Then for the umpteenth time I'd made sure the summit crystals were in my rucksack and clipped on their guardian penguin, Gaius. His puffed-out white chest glowed in the soft dawn light. His time had come!

Pete joined us. "Wonderful to set off in fresh snow!" he exclaimed happily.

And then Jess, "How special is that sunrise! Not something many people see. We're so lucky to be here."

The rest of the team gathered, bundled up in balaclavas, hats and gloves against the icy sharpness of the air. The temperature was well below freezing. It was 6.30am, half an hour later than planned. There was an unusual sense of urgency from the guides for we would need time at the other end of the day for whatever might happen.

"To Kilimanjaro and beyond!" I rallied.

"For Peace!" was the response from Rima and Jess.

I caught sight of Sakimba, holding onto the tyre. He was silent and subdued.

Anthony led off at his usual steady pace, but the way was steeper than we had been used to and a bit of a scramble, so he took a zigzag route, skirting a jumbled rocky outcrop to our left. It crossed a snowscape with rocks interspersed. Rima followed, intense with Rima energy and then Jackie and Ann, plodding. I was pleased to see that they had already given their rucksacks to James and Raymond. Then came Pete. As he turned a corner he looked back at me and crossed his sticks high in the air. This was our secret sign which said "Love you". I acknowledged it with a similar sign. It confirmed for me that all was well with my world on this special day and my last twinge of nervousness subsided.

And it appeared too that Nick and Mary were happy, under many layers of clothes, behind him. Then came Jess as always with no sticks, Nicholas with the lantern, and Gideon and Jacob looking keen to get moving. I joined on behind and after a little while looked back and saw Raymond coming up pulling the tyre and Monisi holding the back rope. Why was Raymond pulling the tyre? Where was Sakimba? Oh no! What has gone wrong this time? Far below, tightening my eyes against the light shining off the snow which was dazzling even though sunglasses, I could see the camp nestled into the rocks. The porters were taking down the tents and loading up in preparation for some to climb to the crater camp and some to set up the retreat camp ten kilometres to the south along our eventual route down. There was no sign of Sakimba. I sighed and headed on after the team snaking upwards on the path to clear blue sky.

We were heading in a general southwest direction across the barren and bleak volcanic desert that we were used to, fast appearing beneath the light snow that was already starting to melt. Now there were awkward loose scree slopes interspersed with ramps of petrified lava flows. This solid base would not be so good for pulling across I detected, though the snow must still be helping. I watched as Felix took over the tyre and decided now was my moment. "Please ... I can take it now," I said in the most ordering-about voice I could muster and held my breath. I'm no good at being commanding. People tend to ignore my attempts. Now was no exception. The guides obviously had it in their remit, after safety, to make absolutely sure their clients make it to the top. To allow a client to use up all that energy by pulling a heavy car tyre was not sound practice; failures don't look good on records. But I was aware that Felix, in spite of all his obvious frustrations with the Maasai warrior our team seemingly brought with us, was at some level sensitive to the greater cause. Whilst his head was battling with his heart I grabbed the rope and set off pulling. Monisi picked up the back rope. Done!

Only then did I feel it safe to ask Felix, "Where is Sakimba?" There was a shrug of his shoulders. Obviously he didn't want to talk about it.

I became hot within a couple of minutes of pulling. The day was warming up fast anyway and the snow around us was becoming very sketchy. Others were stopping to strip off layers of clothing. I noticed the green, yellow and red Rastafarian bands on the London warriors' arms and it struck me that whilst we were all on one journey together, individually our inner journeys, incentives and goals were quite different. All as it should be in the colourful circle of life.

Thank goodness there was a drink stop. I took off my windproof, my fleece, my hat and a thick top thermal. Whew! That was better except now they would make my rucksack heavy. Ah, and now I didn't have a tyre! Monisi had attached it to his sack. Maybe he really wants to pull it, I mused, but I wasn't so sure. Why would anyone else actually want to be quite so daft?!

I heard Mary say, "Our guidebook states that from here on in the chances of failure are high ... and throwing up or passing out are even higher." I figure we must be nearing 5,000 metres. Oh well. This was the place to be daft.

Moving on, we crossed a particularly bumpy lava flow and the first of the porters caught up with us. As always I marvelled at the way the impossible looking load was balanced. But then there appeared a porter who, unusually, was bent over double. Sakimba. Strapped awkwardly to Jackie's big rucksack which he usually carried along with his sleeping bag, were two of the large mattresses. The load looked impossibly heavy. And Sakimba looked broken. He was swaying unnaturally as though waves of nausea were passing through him and he could barely find a smile. "The office said I must carry more," was all he could manage in response to my raised eyebrows. My heart went out to him and I felt his sadness. He'd only come to help us because he believed in our cause. He'd come away from his land where he was master and in harmony ...

I turned, feeling uncomfortable, back to the climb.

The steepness of the rough track eased a little. We were still going southwest and partly across the main slope which loomed high on our right side to the northwest. Underfoot it became loose gravelly scree, not so good for walking up but much better for pulling so long as we kept on the track rather than the heavy loose rock tracts around us. So Monisi said they would let me take the tyre here if I liked. Great! I was a Peace warrior. I would take it for Sakimba too. I clipped in, started off, took the strain and this time Amani felt to be my personal responsibility. From now on I knew I had to think inwards and just concentrate. The Universe had dictated that I was the one to pull. It was my turn.

I tried to get into the steady rhythm, right stick, left leg, left stick, right leg, focus on the movement. Hold the pace. Feel the solid friction of the tyre through my rucksack with shoulders and hips. Inevitably it jumped about. The trail was far from even. Lumps of lava would threaten to not only trip me up but turn Amani upside down with a jerk. Felix took hold of the back rope which helped the stability and the balance. But all was okay. I felt strong and happy. Anyway, how much easier Kilimanjaro was than the harder and more dangerous climbs of Lengai and Meru. And how lovely to do this one in the daytime.

After a while I did manage to settle into a regular movement and was able to focus my thoughts on the job I'd been given. Peace ... Peace on Earth. No small job then ... *Now* was what all the preparation had been for. Helping the world. Everything else fell away from my mind.

Peace ... Peace ... Peace, not just the absence of violence and war. Something far wider, determined by the individual ...

The love and joy which is within us all.

Instinctively, holding myself in balance, I let my right hand push aside my neck gaiter and finger my talisman. There was my familiar *"we are one spirit"*. I laughed to myself fancying it was white-necked raven saying this, flying alongside me squawing and showing off as usual.

And then I had the thought. What if this place of love and joy is also exactly the same place of love and joy in everybody else, in every other form of conscious life? What if we are all in the same place, even if we each describe it differently? What if we are all connected through this place. Could this be the oneness of spirit?

If so, I could see how it was possible for each one of us to make a difference at every moment of life, because everything we think, say or do is affecting everything else. I saw how our Peace Messages, written from the heart of so many individuals, were all intertwined in this way. And with representations from every nation it meant that we were symbolically carrying the entire hopes for our common humanity and the Earth home we all share. Our team had been given the job of bringing them together. Between us we'd brought them this far. And this was the moment to pull them to the highest place.

My thoughts jostled on giving me impetus and keeping me going: left foot, right stick, Peace, right foot, left stick, Peace, heave, onwards and upwards.

It must have been about three hours from leaving camp when we climbed over a lava band into a different valley and our path wiggled down onto a wide open motorway-track filled with countless footprints in the ash. It came from the direction of Mawenzi now swathed in drifting cloud. The dragon breathed smoke again. I turned and my eyes followed the way the track led upwards. Holy smoke indeed! Wooh! That's scary. What a view! The track took huge zigzags up and up and up across a wild moonscape til a thousand metres or so above us rampant clouds shifted just long enough to reveal a dark ridge. The rim of Kilimanjaro's Kibo crater. Somehow I hadn't been prepared for Kibo's size, even though we'd seen it from Meru and been spiralling round it for days. Now that we were up this close it looked absolutely immense. Yes, Kibo's enormity befitted the scale of Kilimanjaro itself, sixty kilometres wide, eighty kilometres long and six kilometres straight up into the sky.

We were merely little ants crawling up it. Any decent wind could puff us away in seconds ... The way ahead appeared to be mostly loose scree and ash with patches of lumpy irregular lava set between the huge volcanic tentacles reaching down from the rim. That was okay. That was expected. What was scary was the steepness. I've climbed Lengai and Meru, yes and they're steep, but I've never pulled a tyre up anything quite this steep and for quite so long. And, of course, at altitude. Is it possible? It's certainly completely bonkers! But there's no way I'm going to bottle out. It has to be done.

I think I'm going to need some help here ... some inner warrior strength.

I am enveloped by my cloak of courage.

We turned west and took the track.

Briefly I joined Jess, Jackie and Raymond for a little hugging circle that Ann was organising to chant 'Om' and speak the Silent Minute prayer every hour as they went. This gave me a boost. Then I set off upwards with Felix still guiding the tyre behind. We were silent now. There was no energy for talking.

It's probably even worse than it looks, I thought grimly. I know that our immediate vision of the mountain is foreshortened. Maybe that's a good thing, otherwise it might look too daunting to even tackle. But hey ho, life is for living. Cut it into bite-sized pieces, and all things are possible. I know I can do the next bit. I can do the next step.

I put my head down and concentrated on the next step. And the next ...

At one of the corners of the zig I looked up for a moment before going into the zag and saw the snake of those of our team who were above me. I could pick out the turquoise of Anthony's sack. It must be Jacob behind him and, the red jumper of Gideon, Mary's pink trousers, so that must be Nick, the green of Jess' sack and momentarily I witnessed a glistening gold light as the sun caught the edge of the Peace Lantern on the back of Nicholas' sack. Ah, who needs matches. We have a slightly larger flame ... It reminded me to hold the light in my heart. And taking a deep breath it gave me the impetus to start a mind mantra: I can do this ... I can do this ... I can do this ... for the World Peace Flame light was leading us onwards.

And somewhere up ahead the highest point in Africa waited.

Convincing my body to move again wasn't quite as easy as I thought it might be. But the reciting of the mantra managed to persuade my legs and arms to find the rhythm, right stick, left leg, Peace, left stick, right leg, Peace ... and this encouraged my brain to put my back into the enormity of the physical challenge. Complicated things, these bodies!

The rest of the team are somewhere behind. We seem to be splitting naturally into a fast and a slow team. Perhaps I can hold everyone together from the middle, like on Meru. I so want us all to be together ... I'll draw the team together as one entity into a bubble of light. Ah this seems to connect me up with everyone. My senses say that Pete is struggling, though I can't see him. He gives out so much strength it's likely that no one else will remember that he battled with the altitude in the Antarctic and that he's been through a cancer operation. But the others will look after him, I'm sure. I'll send him a special bubble of light, like a cloak of courage. I'm pulling the Peace-tyre for him too and for our work with Climb For Tibet. Oh, and of course I'm pulling it for the rest of the team. And on behalf of the whole of humanity.

That was when I saw that if I can draw the team together in this way, then surely I can draw everyone else together too. In my mind's eye I pictured all the people on Earth in the bubble of light. It felt good, though I didn't want to connect up at this moment with those specific nations that I sensed were struggling.

I'll just concentrate on the positives and try and hold the world together. Surely every person doing this inwardly must be contributing to the wealth of love and light which is gathering and making a difference manifesting at a physical level. It doesn't appear so seeing the daily negative news, but something in me says, yes for sure this is what is happening.

We're getting higher. Ah, we know we've reached 5,259 metres. There's a cave over there at the end of that zig up against the lava wall. I don't want to investigate. It would mean stopping. I can just see the plaque beside it on the rock, dedicated to Hans Meyer, the German mountaineer who's meant to be the first human to climb this mountain in 1889. Took him three attempts. Hope we can do it first time. I'd hate to have to come back and do this again. Onwards!

Wooh, my mouth's dry. I could do with a drink. Empact would be great. It'd give me some energy. Daren't stop though. Too hard to get going again and anyway I'd have to take my sack off to get the bottle. Should've got one of those water-sucking things like Nicholas. At least I haven't got a headache, well, it's more a sort of nauseous feeling in the brain, but nothing to worry about. Stomach feels a bit dodgy though, probably some food would help, maybe I've still got some dried mango in my pocket. Oh, no, wrong pocket, I've got my ski trousers on. At least they're pink, so I'm in fashion now too. Very important. Can't climb to the Roof of Africa in just any old trousers!

Wooh, it's hard work, this pulling a tyre bit. Whose idea was it anyway? I suppose I have to put in great effort to make it worthwhile. I can't remember why, oh yes I can, it's cos it's a giving of self. I have to give of myself. It's the African way.

The tyre yanked me backwards caught on a rogue piece of lava and would've tipped and tumbled steeply downwards off the more flattened track but for Felix holding the back rope taut. "Come along, Amani," I mumbled, "stop fooling about." My brain sent another message to my mouth to say, "Thank you, Felix," his strong calm presence was so comforting, but somehow not all the messages were getting through. And I didn't like to turn round and smile as I felt better if I kept my head steady and my eyes focussed on the track immediately ahead. Somehow as long as I kept the movement going I knew all would be well.

I must not stop. Each zig we traipse laboriously across seems to only bring us upwards a small bit, but we cannot leave one out. Each step along the way has to be undergone. Onwards, onwards ...

I need positive thoughts. What about the funds? Ah yes, all this effort is helping raise sponsorship. Thank you, all you lovely people who have donated to our list of causes. For the school children at Ngongongare, so they can have water, for the planting of trees with Tree Aid in Ethiopia so famine will be reduced. For the African Initiatives work to help the Maasai hold onto their traditional land. The ongoing Tibetan struggle to help those who lost everything in the earthquake, and Pete's prostate cancer charity. Thank you. We do this to help all of you. I will not stop. On. On ...

It's becoming steeper still. But my chest is hurting. It can't seem to take in enough air. It's my upper chest, no it's the lower. It must be the lungs. C'mon, take in a deep breath. Take another one. Make it long and drawn out. Breath out the tension. No, I know it doesn't help the body, but I can't relax. I have to hold onto to this. I cannot let go. I have to hold it together. Of course I already knew that it would be tougher doing something intensely physical at altitude rather than at a steady plod. But this ... this is a geometric difference. It's crazy. How can I hold it together?

I can do this. I will not let it beat me.

On, on ... the sky awaits ... on, on ... heave, heave ... step up, step up ...

My lucidity comes in waves. Ah, I really do feel good now. 'Cept, it all feels so timeless. There's a sense of the sun high overhead, but how many hours is it since we left camp? How many hours since the junction ... since the last drink ... I've no idea how far we've come, or how much further to go, there's all that cloud ahead and anyway there's only rock to see up there ... and scree here. At least the footing's good, though as it's loose I do slide backwards a bit on every step. How much worse if this was all iced over? Pictures I've seen show most of the upper reaches as white, covered in snow and ice. And there's tales of wading through knee-deep snow. Where is it all? There's no snow at all from yesterday's fall. Is it global warming? Is it caused by man? Certainly Freddie thought so. Or is it perhaps just part of nature's cycles? It makes climbing easier, yes, but what will become of all those dependent for their crops and livelihood on the mountain's streams and rivers if the snows are no longer here?

Great Kilimanjaro, where is your white beard?

I give you the strength of my body, pull, heave, step, stick, step, stick ... I give you my life's blood on its mission of searching for oxygen, I give you my sweat, tasting sour on my dry lips, mingling sticky with the dust. Sweat! Oh, should I be taking my mid-layer thermal off? No, bare arms would be stupid. My body warmth is keeping me going. It's hugging my aching shoulders and the pain of the weight of the tyre on my hip bones. Ah, I can adjust the straps of my sack so that the pull is more from my waist, less painful but needs more energy and more sweat ... I'll just have to sweat ... can't be much left to come out anyway ...

How am I keeping going, hour after hour? Maybe it's not me but the mountain that goes on forever. It passes me by as I stand here with the Peace-tyre and with Felix. I'm beginning to feel dizzy and I'm obsessed with water, but my brain cannot make decisions like, get sack off, get out water bottle ... too much effort ... can't do that ... as though it's the most stressful job imaginable ... The brain's not even doing the work. It's the legs. They feel like jelly. The calf muscles are crying out ... they've had enough of this pulling business ... They're going to go on strike!

My confusion grows as the way becomes steeper still.

At around two in the afternoon there are voices from above. We negotiate a patch of well-polished lava and come out onto the edge of an eerie-like sheltered hollow surrounded by large rocks, a place called Gillman's Point. We are on the rim of the crater. Many people give up here and call this the end of their climb. I could see why. I was sure the supreme effort to get here in this rarefied air is more than should be endured. I could hear my mother saying, "Well, if you will pull a tyre ..." and that made me smile.

For the first time it was possible to see into Kilimanjaro's inner sanctum. Wow! What a privilege. The huge circular crater went steeply down and stretched across our vision, two and a half kilometres wide. The floor was virtually all grey hilly volcanic deposits. A handful of snow patches and a couple of small ice waterfalls were all that honoured the expected polar zone, all that is except for the amazing glaciers around the outside. To our north we could see the white tips of the Eastern Icefields and to our west the towers of the Southern Icefields. It was extraordinary, as if someone had decided to try and daub ice cream on the outside edges of a bowl. It was incomparable with anything else I'd ever seen. The volcano's mouth itself was a gentle rise in the middle, an inner crater. Even when the shifting cloud cleared it was not possible to see within that, though it's said that sometimes the fumaroles there in the ash pit let off sulphurous smoke, showing that Kilimanjaro is indeed alive.

Around the rim little more than two kilometres away, the ridge led to the highest point in the sky ... the summit.

Even in my shattered state it was impossible not to feel a burst of excitement. We were so nearly there. But first a rest. The stopping of the physical effort, allowed some rational thinking to come back. Whilst I had the energy of movement I delved into my sack and found my thick top thermal, fleece and windproof. Then I crumpled down alongside the Gillman's Point sign reading 5,681 metres. A stupefied smile on my face. Made it this far!

A couple of the porters were here and also the fast team. They'd been waiting for us for well over an hour, so were stiffening up and cold and keen to get going again. They set off along the ridge once Jackie and Ann, supported by James and Raymond, came up not far behind me. Wow, look at these mountaineers. Who'd ever have thought they'd be able to achieve this! Jackie seemed in a dazed zombie state, but Ann settled down to eat and drink as though she did this every day of the week.

Monisi gave me biscuits and held out a can of red-bull. In spite of my desperate thirst I hesitated, remembering how sick it had made me feel on Lengai. He leaned over and gave me a big encouraging hug. The red-bull spilled down my leg and went through the thigh split in my ski trousers. Ah, I would it have anyway. The chill went right through me and became part of the exhaustion. I knew I couldn't sit still for too long or I'd never move again ...

But I wanted to wait for Pete. He, Rima and Freddie eventually appeared, climbing into the shelter of the hollow. I could see that Pete wasn't with it at all. There was a lethargic aura wrapped tightly around him. Rima was inciting him on, telling him how well he'd been doing, how we were nearly there. Jess joined in, calm and steady. She had waited to do the last bit with Rima.

There was no sign of Sakimba. But his warrior spirit climbed with us.

I stood up shakily and swung on my rucksack. Felix picked up the tyre as though it was nothing. Had all my struggles been for something that light? Of course he was completely acclimatised and worked at these altitudes. Breathing heavily, I followed him off along the ridge, the path starting off inside the rim and then taking both an inner and outer way. I felt like throwing up; it had to be the red-bull.

"We should be there in about an hour and a half," he encouraged.

"Good. I'm fine to take the tyre again," I said. I would finish what I'd started. This was my way of service. It's for humanity. Our ultimate symbolic act, all nations pulling together for Peace. I remembered then that as well as drawing the team together, it was important to keep drawing all people together in my mind. Today was UN Peace Day. The world is being enveloped by Peace thoughts and initiatives. There are others doing Peace Climbs and tuning in to us. We are part of the Peace movement right across our planet.

Felix stared intensely at me as I fixed the tyre rope to my sack. "What religion are you?" he asked.

"Nothing specific," I replied. "I kind of accept what feels right for me as ideas come along."

"Whatever you are, I want to be it too."

The accolade of these words passed over me like the echo of a wind-song.

Not much wind though. This is extraordinary. Surely there should be strong gales here with nothing else to stop their wild paths blowing around the world? And freezing temperatures? Every picture of the summit I've seen has shown icy cold conditions. But now although the Earth in all directions is covered in voluminous cloud, here we are, uniquely just the crater and us, basking in warm sunshine, above it all. I'm sure it's warm sunshine. Thank you, Great Kilimanjaro. You are looking after us.

Things changed as soon as I started pulling the tyre again.

I feel completely horrendous. It's the physical exertion demanding of the body what the body's unable to give. I know that as long as I can hold some semblance of my mind together, then my body will have no choice but to come along too. But my head feels really weird, like my brain is exploding and burning my mind. Not so much a headache as a headfire. If my mind has been holding my body together, but now is on the way out, what will hold me together? I'm drifting in a timeless ocean ... both time and space have ceased to have any meaning.

The track hugs the ridge-top. A place of crossroads marked Stella Point at 5,730 metres comes and goes. On an outward facing part of the path an enormous glacier looms to our left, a huge lump of ice cream carved to perfection like a curtain across the sky.

The ridge, now with only gentle undulations, curves upwards to the horizon ... til only a few hundred metres away in the distance is what looks like a sign-post touching the sky. Nearly there.

My struggling mind is overridden by a waterfall of knowing that I will pull this tyre from here to there.

Pull, pull, pull ...

My body forces a long drawn out breath and holds open my arms in an instinctive heart opening movement.

Pull, pull, pull ...

Closer, closer ... here are the welcoming faces of the fast team and the Peace Lantern hanging on the summit sign: 'Congratulations. You are now at Uhuru Peak, Tanzania, 5,895 metres above mean sea level. Africa's highest point. World's highest freestanding mountain.'

I come in service for all nations, all people.

I am exhausted ... vulnerable ... humble ... I have given everything. There is nothing left to give ... except love.

I am enveloped in loving compassion, like the warrior cloak, only this time I am part of it, there is no separation. It lays bare my innermost being to be with unconditional love.

My outstretched hand touches the sign, then tears the rucksack from my back. I release Amani the Peace-tyre to settle by the summit post and collapse beside it onto the well-worn rocks.

Everything goes blank.

Somewhere on the edge of the dream between now and eternity, an African voice is saying, "I'm going to take her down *now*."

THE PLACE WHERE
ALL MEET

I am out of it.

An observer. Above my body as though flying like white-necked raven. I am watching what my body is doing, but I am not there. I have stepped aside. I see myself lying writhing on the ground on my back, one hand over my face, sobbing though there are no tears. My chest is heaving uncontrollably, breathing fast with harsh rasping sounds. There is a sense of trying to fall into the Earth, to be swallowed up as though this is a way to be hugged and held.

And then I see ... from this higher perspective ... and I know. I know because I am. All things ... And nothing. It is simple. I know that this is the place where all meet ... and that this place is one spirit.

I don't feel love and joy. I *am* love and joy ... for I am all things.

I am light. As is every other being; for I see chords of light reaching down from an infinite expanse of light into every one of the bodies of the team, like a flattened translucent jellyfish with tentacles.

I see how we're all connected ... like each individual is one cell of the body of humanity, each being one cell of the Universe.

I look down as the light directed towards and into each

member of the team comes together in a hugging circle. Prayers are causing puffs of light to emanate. And light is wafting from Monisi who is laying down his precious coming-of-age bracelet in a hidden rock crevice. The Chagga people have been honoured. Their bond with the mountain is in trust for a bond with all humanity.

I am aware of Ann beside my body. She is saying, "C'mon, breathe with me. Think light into your solar plexus."

Felix is saying, "I'm taking her down now."

Ann responds, "No, she'll be okay." She helps me sit up and offers some of her holy water to drink.

My body is saying, "Can't go down. Things to do ... photos ..."

"It's urgent that we get her down."

"No!" says Ann firmly, finding a piece of muesli bar to feed me.

My body starts shivering from cold, a deep searing cold that is seen rather than felt. Ann helps me rummage in my rucksack for my duvet jacket and hat to put on, in addition to three thermals, a fleece and a windproof, far more than the others are wearing. My hands are grasping Gaius and my little summit-bag as though tightly holding onto their significance. Then the flags are found and my body is staggering to its feet and as though in a dream holding up the Tibetan flag, the nutritional sponsor's flag and the small Welsh flag. Jackie is taking photos. Raymond fixes the UN flag and the Peace sign to the summit sign, so that it reads 'Congratulations. You are now at Peace.'

With dragging steps, Pete walks up to the sign. He is hurting. Somehow my body is holding on to him and there is comfort in sobs of relief, born of long years of affinity and togetherness. Grounded even now, he looks at his watch: "4pm," he notes.

Then Rima is giving me a long soul sister hug and telling me, "I really struggled at first. Couldn't get my head together and was way behind everyone. Freddie stayed back with me. Then I caught up with Pete who's been going through a nightmare, unable to breathe. Monisi took his pack for him, but every one of his steps has been tortuous. I've no idea where he found the courage to keep going. On the ridge I went back to find him, gave him a hug and he burst into tears."

There are more hugs and photos with the tyre and the Peace Lantern and just for a very short while the Peace Climb team – on behalf of all the nations of the world – stand together on the summit of Kilimanjaro.

Mary, Nick, Jacob and Gideon, chilled from another long wait, are led by Anthony towards the inner crater rim.

More photos, then Freddie and Raymond take Nicholas, Rima, Jess and Pete along the same path. My body shouts "Pete! Wait!" But the sound disappears into thin air.

As if guided by unseen hands those remaining know what has to be done. Also, the exact place.

Ann is kneeling and clearing a circle half a metre wide to create a shallow bowl. My body unwraps the parcel of sacred crystals and hands them to Ann who places the large shiny golden iron pyrite in the centre, the three beautiful intense blue lapis lazuli equidistant around it, the six clear glass-like quartz crystals around them and finally, the six whirled-chocolate fire tiger's eyes surrounding them. The figure resembles six spokes of a wheel coming into a golden hub.

A small pink-flecked picture jasper crystal is given to each kneeling person: one, two, three, four, five, six. There are six people representing the Peace Climb team. Each speaks a message and together chant the 'Om'. We are blessed with the power of Master Advarr from the world of light. Nearby, the faded colours of prayer flags on my rucksack flutter and light emanates from the Peace-tyre.

And I watch, from this position of skyness, the shimmering translucent light that emanates both from the hearts and from the prayers of this circle of six. There is a complete balance: Monisi's compassion and giving nature, James' devotion and Maasai Earth sensitivity, Felix's faith and drive for Peace, Jackie's sweetness and purity of nature, Ann's wisdom and selflessness. And from my body, service and, thanks to the pulling of the tyre which had done its job of bringing me to my knees, unconditional love.

I am seeing the figure of a shining, six-pointed star.

The final piece of the jigsaw has been placed. There is a sense from deep within that all my life has been for this.

Gaius sits beside the ceremonial site, looking smug. Mission complete!

We six head north off the summit ridge into the crater, Felix carrying the tyre over one shoulder. As the path falls away I see Jackie experience fear, looking down the sheer drop of fine scree. James turns to face her. "Trust me," he says. Using his arm to support her on the side of her weakened ankle they descend rapidly, fear abated.

Ahead within the desert landscape of the crater is one huge glacier shining fiercely in the evening sun. It is a mighty wall of ice dwarfing the tiny tents incongruously pitched nearby at 5,729 metres, the crater camp. Here there is consternation within the team. Some need to descend fast and cannot wait til morning. Freddie and Anthony lead Mary, Nick, Jacob, Gideon and Jess, plodding at a snail's pace, over to a low part of the ridge for five hours of tortuous descent through darkness to the retreat camp, where they can begin to breathe freely again.

Those who are more acclimatised by having done the Lengai climb remain. Plus the ever-brave Rima. "The pensioners have stayed the course," Nicholas says shivering as he moves in to share her tent, "though we forget we feel the cold far more."

The temperature is down to minus 10°C.

My body is crawling into the tent with Pete. My head in a vice. It is burning ... calmly because it has no mind to express itself properly. My brain wants to be sick, but there is no place for the vomit to get out. Anyway, all is focussed on the one crucial job. To operate the satellite phone. Everything happens in excruciatingly slow motion, but the vital phone call to Ivy in London is made. "The crystals have been placed. The grid is set."

Continually sending light and prayers, Ivy now has the information she has been waiting for and is able to activate the star grid. Everything slots easily into place. Having previously programmed these crystals to the frequency of the Kilimanjaro grid, she is able to connect this grid up with the other five crystal grids that we have placed across the globe over the last thirteen years and which she has been holding as beacons of light. The six individual zones connect now via a greater whole, into completion state.

The six-pointed star of Peace shines!

Twenty-four people at Ivy's Wattle centre in London undergo prayer vigils in shifts to hold the energy.

The Earth turns on her axis and shows her other side to the light for warmth, whilst in the crater a Universe of stars stays on watch.

Tonight, there is one new star.

I am even now in this observer space wandering peacefully above everything. Somewhere lost in the crater at 6,000 metres my mind is shouting, "Speak out the Nation Messages! Speak out the Nation Messages!" But my body doesn't get it. All it can do is say, "Get me out o' here. Get me out o' here fast!"

Pete's brain has lucid moments. With great effort he says, "Every action seems impossible, doesn't it? Let's bury the Peace Message tubes here in the crater as we've always planned, but remember we've already spoken the Nation Messages out along with all the General Messages on the way up the mountain, so we can speak them out specifically later when we're with everybody lower down and in a sane state. It'll still be on the mountain." My body nods listlessly, not connected. It has lost the vital passion that has been driving it for so many months – years – along with any desire to get involved mentally or take action physically.

Andrew, one of the few remaining porters, brings soup and popcorn to the tents. Though all our drained bodies are badly in need of sustenance, nobody feels like eating. Pete's soup spills all over my sleeping bag. Hakuna matata.

Ann is in a bad way. She is struggling with a damp sleeping bag, deeply chilled, shivering, delirious and breathless. Her thoughts are calling out to Ivy in London.

Rima is anguished with an excruciating headache, vomiting and thumping heart.

Nicholas, in spite of breathing difficulties and a thin sleeping bag, guards the light that comes from the Peace Lantern.

Jackie sleeps.

Pete sleeps, though his light dims.

Everyone is cold and waiting for morning.

As the sun peers over the eastern edge of the crater rim the camp stirs.

Felix chivvies us all as though we are children to make ready to leave. My brain is still trying to explode out of my head. Pete's brain is wandering. He actually lets Felix get the tubes out of the tyre. I can see his inner conflict. He doesn't like anyone else touching his precious bolts.

We creep haphazardly but slowly as though walking in meditation across the floor of the crater towards the place of more gentle incline onto the ridge. The light is shining from the Peace Lantern on the back of Nicholas' rucksack. There is silence save for the boots crunching on the grey volcanic ash, loose and inviting. "Here," says Felix, moving away from the track, "how about here?" My body nods zombie-like and tries to dig with my feet but can't manage it. Nicholas moves in and works his foot into the dirt. He creates first an indentation, and then enlarges it to become a little well to take the precious gifts we are to leave behind. Pete places the two golden tubes into the waiting hole. One filled with 2,600 General Messages, one with 220 Nation Messages, representing every nation on Earth. Light streams from them as my body persuades itself to tackle the reading out of the Message from the United Nations Secretary General:

" ...Peace is our mission; our day-to-day quest ... I salute you activists and ordinary people for your courage and determination to build a better future ...To all those seeking Peace, this is your day, and we are with you."

It was one Message spoken out loud to hold the others safely together in their resting place.

"Anything else you'd like to bury?" Felix asks seemingly much amused by the habits of western clients.

Pete shakes his head, covers everything up with his feet and smoothes the spot with his hands, so there appears to be just a jumble of volcanic debris.

All the Peace Messages will stay here – touching the sky. For all time.

A soft glow comes from the large circular mound of the inner crater. Kilimanjaro's heart beats.

There is now only downwards.

Wow, this is fun! I love running down this loose scree, taking quick short strides, digging heels in, turning from side to side as though skiing ... now slipping and sliding on the scree ... feeling freedom, exhilaration, joy. I feel joy! I need to stop. Can only do this in short bursts. Slowing my headlong descent with my heels and sticks I came to a halt and sat, breathless.

I looked at my hands and turned them over, checking, smiling. Then stared back up the mountain. And took a deep breath.

I think I'm back together.

Where have I been?

It feels like I've just woken up from a night's sleep, having been busy in my dream body. Wooh! Maybe it was one of those meeting points of Heaven and Earth. Whatever, that was one heck of a senior moment!

How lovely to be able to feel again. I feel joy not only at the movement but a deep-rooted joy at what we've achieved.

Rima flew by pulling Amani, obviously having recovered too. "With Peace comes joy," she shouted and then stopped lower down to help a couple of stray porters, one of whom was Andrew who had looked after us in the crater. He was struggling with exhaustion and an excessively huge load. There must have been lots of reorganising along the way, I thought, especially when Sakimba had to leave his load somewhere when whatever happened to him happened. It must be a standard problem on the mountain. Through the clouds I could see plenty of other teams coming down like us but also a little way to the west a steady stream plodding upwards. Where have all these people come from?

That was when it hit me. There were hundreds of people on the mountain. All trying to climb Kilimanjaro. They must be queuing up at the summit. This was the South East valley, not only one of the main ways up but also the main way down over the steep crater wall. We were in a bottle-neck. Because of our well-chosen route we had barely met more than a handful of people over our entire nine days. And because of sleeping in the crater, the timing of our summit bid had been perfect to seemingly have the mountain to ourselves. Wow, how lucky were we?

Nicholas was having a go at pulling the tyre so I joined on as wingwoman on the back rope. How well he had held his energy throughout, in spite of the cold. "Pensioners can do anything!" I shouted as we followed on down the scree valley slipping and sliding on our downwards flow til Rima happily took over pulling Amani.

I thought of all the things I'd wanted us to do but hadn't managed in the summit crater, particularly speaking out all the Nation Messages and lighting the World Peace Flame.

So vital to have been done there. But then I realised our whole journey was the Peace Climb, and yes we would speak the Nation Messages tonight. And we had lit the lantern on Meru's summit and held the light in our hearts.

Maybe, sometimes the intention in the right focus is enough without having to actually do it in the physical. Which perhaps someday at some higher vibration we will all be doing anyhow. Hmm, much quicker and easier if we can get it right! Yes, things ended up different than planned. That's change. That's what's going on everywhere. To stand still is to go backwards.

Hakuna matata.

We came down into Millennium camp at 3,810 metres amongst the welcoming green of giant heathers. From here I could see the crater rim showing more glacial ice tongues than from the other side of the mountain, but already it all seemed small and far away. Anyway before us was a table set with a lovely lunch of soup, fried bread and fruit. We'd barely eaten since yesterday breakfast; I could only manage six bowls of soup. White-necked raven appeared, looking as though he could help out. He strutted around on the ground, head on one side. "So, how did you get on?"

"Yeah, survived!"

"I know. I was there."

I threw a piece of bread at him and he dived to pick it up in his beak and though almost half his size managed to become airborne. Quite remarkable he is. He left a farewell feather to place in my hair. No, I wouldn't forget him.

Then we moved further across the open moorland of his territory down, down, forever down with knees shouting to find our tents at Mweka Camp on the edge of the forest at 3,090 metres. It had been twelve kilometres from the crater. Now we could take in all the oxygen we wanted. Now we could breathe easily. We missed the fast team, but it was good to catch up with the rest of the porters. One came to me and asked, "Please give me some light," and I saw deep respect in his eyes. Porters from other groups were also greeting us with "Is that the magic lamp?" "Hey, Peace Bibi"(a nice name for Peace granny), "High five!" "Amani!" It was clear that the essence of our Peace Climb was spreading out and having far-reaching effects.

The porters and guides gathered enthusiastically in the mess tent for the reading out of the Nation Peace Messages. The Peace Flame burnt brightly sending light into shadowed corners. Monisi did a special prayer, Rima sang and then each and every people of the world were given a voice, everyone in the room taking a turn to speak. How fulfilling to share this with the Africans. It made all the effort seem worthwhile.

Raymond did the one from Kiribati: "On behalf of the people of Kiribati, Greetings and Peace to you all ... We are one of our world's most Peace-loving island nations, but world pollution is causing ice caps to melt, sea level to increase and our islands to become flooded and disappear beneath the crests of the mighty Pacific Ocean. Please help ..."

Sadness swept through me. Is it all too late? What can we do? I thought of all the strangely-isolated ice cliffs that we had seen, standing sentinel to a previous time of snow and ice. I felt a surge of determination. No! It's not too late. We can each do something to make a difference, however small. We can value our precious planet, finding harmony and balance. We can put love as the priority to replace greed. All nations have their problems but surely together they can be resolved.

These were powerful Peace Messages.

It got us thinking that it'd be good if we could set fire to them, to leave their ash essence here as part of the mountain like we had done on our Arctic Peace Climb. Ann found a large empty hot chocolate tin. It wasn't the most glamorous of sacred urns, neither did it appear to want to burn the Messages, however it did catch fire itself and create a lovely smoke-filled tent, which gave a certain sense of mystery to the ceremony. Perhaps leaving the tubes in the summit crater was enough, we weren't meant to be doing this here. Though possibly somewhere else ... ?

We still had to get off the mountain. After an amazing night's sleep everyone seemed to have recovered their energy.

Even Pete. My knight in shining armour was back! He attached Amani and went flat out, like a charging jouster, down the track for the nine kilometres to the National Park exit, Mweka Gate. The good thing about being a pensioner is that, in spite of sometimes extended senior moments, it's easy to forget all the things you're meant to be worrying about and get on with enjoying the now.

I felt honoured to carry the Peace Lantern on this final journey down the mountain, through the beautiful rainforest with towering tree giants, vibrant flower colours, bird calls and the smell of thick rich soil producing a profundity of life. Thank you for all things, Great Kilimanjaro.

Along the well-kept track, a guide rushing down stopped to ask about the lantern. He told me about the Torch of Tanzania known as Mwenge. This kerosene torch is a national icon and even appears on the back of coins. It was first lit on the summit of Kilimanjaro at independence in 1961, and is now lit every year and taken around the country amidst great celebrations symbolising light and freedom.

"Yes," Monisi confirmed, "I believe both light and freedom are more important than money."

Perhaps this was why our extended Tanzanian family was accepting the World Peace Flame so easily and with such understanding as a symbol of hope. It was already in their national psyche. And it showed the power of a little flame.

I proudly carried our Peace Lantern with the flame burning brightly into Mweka Gate at 1,641 metres. Here we met up with Mary, Jess, Gideon and Jacob. We barely recognised them, they looked clean and lovely. Sadly, Nick wasn't there. Having constantly supported Mary and energetically kept strong for the whole climb he had now crashed, suffering exhaustion after-effects. We missed him. He was the only one in the group to have kept up appearances by making sure that he always shaved!

A group of ragged and dirty children with big smiles on their little round black faces ran along beside us as we walked down the road beyond the gate past small tin-roofed huts and bright green farmland. I thought of all the stuff we had and how little they had. It tore at my heart-strings not to be able to give them anything. We had no sweets and all the cash was allocated to give as tips to our support team.

I remembered the time on our Millennium Climb high in the Andes when I was asked to make an offering to the Earth of something which was most important to me. Only if this was a true sacrifice by me would it be a worthwhile offering. Only if I could give away my most treasured possession would the gift be heartfelt enough ... and give enough honour.

There was one thing ...

Freddie gathered our team for the final song and dance with everyone joining in the hip-swaying routine. There was Sakimba milling in the crowd and looking somewhat recovered. The tips were presented from the clients to the guides and porters and it was farewell time for our little family that we'd become close to over the trials and fun of the journey.

How would it be if we thought of all people as our family? A better world?

And that would apply to penguins too.

Ah ...

I turned to three little girls who were quietly watching the proceedings. The oldest, perhaps eight, was caring for the other two. The second, maybe aged six, gave a shy smile showing half-grown adult teeth. And the tiny one who looked as though she might be disabled in some way, was peering out from behind the scruffy skirts of the others. I reached for my rucksack to give them a gift. Gaius had decided that his job was done and that he was going to go off with the little girls. Personally I believe that it wasn't so much a defection as his cover to still remain close to the mountain to guard the crystals. Forever ...

Gaius had been named after a wizard who knew the answers to everything, so I had to trust his judgement. He may be the only penguin to have actually travelled to the South Pole and possibly the only penguin to have climbed Kilimanjaro. This would mean nothing to the little girls, but the love he came with would mean everything.

He left his collar hanging empty on my rucksack and went to hug his new family. My last view of Gaius was of him tucked under the arm of the middle-sized girl who skipped excitedly along a mud path winding between maize plants and banana trees dripping green and lush.

That broke my heart.

Rain started bucketing, so we were all put onto a bus. Not everyone could fit, so we had to leave behind some of our family of porters, waving a sad goodbye. The park exit road was blocked by a mudslide, so we took a less-travelled route, which involved climbing a hill in a banana grove. The bus couldn't manage it and skidded off the muddy track. After much pushing and shouting everyone that was clean wasn't any more and the bus ended up deeper still in mud, tipping at a dangerous angle. Mary jumped out of the window and marched off into the banana grove, pulling her bright-pink polka-dot suitcase along the muddy track. The Africans stared at her. Ah, what would these westerners find to pull next? Well, it was much more fashionable than a dirty old tyre!

We all followed Mary back down into a village where another smaller bus was found. Piling everyone in may have been the African way, but after much jolting it was decided there were just too many bodies for it to go, so amidst heated debate some were chucked off. One of them was Sakimba. There hadn't even been time to speak with him properly; all we had gathered was that he'd been sick whilst on the mountain.

That was the last we saw of our Maasai Peace warrior. He disappeared into the thick liquid air of the lower slopes of Kilimanjaro.

OCEAN FIRE

Against all the odds, the entire team had completed the Peace Climb to the top of Africa's highest mountain, giving us exciting individual and collective achievements. Much was due to the guides looking after us so well, under Freddie's excellent leadership. In farewell they presented us with certificates. Just in case we might forget!

Guides aside, in the end surprisingly it had been the strong experienced ones who had struggled the most with the altitude. You never can tell. Anyway, each person had been on their own growth path. So there were differing personal legacies.

Jackie and Ann had both lost loads of weight and also proved to themselves you don't know what you can do until you try. Jacob and Gideon, though nervous at first, had been forced to face themselves and find strength. Mary had confirmed to herself that material wealth is not the real wealth. "It's what we hold in our hearts," she said. Nick had discovered the importance of health. Nicholas had decided to pursue his renewable energy work, partly in Africa, to make a difference in the world. Rima was just happy that we'd completed our six-pointed star to spread light. And Jess knew that her trip would always give a sense of calm that everything in life would work out okay. Well, maybe not so okay for all the men chasing her.

Pete loved the emphasis on one human family, all distantly related because of early-man's roots here in Africa. And the unusual achievement of everybody reaching the top, reinforcing the willingness of us all to work together. And yes, my knight had been through cancer and was still experiencing life to the full.

For me, what I went through on the summit was a real surprise. It was as though I couldn't feel any emotion, couldn't experience things. In this respect it was actually quite boring! From now on I intended to appreciate more this opportunity of being in a body ... But it was also beautiful, with teeming light and showed me how we're all interconnected as one. Because of this I felt a kind of responsibility for everything, so will commit to keep going with the Peace Message work in some way. No doubt life will show me how. But I know now it's important as part of the critical mass of individuals opening hearts to love and light ... the new birth of Peace.

There was a sense of everyone having been enriched and having grown at an inner level, because of the experience ... because of the fight ... because of the adventure. And yes, I was sure we would all carry Peace in our hearts as we returned to our everyday lives.

This included a most important event, taking a shower at the Outpost. From here Ann, Jackie, Pete and I set off on a little bus. There was one last job to do to tidy up the work of the Peace Messages.

From the bus window we watched as Mount Kilimanjaro passed by, cloaked in excessively shining cloud. Farewell, Great Kilimanjaro. I have given of myself to you, you have given of yourself to me. It seems we have exchanged vital energy. I will remember to hold humanity together in my mind light bubble.

All felt harmonious.

Just as the flow from a mountain is naturally to the sea, so we left the high country of Tanzania, crossed the great savannah plains of Kenya and came down to the coastal lowlands at Mombasa, there to following the beach road up to Malindi. Our driver Earnest kept going almost nonstop for twelve hours, much on rutted dirt tracks. The Indian Ocean was waiting for us to explode our high-desert starved senses. We could taste a salty tang in the warm night air, smell a powerful fragrance of tropical flowers and hear an endless crash of waves on a shore in tune with a wind singing around ancient baobab trees. It was like being in a dream, balmy and wafting ...

We awoke to paradise. I opened my eyes and through the fine net curtains of a huge bed looked across the tops of casuarinas and palm trees to a deep turquoise ocean playing with white horses out on a far reef. Bright plumed birds darted by and cicadas strummed in rhythm with the ocean song. Our accommodation was an integral part of the enchantment with no windows or doors and even open plan bathrooms, to share with twittering birds, scampering monkeys and the odd lost snake. This was a tall circular tree-top house perched above native forest, with palm-thatched roofs and walls decorated with light-bringers in the form of mosaics made from coloured glass bottles. The rooms were connected by little walkways as though part of the tree branches themselves. It was unique and totally beautiful.

Hospitality came courtesy of Peace Flame Paul who had organised for us to receive the lantern and then invited us to stay with him. What a gift from the Universe! So we were able to return the Peace Lantern to its rightful African guardian. But not before it had undertaken its final assignment for us.

Paul led us down a little winding path, soft fine sand squidging between our bare toes, to an expansive white sandy beach, decorated with lines of seaweed where the daily tides had left their offerings. It was deserted, save for a handful of distant figures and a few gulls watching over the waves. Pete and I ran into the sea to be enveloped like a warm hug and to float drifting in the water as though accessing the essence of life itself, connecting to the Earth's cycle of rivers running from Kilimanjaro to the sea flowing out endlessly across the oceans of the world before returning to the sky.

Paul had dug a deep pit and filled it with sun-bleached driftwood. The rim of the pit was protected by a battered down rampart, like the ridge around Kilimanjaro's crater, and displayed six rays which extended a couple of metres in length from the pit, like the mountain's lava tentacles. From the end of each of these he had brought out six small tentacles. A narrow channel was carved through the defences from the seaward side. It was ideal moulding sand for this special sand castle.

Our stage was now set. All felt perfect as I laid out the special objects, the UN flag, the prayer flags and the small Welsh flag which stated 'Peace to the people on Earth'. Nearby I put the Maasai container and my little summit-bag, which held an item from each of our six points of the Earth, including now the little piece of obsidian from Kilimanjaro. Oh, no! We seem to have lost our Antarctic representative, Gaius. I moved Pete's rucksack closer as on it was sewn a South Pole badge. All was ready.

I brought out my tingshaws and twanged them together, walking around the ceremonial pit, sending out ringing vibrations like bells from a church. Paul poured a little of the lamp oil from the lantern into the pit. He then ignited the World Peace Flame and placed it near the wood. The fire burst into life.

Next, the Message from the UN Secretary General was read. Then we each took paper sheets of all the Peace Messages, speaking out some on the way and scrunched them up to be thrown steadily, sheet by sheet, into the fire. We added the beautifully drawn originals from children we had brought, which included the precious ones from my granddaughters Elsie and Bess.

I feel the energy winding round and round in a spiral, higher and higher, as the vibration lifts and I feel fuller and fuller ... and the sound of the ocean is louder and louder and I clash the tingshaws and we chant 'Om'. And I'm full to overflowing and our hands open to the ocean and Peace Message essence is coming from the mountain and going out and out to the world as rays of light.

In the sky above, the clouds play and two enormous angels appear in the whiteness with huge wings and as we 'Om', a six-pointed star dances in the clouds. They are there and then they are gone.

Each in our own thoughts, we waited for the ocean to come. Free and flowing ... spacious as within each tiny cell, graceful as the dancing wind, as unchained as the sky itself. We waited ... and the waves rolled and swayed closer and closer ... til the water touched the channel ready to welcome the incoming tide. Gradually, gradually, wave after wave, the water came up and the anticipated moment arrived when it tumbled over into the pit, dousing the flames. The potent cauldron mix swirled til the next wave came and sweeping back, took the ashes of the Peace Messages and set off into the forever of the waves, as is its calling. We knew that this was what was meant to happen, which was why we couldn't burn them on the mountain, and so all was perfect. I felt a wonderful sense of completion ... yes, finally the work was done.

The waves smoothed and flattened and drew back. All went into one. The Peace Messages became part of the ocean. Finally, I placed the little pebble from Tibet whose brave spirit had led our inspiration and my granddaughters' two tiny stones to represent new life. These fell effortlessly to the waves. We stared at the saturated flat piece of shimmering sand, all that remained.

I smiled.

And the ocean in its beauty kept rolling on without drawing breath ...

The waves lapped at my feet and held me in Peace.

Now away from the mountains, I could stand back and see my own journey more clearly and where I had grown. I had overcome fear and found harmony with myself on Oldonyo Lengai. I had worked with service and experienced harmony with the team on Meru. I had perceived oneness and felt harmony with all people on Kilimanjaro.

I could see that by following my own passion I had been true to myself and with better understanding about everything being interconnected as one spirit I could see that I'd also been true to everybody else.

The challenges I had faced had helped me learn.

I know that life will continue with its changes and challenges in its perpetual movement like the ocean ... whether I wait for them to come looking for me or grab challenges of my own choosing, which is considerably more positive and fun. I cannot run away, though I can gather extra energy and strength to cope with them, simply by asking for help inwardly. And if I'm following my own passion, then the extra energy flows naturally.

I believe that in spite of all the disasters in the news and touching our personal lives, that there is an exciting sense of awakening around the world. That humankind is in the process of evolving further, of rebuilding itself ... to become *homo luminous*, man of light, as the old prophesies like those of the Mayans have always foretold, where decisions are made for the greater good, where people do things for the world, looking after each other and our Earth.

By bettering ourselves we really are bettering humanity. We're all in this together. It is time. Each and every one of us is needed to take part, in our own way. To allow our visions to come so that we can see them clearly. And then hold onto them. To follow our dreams and stand up and be counted. Yes, dreams really do come true; we just have to dream them and trust. And aim for the highest we can imagine, send prayers, give love, take action and not give up.

To go climb our mountains.

To go pull our tyres.

To be brave, finding our own cloak of courage ... and that Peace warrior spirit within.

To reach up and touch the sky, shouting, "I'm in!"

"No worries! Hakuna matata!"

"I'm in!"

EPILOGUE

Six months after the climb, Pete received a phone call from the UK police whilst we were skiing in the Alps. "Morning, Sir. We wish to inform you that your house has been broken into and been set on fire. Most of your things have been wrecked." Oh dear! So we returned to England and Pete, bravely in his usual matter-of-fact way, began the long process of renewal. It was as though his path was to let go of the past and start again. I should have noticed the warning.

Five months afterwards, Pete, Rima and I pulled five gaily coloured tyres through the streets of London during the 2012 Olympics to honour the spirit of all nations coming together in Peace. The tyres beautifully symbolised the Olympic rings. We pulled them down the River Thames to meet Ann and Jackie at the Peace Pagoda in Battersea Park, where we spoke out our Nation Peace Messages. The Peace Focus of our African Climb continues to do its work in the world. Yes, we can all pull together for Peace.

But perhaps the concept of 'together' has a wider meaning than I had previously thought. A further four months after the Olympics, on 21st December, 2012 – the time when the old world was meant to end – my Pete informed me that he was in love with another woman. For fifteen years, ever since we had been together, I had thought that we would be forever, he and I ...

I was to need all the strength I had gleaned through our expeditions. I was determined, somehow, to accept the cards that had been dealt to me and which no doubt I had a part in attracting. Obviously there was one simple fact: I hadn't made him feel loved enough. But I could move on in a loving way, so there would be no ill feeling between us. After all we had been through so much, so very intensely together.

Egbert had a field day playing cruelly with my emotions. "How could you do this to me? How could you abandon me? I'm the victim here. What about the lies? What about the betrayal? It's only your male ego that you're pandering to. I should know."

"Shut up, Egbert. Anger only hurts yourself."

"Ah, but it feeds the internal anguish. Then you can justify things and feel like a winner."

"Shut up, Egbert! There's enough to fight in the world without fighting myself too."

I realised that when I hid within myself, wallowing in my sadness and allowing critical and negative thoughts and feelings, that I felt dead. When I was able to say "thank you" and "goodbye" in a loving way, I became alive again. And then the wounds were able to begin the healing process.

This was an important discovery. I now knew that it is within myself where all things happen. It's not so much what comes at me in life; I am the one who dictates what I feel. I am in theory in control of myself. I was reminded of that old maxim: 'As a man thinketh so he is'.

Ah, easier said than done perhaps. But to know it at a mind level can only help its manifestation at a physical level. Was this experience opening me to a deeper part of myself? Awakening layers that had lain dormant? Perhaps it was bringing up stuff like gratefulness and humbleness.

My heart is heavy as I write this. But more than anything, dear reader, I want to show that it is also uplifted and inspired.

D'you know, there is so much beauty in all this.

You know when you are deeply sad and struggling through some major trauma and pain, be it grief, or illness or loss ...

and people are truly compassionate. You know the sort of thing ... "Oh, I'm sorry to hear about your break-up. I thought you were such soul-partners". And it makes you go straight into the hurt, kind of opens the wound, much more than if someone was nasty .... and it moves you close to tears. This brings it to the surface. So you have to face it ... face yourself, but lovingly. You cannot hide it away. Somehow it seems to be the genuine compassion that actually brings the hurt to the surface that exposes it. And then it is able to be healed and slowly, slowly there is a transformation. Sadness does cleanse the heart, though it takes time for the emotions to catch on.

Even though at the time I was so wobbly and vulnerable, I found looking back that it was the compassion of family and friends that sustained me and gave me the strength I needed. My heart was held in the strength of others' compassion. Humbly with no ego ... along with the Dalai Lama's example of loving those who hurt you. The strength of other's compassion actually helped me open my heart to find unconditional love. This was akin to my experience on Kilimanjaro when I was so exhausted and vulnerable.

What a gift it was to experience the receiving of compassion. To be held by the tenderness and love of family and friends. Those who were thinking of me and supporting me and surrounding me with light.

And I was deeply touched by Sakimba, who on hearing our news, emailed me. I could see him in my mind's eye in his mud hut. "I am here for you, no matter how far you are, but in spirit always together. Enjoy each day of your life. Delete all stress and all bad thinking in your head. And accommodate all good things, so that you will get happiness in your life."

Okay! I have pressed the 'delete' button in my head, the one that held the file of 'break-up of relationship'. Anyway, soul partners have certain agendas, maybe from pre-life agreements, though these can be tempered by choice. And I suppose not just any sort of soul could give me the gift of opportunity of growth like this. I have had to accept, to let go and to see the positives and joys of new beginnings. So, yes, I am grateful to Pete.

My spiritual guides tell me that all is as it is meant to be. That it is merely the ending of a chapter. That on my course into the new world era I will now not be held back. That I must stride boldly onwards with no fear. I have my cloak of courage.

And thank you Sakimba, peace warrior. You speak as a voice of Africa for harmony. We are under one sky. I have tested your Maasai and very human wisdom and found it not to be lacking. May your new tree-planting programme, Green Africa Restoration, go well and fulfil its dual purpose of providing security for the Maasai people and vital environmental benefit for the Earth that we all share. How lovely to dedicated your work to our little Peace warriors, the baby Sakimba in your village in the dry savannahs of northern Tanzania, and to my grandson Bodhi in his home on the surfing beaches of southwest England.

My new but different space continues with joy along the journey of life's path, not the least of which is spending precious time with my grandchildren. And making sure I play my part in leaving them a beautiful, Peaceful Earth.

C'mon. Let us, all together, bring on a bright new world!

NATION PEACE MESSAGES

TANZANIA: "We the people of Taganyika would like to light a candle and put it on the top of Mt Kilimanjaro, which would shine beyond our borders, giving hope where there was despair, love where there was hate, and dignity where before there was only humiliation." Julius Nyerere

AFGHANISTAN: I promise to turn things off when I'm not using them, to help the Earth (age 8).

ALBANIA: May we keep animals safe (age 4).

ALGERIA: We shall take care of our planet to make our society greener and peaceful for our children.

ANDORRA: I will keep the World Peace Flame candle with me and light from it as many candles as possible with love.

ANGOLA: I wish all the nations peace and harmony and lots of love.

ANTARCTICA: Love shine a light in every corner of the world.

ANTIGUA & BARBUDA: Much love to all peoples of the world.

ARGENTINA: Live every day like it's your last, 'cause one day you're gonna be right (age 15).

ARMENIA: Peace and Health to the world!

AUSTRALIA: 'If we have no peace, it is because we have forgotten that we belong to each other' (Mother Teresa). May we see only a peaceful, joy-filled world as we unite in love.

AUSTRIA: Appreciate the luxury you are living in.

AZERBAIJAN: For many years Azerbaijan is under aggression. Mothers of war martyrs, war widows and orphans sat with the World Peace Flame, focusing on our own inner peace and on world peace. We honoured, by a minute of silence, victims of armed conflicts in our country and all over the world. A new peace network is founded.

BAHAMAS: Forwards… upwards… onwards… together.

BAHRAIN: I think that people need a constant reminder that peace is achievable in the little ways as well as in the big issues.

BANGLADESH: I wish for every-one to be friends (age 10).

BARBADOS: It is you who is weaving threads of gold into the tapestry of life.

BELARUS: I am grateful for the World Peace Flame candle. This does me credit to light it because I know that people in the whole world will do the same.

BELGIUM: Let's work together and become one big unit in which we add to each other and celebrate our differences, enjoying the richness of each other's culture.

BELIZE: Honouring our history, celebrating our culture, uniting for peace. We who celebrate our 30 year anniversary of independence on UN Peace Day this 21st Sept.

BENIN: Hello! Good Morning to Everyone! Peace to All!

BHUTAN: May we be united in a single flame of hope. May peace prevail on Earth.

BOLIVIA: Defend Mother Earth's Rights!

BOSNIA: Love and light from Bosnia. Wishing peace, love, health and prosperity for all countries and their peoples.

BOTSWANA: Coming from Botswana which is one of the most peaceful countries in the world, peace and prosperity for all should definitely be the epitome for all governments.

BRAZIL: I wish everything that was made from wood, such as this paper, is only if they plant more trees than they cut down.

BRUNEI DARUSSALAM: We wish the entire world to be an abode of Peace.

BULGARIA: I wish that the world is nice and spotless (age 5).

BURKINA FASO: When we are united, we have much more force. We can exchange ideas and reach a much better consensus than we would on our own.

BURMA: 'Use your liberty to promote those without.' Aung San Suu Kyi.

BURUNDI: I have a dream that one day my country can be a peaceful one. Could you help me in that goal?

CAMBODIA: 'The suffering of Cambodia has been deep. From this suffering comes great compassion. Great Compassion makes a peaceful heart. A peaceful heart makes a peaceful person. A peaceful person makes a peaceful family. A peaceful family makes a peaceful community. A peaceful community makes a peaceful nation. A peaceful nation makes a peaceful world. May all beings live in happiness and peace. (Venerable Maha Ghosananda).

CAMEROON: All we need is Love. Love can overcome all boundaries. LIVE, LAUGH, LOVE. Peace.

CANADA: May we open our hearts to the world!

CAPE VERDE: Peace and love to all from the enchanting islands of Cape Verde.

CENTRAL AFRICAN REPUBLIC: We send greetings for peace, and wish unity, dignity and work for all people. Let us unite in the greatest love and work together for peace for all humanity.

CHAD: Peace from Chad is shared with the world.

CHILE: All our energy and love in the search of a fraternal global communion for the evolution of all mankind.

CHINA: I will play my part by planting more trees and looking after all the flowers (age 10).

COLUMBIA: I wish all the people in the world have food and drink whenever they want (age 12).

CONGO (Democratic Republic): Arise world and make peace!

CONGO (Republic): We send our best wishes for peace and non-violence, and greetings for the whole of humanity.

COOK ISLANDS: Keep up the good work. Wishing you every success.

COMOROS ISLANDS: May peace prevail in the world. Peace and good luck upon you.

COSTA RICA: Costa Rica desires to share its immense love for nature and peace. We hope all the people learn to put Mother Earth interests before their own. Care and love all creatures as equals!

COTE D'IVOIRE: Reconciliation and Peace.

CROATIA: Let there be Peace in the World.

CUBA: Cheers! Sending good vibes, love from the people of Cuba.

CYPRUS: Peace be with you!

CZECH REPUBLIC: Please pray for President Vaclav Havel who has supported the Dalai Lama's way of peace for many years.

DENMARK: I pledge to plant a flower (age 7).

DJIBOUTI: Unity, Equality and Peace.

DOMINICA: World of beauty, world of splendor. Let us care for nature's beauty.

DOMINICAN REPUBLIC: From Pico Duarte, the Caribbean's highest mountain, we send our most positive thoughts for peace.

EAST TIMOR: I will say a little prayer for peace.

ECUADOR: We had a war between Ecuador and Peru but now we are in peace. I wish to continue this way for ever and ever. Stop killing other humans! No more!

EGYPT: I wish that every animal is not in danger and Earth can live in Peace (age 10).

EL SALVADOR: Peace to all people of the world.

ENGLAND: People! Just be kind to each other. (Joanna Lumley).

ERITREA: I wish there were no litter or wars but more animals so we can live in a better environment. Let's take care of our environment (age 10).

ESPERANTO: With universal responsibility, it becomes possible to support peace and non-violence. Where does peace begin if not in our hearts? The world is more than ever in need of peace. It is the responsibility of us all.

ESTONIA: There will be lights of peace in Estonia on 21 September.

ETHIOPIA: Now is the day for the dream of lasting peace, world citizenship and rule of international morality.

EQUATORIAL GUINEA: Let us walk the Peace-path. Everybody wants Peace.

FALKLAND ISLANDS: 'They shall beat their swords into ploughshares, and their spears into pruning-hooks; nation shall not lift up sword against nation, neither shall they learn war anymore.' Isaiah 2, the Bible.

FIJI: May the beauty of our islands be reflected in the beauty of our Earth.

FINLAND: Peace to all peoples and nations in the world. May there be peace in your heart. We wish peace and harmony everywhere in the world.

FIRST NATION CANADA: To the wise ones, the elders who hold and keep bright the light of the one true tradition, no matter the color of their skin or the name of their religion – I honor you. And also to the generations who follow, that you may remember and honor those who have gone before you. May Great Spirit watch over all the people of the earth, May peace love and forgiveness follow for the new time to come. Aho!!!

FRANCE: For me, peace is about sharing everything which is vital for man: Water; Forests; Education; The pooling of research on health etc; Respect, everywhere, of human rights; And the duty to ensure that every one has work, food, shelter and instruction. Peace, for me, is also the source of creation... permission for everyone to express themselves by: speaking, art, music...

GABON: Peace from our land which expresses the beauty of Africa.

GAMBIA: A proverb from the Smiling Coast of Africa... 'If there's one donkey in the room, don't make it two' ...So smile!

GERMANY: Let's talk to each other.

GEORGIA: Strength is in unity.

GHANA: I pray that all children in need will find peace and joy! And that every child will smile. I want every child to have an opportunity to be happy (age 12).

GIBRALTAR: The Rock of Gibraltar, one of the Pillars of Hercules, sends a message of love and peace to all its neighbours and citizens of the World. Let us unite as one family in creating a haven of peace for all our children around the world.

GREECE: From the East, House of Light, may wisdom dawn in us so we may see all things in clarity. From the North, House of Night, may wisdom ripen in us so we may know all from within. From the West, House of Transformation, may wisdom be transformed into right action, so we may do what must be done. From the South, House of the Eternal Sun, may right action reap the harvest so we may enjoy the fruits of planetary being. From Above, House of Heaven, may star people and ancestors be with us now. From Below, House of Earth, may the heartbeat of her crystal core bless us with harmonies to end all war. From the Centre, Galactic Source, which is everywhere at once, may everything be known as the light of mutual love. Oh Yum Hunab Ku, Evam Maya E Ma Ho! Oh mother source –the harmony of mind and nature.

GREENLAND: The Greenland air is clean, cold and crisp to breath, colours are extremely vivid, our guests who visit are completely inspired and this simply restores your faith in this world because you see the world for what it should be ... a peaceful place.

GRENADA: Country of my birth, beautiful jewel of greens, blues and sunshine, I offer you this humble prayer for peace; that your beauty, simplicity and peace may continue to be felt and appreciated by your people; that they may cherish and nurture what they have been given in nature, and by a bountiful God. That they may continue to live in peace and harmony with each other with all life forms within nature, and the land itself.

GUATEMALA: I want that all countries of the world have peace and love, and the whole of the people have water and food, and no longer wars any more.

GUINEA: I welcome from my heart all people to our beautiful land. Ah! It is beautiful…

GUINEA-BISSAU: Wishing you success in your project.

GUYANA: I will respect the world like I respect my parents, sisters, brother and myself (age 9).

HAITI: From the Mission of Haiti we send greetings to our brothers and sisters in Africa, and best wishes to the world for peace, security, development, education and care of children. We love you!

HAWAI'I: Love and Thankfulness.

HERZEGOVINA: I will educate more people in my country on recycling.

HOLLAND: May the Light open everybody's heart to share love and compassion with each other.

HONDURAS: Honduras, as a founding member of the United Nations, wishes to express its solidarity and pledge with world peace. A peace based on democracy, respect for Human Rights and fundamentally the dignity of human beings. Our people have the duty to reach their levels of progress based on a human coexistence of respect, equality and tolerance in every aspect of daily life. Only with the promise of a fair and egalitarian society can we reach the peace we long for in our world. We reaffirm our pledge to peace not only as means to an absence of war but moreover as a peace based on education and the integral development of our society. Peace for everyone and everyone for peace.

HONG KONG: The Pearl of the Orient. Let the wisdom and the wealth of the Orient be shared throughout the world, that peace and harmony may touch all humanity.

HUNGARY: Let us build a just and peaceful world.

ICELAND: Let us treat strangers like they are part of our family. To protect and defend those who cannot defend themselves. To love our planet and all who is in it, no matter what color, race, religion or age.

INDIA: I pray people will see in each other what they have in common, not what is different.

INDONESIA: May all human beings live in peace and harmony, sharing and caring.

INUIT: Let all people of the world work together as a team (children age 9).

IRAN: Dear God, I wish that you save the Bahai's in Iran. Oh God, guide me, protect me, illumine the lamp of my heart. And make me a brilliant star. Thou art the Mighty and powerful (age 15).

IRAQ: Please give particular thought to the world's oppressed people who are in need of true and real peace. Also give special thought to those people who are suffering from man-made disaster and oppression in the name of international and national institutions ... People of Cuba, Sudan and Iraq are suffering from human imposed sanctions and the target is the people. Such people need to have true and real peace of mind so they can enjoy proper development. People in the Third World Nations are in quest for real and true peace.

IRELAND: I hope that everyone in the world finds a great team to help them live their dreams!

ISRAEL: Everything is possible. Say out loud 'Shalom!' to the world. (Uri Geller).

ITALY: We must ensure that our presence on this Earth is beneficial to others. Remember, while living, that we are all guests on this earth – we came with nothing and will leave with nothing. Therefore let us live life to its fullest in full respect, peace and harmony with all living beings and let us expand our vision of unity beyond our four walls.

JAMAICA: I pray that everyone in the world will work together to make it a better place (age 10).

JAPAN: Everyone of the world! We are one family.

JORDON: We wish for everyone in the world to have health and wealth, to drink clean water, and to be able to walk the streets safely.

KAZAKHSTAN: People! Try to be wise and live in Peace! Be tolerant and kind! Enjoy life, laugh and love. Try to be helpful for your community!

KENYA: I wish the world could be a happy place for everyone and I wish that everyone is happy where they are (age 7).

KIRIBATI: On behalf of the people of Kiribati I would like to say Greetings and peace to you all. The people of Kiribati are one of the world's most peace loving island nations on this planet of ours but their total existence is on the brink of disappearing due to increases in world pollution which is causing the ice caps to melt, the sea level to increase and the islands to become flooded and disappearing beneath the crests of the mighty Pacific Ocean. Please help to stop the pollution and help to preserve and protect these beautiful pristine islands and its peace loving people. We wish you all Peace, Happiness and Prosperity.

KOREA (North): Greetings from the Korean National Peace Committee! I hope that we can contact and co-operate each other for the world peace and justice. Yours in peace.

KOREA (South): I would like to see the United Korea during my lifetime.

KOSOVO: I stopped the truck a few hundred yards past a mass grave and we lit a World Peace Flame candle and sat quietly for a while.

KUWAIT: Peace is the Foundation of all Human Potential.

KYRGYZSTAN: Life! Like driving a bicycle. To keep your balance you must move.

LAOS: May the peacefulness of Laos touch the rest of the world.

LATVIA: Shalom to all living beings, especially those on Kilimanjaro!

LEBANON: We hope things get solved in all Middle-Eastern countries, especially Syria and Lebanon, as with a more peaceful atmosphere we could all enjoy living our lives happily and building a better future for ourselves and our families.

LESOTHO: Peace, rain and prosperity for all.

LIBERIA: In union strong, success is sure.

LIBYA: Democracy in the Middle East is not impossible…

LIECHTENSTEIN: Peaceful greetings to all the world from Liechtenstein, which manages to live peacefully without an army!

LITHUANIA: I promise to not waste water (age 6).

LUXEMBOURG: Peace and joy to everybody.

MACEDONIA: I wish everybody could be eco-friendly and care for all animals and Earth, and we can be in Peace (age 10).

MADAGASCAR: Keep the peace and friendship bond.

MALAWI: We lit the World Peace Flame candle and my family members were interested. I explained to them the meaning of lighting the candle for Peace. One of my neighbours admired this and did the same at his house …

MALAYSIA: I wish for freedom … in mind, in heart and in soul … to all those in the world!

MALDIVES: Gunam has been doing yoga since the age of 9 taught by his grandfather who lived until 96!! His dream is to teach yoga to children but at present he works to support his mother and sisters as a cook in the holiday resort. He never misses his yoga and meditation and it would be lovely to see his dream materialise.

MALI: Trees are important to me because they are in the heart of my life. They provide us with food, energy through firewood, medicine, shade and daily tools.

MALTA: May the breeze of love flow through the trees and across the ocean to envelop the world and create peace and goodwill among all.

MARSHALL ISLANDS: Accomplishment through joint effort.

MAURITANIA: I will light a Peace flame in Mauritania. I will do all my efforts.

MAURITIUS: During my visit to Scotland I promise to put down a piece of corrugated iron to provide a shelter for adders, an endangered snake (age 10).

MEMON ETHNIC GROUP: I wish that people understand everybody and stay calm when there is a problem (age 10).

MEXICO: We will teach our child to care for the world and the people in it.

MICRONESIA: Peace, Unity and Liberty!

MOLDOVA: Peace and harmony from Moldova.

MONACO: Be Green! Through trying to repair some of the damage we have done to our sacred Earth hopefully we can find peace.

MONGOLIA: From the open spaces of Mongolia we send peace and freedom to all people.

MONTENEGRO: May All Our Dawns Be Bright! And 'Imagine all the People Living Life in Peace ...' (John Lennon).

MOROCCO: I will help grown-ups and children (age 5).

MOZAMBIQUE: Our Earth is the 'Beloved Homeland' for each and every one of us.

NAMIBIA: From the land of the brave, we share our spirit with the world!

NATIVE AMERICAN: O Great Spirit of our Ancestors, I raise my pipe to you; to your messengers, the four winds, and to Mother Earth who provides for your children. Give us the wisdom to teach our children to love, to respect, and to be kind to each other, so that they may grow with peace of mind. Let us learn to share all good things that you provide for us on this Earth.

NAURU: Peace, love and hope for all nations.

NEPAL: Tashi delek, peace, love and prosperity from our country Nepal. Lots of prayers. Namaste.

NEW ZEALAND: I wish that there were no bullies in the world (age 13).

NICARAGUA: We Nicaraguans feel linked to this place where our origins are.

NIGER: We need every effort for peace. God Bless.

NIGERIA: I wish Nigeria was safe for everybody, so they cannot be dead (age 6).

NORTHERN IRELAND: If we can do it, so can you!

NORWAY: I hope we all could try to take better care of the environment so the Earth can take care of us for many years to come.

OMAN: I wish for peace for the Sultan of Oman and that the water in the mountains of Oman keeps on flowing. My wish is for humans and nature to prosper side by side.

PAKISTAN: I wish for a world that has peace; no fighting or hurting each other (age 9).

PALAU: We send you a message of peace and hope for the world.

PALESTINE: We will ask for peace from now till forever… it means living peacefully… it means no more blood, no more violence, nor more new orphans, and widows… Although there are lots of challenges, there is still hope to live in peace one day.

PANAMA: Let there be peace in every heart, family, community and nation in the world.

PAPUA & NEW GUINEA: I am from the land of Papua & New Guinea which is diversified in the cultures of our traditions, giving us strength. 'There is Unity in Diversity.' We wish to extend best wishes to the world.

PARAGUAY: From the heart of South America we send peace to the heart of the world.

PERU: The World Peace Flame shines from an island in the middle of Lake Titicaca – the worlds highest lake.

PHILIPPINES: May the warm hospitality of our country be experienced by all nations.

POLAND: I wish all the children in the world would not suffer anymore; and I wish that everyone would be more positive about things and I wish I was more smiley (age 15).

PORTUGAL: Love the planet and all living creatures so that it can continue to turn forever.

QATAR: People should want peace.

REUNION: Thank you for letting us participate, my friends and I from the Island of Reunion with the World Peace Flame.

ROMANIA: Be a friend for the others, but do not forget to be your own friend.

RUSSIA: For peace to happen we must learn to walk the Earth together (age 13).

RWANDA: God visits the earth and rests in Rwanda, it's a new Dawn in Rwanda, we own our Peace.

ST KITTS AND NEVIS: In times of struggle and strife, we wish strength; when souls become lost, we wish direction for an island so rich in pride and so close to our hearts; for a place that raised our ancestors so that we could make a start. St Kitts, we owe you our all; we send peace and love to the island and all of its children – from a proud son and daughter.

ST LUCIA: Dear God, please bring peace to all hearts, and harmony and balance to all things upon this beautiful island, brought about by the will of all people. Amen.

ST VINCENT & THE GRENADINES: From 'the land of the blessed' we send blessings of peace to the world.

SAMOA: On the 21st so we are going to have a little moment of silence for peace.

SAN MARINO: From the Serene Republic of San Marino we send serenity to all beings.

SAO TOME & PRINCIPE: Peace to the whole world!

SAUDI ARABIA: I wish and pray for peace for all the world, and that one day we will all be united.

SCOTLAND: Sacredness guide us. Sacredness flow through us all.

SENEGAL: I give you the small light to celebrate the international journey of peace.

SERBIA: The people of Serbia wish peace, happiness and prosperity to all peoples of the world.

SEYCHELLES: May we take this opportunity to wish you success in your endeavours to make a difference in this world.

SIERRA LEONE: I am sending this message from my country, Sierra Leone to the rest of the world. I pray that God, God of peace, continues to bring peace on us all.

SINGAPORE: Peace is not something you wish for. It's something you make, Something you do, Something you are, And something you give away.

SLOVAKIA: Mother nature has got everything we're looking for – love, stability, health, happiness… Get connected with her and we will be content and at peace.

SLOVENIA: Peace to all people on Earth!

SOLOMAN ISLANDS: Peace is a good cause!

SOMALIA: I want to help the tigers (age 4).

SOUTH AFRICA: Respect all living things and the Earth for the benefit of all future generations.

SPAIN: Believe! (age 12).

SRI LANKA: I wish everyone can eat food (age 4).

SUDAN & SOUTH SUDAN: The World Peace Flame is lit in Khartoum.

SURINAME: I wish you a lot of success with the project. With love and light.

SWAZILAND: We wish peace, health and prosperity to all people.

SWEDEN: May there be peace between all beings, everywhere on Earth.

SWITZERLAND: Respecting each other is most important. Use your own thoughts and judgements following your heart's way to make this a better place for all of us. Let love rule!

SYRIA: It doesn't matter which religion you believe in. Everybody believes in something else. It doesn't matter whether you are Christian, Muslim, Jew, Buddhist or someone other; we should all respect each other, because a human being is a human being. It doesn't matter which faith he or she has.

TAIWAN: Smile, be kind and considerate – a little warm gesture from everyone gives the world more hope.

TAJIKISTAN: We send peace and prosperity to all nations.

THAILAND: Dream for peace. Peace made the world beautiful. We want peace for the entire world. Keep peace always. Santi.

TIBET: I wish for nothing else but peace, love and understanding. No hatred in the name of race, religion or culture. May all living beings be free from suffering.

TOGO: In difficult life situations there are rays of light. The Lord does not abandon you. The candle burns with the Blessed Virgin, praying for peace.

TONGA: From the Friendly Islands we extend friendship to all people.

TRINIDAD: I wish there are no more wars (age 5).

TUNISIA: We send love from the beauty of Tunisia and the warmth of our people.

TURKEY: My Peace Message is for my family to be happy. And everyone smiling (age 10).

TURKMENISTAN: From sunny Turkmenistan we send warmth and peace to the world.

TUVALU: From our small beautiful island home we send much joy and peace to the world. (Dr Iftikhar Ayaz OBE, who climbed Kilimanjaro in 1956).

UGANDA: 'Returning hate for hate multiplies hate, adding deeper darkness to a night already devoid of stars. Darkness cannot drive out darkness: only light can do that. Hate cannot drive out hate: only love can do that,' (Martin Luther King Jr). My one wish for this world is for people to love one another because Love conquers all things.

UKRAINE: I wish that our world could be a better place (age 13).

UNITED ARAB EMIRATES: 'Love is but the discovery of ourselves in others, and the delight in recognition,' (Alexander Smith). Love in its many forms, from simple friendship to deep connection is often started with the most unlikely bond, a common thread no matter how small. Maybe as humans we all need to try a little harder to search for that common bond of kindness and understanding for there to be greater peace on this Earth.

URUGUAY: As a founder member of the United Nations, Uruguay is pleased to send peace and best wishes to the world. We are respectful of peace and international relations.

USA: I wish that the endangered animals could stop being hunted, especially dolphins (age 10).

UZBEKISTAN: Let us all care for the world's precious water resources.

VANUATU: Best wishes from the island of Efate in the archipelago of Vanuatu.

VENEZUELA: All that glitters IS gold.

VIETNAM: I will look after the world (Emma age 4).

WALES: Let There Be Peace Across The World.

WESTERN SAHARA: Our de-miners have the World Peace Flame candle as a token of our peaceful work in cleaning the land of anti-personnel mines and other lethal devices, and we want to embrace the candle and send this message of peace to the world.

YEMEN: I wish freedom of choice and world peace.

ZAMBIA: I would like to see every child have enough food and basic needs.

ZIMBABWE: Hopefully the South Pole won't melt any time soon (age 14).

UNITED NATIONS: "To the Kilimanjaro Peace Climb Team. Every year on the International Day of Peace, people around the world commit to non-violence... and to harmony among all peoples and nations. Peace is our mission; our day-to-day quest. This year's theme focuses on the timely issue of peace and democracy. Democracy is a core value of the United Nations. It is crucial for human rights. It provides channels for resolving differences. It gives hope to the marginalized... and power to the people. But democracy does not just happen; it has to be nurtured... and defended. The world needs you to speak out... For social justice and freedom of the press... For a clean environment and women's empowerment... For the rule of law and the right to a say in one's own future. I salute you activists and ordinary people for your courage and determination to build a better future. We at the United Nations will work in common cause to realize our shared aspirations for dignity, security and opportunity for all. To all those seeking peace, this is your day, and we are with you." United Nations Secretary-General Ban Ki-moon

GENERAL PEACE MESSAGES

Peace is the perfect posture of the soul, seek it and it will affect all those around you like the sun gives life. MARY • Let a spark of light ignite in the hearts and minds of humanity to bring LOVE AND PEACE upon all of creation. ANN • Our hearts and minds may at times be in conflict, but if we look into ourselves and find the light we can find inner peace. Follow the light and may this lead the way for peace. JACKIE • Our trash is poisoning the world (e.g. estimated 72 million tonnes of plastics in the oceans). Reduce your trash by refusing single use plastics (coffee cups/take away containers) and reusing by fixing things or by giving it away to someone else! RIMA • We live in an unsustainable world with an ever increasing population, where almost half is suffering from excess and other half from scarcity, and a climate that is threatening to engulf us. An enormous amount of the world's annually generated wealth is consumed by armaments and the cost of war, waged across the world with no apparent visibly beneficial results to either side. Let us hope and pray that, ultimately, common sense and wisdom will prevail so that the funds for war may be diverted to the creation of peace and nourishment for us all. NICHOLAS • In order to live in harmony we should all be aware that we are one human family no matter what the colour of our skin is or our religious beliefs. As such we are all related, albeit distantly. Any problem or conflict can be solved if we apply enough love. PETE • Mother Teresa said 'Peace begins with a smile'. I smiled plenty on our African journey which will be etched in my mind, forever. NICK • My peace message for the world is for all nations and all things to find harmony amongst the chaos. To embrace each other, love one another and stand united as one. I pray we turn away from violence and seek understanding. The idea that we belong to one another should be shouted across the world until we can all open our hearts and truly see. JESS • May we remember the inter-connectedness and equality of all. • May all Beings experience Peace and Happiness in their hearts and share this at times with others. • From the highest mountain in Africa we send messages of hope and love to the Earth's darkest corners, to ease the pain of all creatures that suffer. VIRGINIA MCKENNA • I am wrapping my arms around the Earth enveloping her in a beautiful shining white light sending her healing and protection. • My mountain message is … Never spit into the wind and each breath you take is the breath of life; to give to another human being. • One day mankind will live in balance with the natural world, when that happens there will be harmony, happiness and peace, both physically and spiritually for all. • My dream is for every man, woman and child, in every nation and country, from every religion and creed, to be united by the World Peace Flame. MANSUKH PATEL, co-founder of the World Peace Flame initiative • Peace cannot be delegated but begins with you and me and the choices we make today. SAVITRI MACCUISH, co-founder of the World Peace Flame initiative • Peace Strength and Love. Be glad for work that's difficult. For tasks that challenge you workers find a thousand blessings the idle never knew. • Children of the World Unite; We alone can make it right. • Happiness and smiling costs nothing, but reward many. • Love, Happiness, Joy and Peace to all who live on our Mother Earth. • I give thanks for today I have a vision … Where all people are at peace, fed and housed: Every child is loved and educated to develop their talents: Where the heart is more important than the head: And wisdom is revered over riches: In this world justice, equality and fairness rule: Nature is honoured, so the waters flow pure and clear: And the air is fresh and clean: Plants and trees are nurtured: And all animals are respected and treated with kindness: Happiness and laughter prevail: And humans walk hand in hand with angels: Thank you for the love, understanding, wisdom, courage and humility to do my part to spread the light: May all the world ascend: So be it. Vision Prayer for 2012 • You may have had no part in choosing to live, but you have the right to choose how to live. • May there be peace between nations and harmony between humans and animals (age 12). • My peace prayer is:- peace, peace, perfect peace. May all people hold love and light in their hearts and show kindness to each other and all animals, four-legged, furied ones, winged ones, the bees and other insects. • Of all the things you wear, expression is the most important. • Peace be with you all, wherever you are. • Dear Earth, help the Africans and other parts of us (age 12). • May everyone's dreams come true (age 13). • Dear Earth, you are a planet and home and supplier for all our needs, but we don't always take care of you. I promise to try harder to look after you and be more eco-friendly (age 14). • Thank you for this Earth that I love (age 11). • Dear Earth, you are a planet and home and supplier for all our needs, but we don't always take care of you. I promise to try harder to look after you and be more eco-friendly (age 14). • I pledge to forgive people for the bad things people have done instead of making it worse (age 10). • I promise to respect the earth with all my heart and soul (age 9). • 'And this shall be a bond between us; That we are of one blood you and I; That we have cried Peace to all and claimed fellowship with every living thing: That we hate war and sloth and greed, and love fellowship. And that we shall go singing to the fashioning of a new world.' William Morris • Dear wonderful Earth, I promise to recycle every day; to not waste food; and I'll turn off lights and plugs when not being used. Thank you for our great world (age 9). • I wish that everyone will get along regardless of religion or race (age 10). • I pray for less landfills and more eco-friendly houses and cars (age 11). • I pledge to plant a plant in my back garden every summer to help our environment and to symbolize peace in our world (age 11). • I wish for every child in this universe to be fed. I also wish for no wars, no crime ... and every special valued cared-for person to always smile (age 10). • I want African children to drink clean water, and have home meals (age 7). • I want the people in India to have homes and schools and food (age 7). • Dear Earth, I wish the children who don't have toys, do (age 7). • I pledge to look after my world age 8). • I wish for more stars in the sky. from Denmark (age 16). • Just look around you, Mankind. Selfishness is destroying what you see, but it is only mankind who can stop it ... We ALL need to help (age 13). • To make the world a better place by stopping war, global warming, starvation, abuse and to keep our generation healthy (age 11). • May any man or woman have the right to an education, food, water and shelter (age 14). • Make everyone happy and spread happiness like a breath exhaled from the Earth (age 16). • I wish for world peace, to heal the world (age 15). • May all people be fed equally and may there be no greed (age 15). • I wish that racism would stop and that all human beings were treated equally across the world. • I wish for everyone to have a chance (age 16). • May everyone respect the beauty of Earth, and try and preserve the stunning sights and sounds of our mother nature (age 12). • May all those who have been scared, feel safe. All those who have shed a tear, be happy. And all those who gave their lives be legends (age 13). • Please let all people in the world enjoy little things • May all the children of the world be able to drink clean water (age 13).

• I wish all the kids in Africa could have food and clean water (age 12). • May the Earth Mother smile upon us.• I would like to help the tiger and stop them from dying by stopping the hunter (age 6). • There's a hero when you look inside your heart. You don't have to be afraid of what you are. • I wish the world could stop war and unite everyone. • I wish for world peace and if it didn't work at least for violence to stop (age 13). • I promise to love the world and never do the people of the world harm (age 15). • May all people be blessed into health, happiness and free opportunity to fulfill their aspirations, with a planet we all strive to look after and protect. • I wish that I could visit poorer countries in the world and give them happiness and peace. • I wish for peace of mind for every person on Earth. That we will all have peace, perfect peace, in our lives (age 12). • No hunger (age 13). • May there be no more war ever. 'Bread not bombs' (age 13). • To stop destroying wildlife and no war so the whole world can get on and to stop littering and to sponsor poor people and to help them by giving them better education and things for them in the future and to help the environment (age 13). • Believe (age 12). • With light comes hope. Never give up. • I come from the UK! I wish the world would discover a new revolution in human beingness! • Shoot a smile not a bullet.• I want everyone to be able to believe what they want to (age 10). • I hope that everyone who is being hurt will be better. And poor people will be richer! • Here is my heart. • A miracle happens every moment, each time a good thought is sent. • We are our ancestors and we are our children. We are the river of life flowing through the world as it is today and we will inherit the world of the future. Let us step out of the small ways we see ourselves into the vastness of how we really are, and grow a healthy, conscious and wise world!

For more Peace Messages or to post you own, please visit:
www.climbfortibet.org

ACKNOWLEDGEMENTS

Warm and heartfelt thanks to all who have given of themselves to support Climb For Tibet and our work for Peace with sponsorship and Peace Messages, particularly the school children at Woolmer Hill, St Bartholomews, Cranmer Primary, Royal Alexandra and Albert, Woodcote House and Dunhurst.

With special thanks to:

His Holiness the Dalai Lama for his inspiration and universal love. Our other patrons – Joanna Lumley, Uri Geller, Doug Scott and Princess Helena Moutafian for their belief in the spirit of Climb For Tibet.

The Kilimanjaro Peace Climb Team – Pete, Nicholas, Ann, Jackie, Jacob, Gideon, Mary, Nick, Rima and Jess – for the great joy of sharing the entwining of our different paths as we travelled together. Especially Pete for being there for me across the years with so much love.

All the wonderful Tanzanians, guides and porters who became part of the Kilimanjaro Peace Climb Team and who now sing and dance through these pages. Especially Philip, Freddie, Felix, Monisi, James, Raymond and Anthony.

Sakimba whose warrior stick carries his Maasai spirit onwards, enticing out the Peace warrior heart from those on far off shores.

Henry Stedman of Climb Kilimanjaro for organising the adventure so well and Team Kilimanjaro for making it happen efficiently.

My sons Paul, Scott and Mark who with Nella and Chloe give the unending support and immeasurable love which makes all things possible for me. Including sketching the talisman and map. The family rock-like strength of my brother and sisters. And Lawley for his continued loving support.

Also: All at the White Eagle Lodge for unconditional love, Maureen for homeopathic help, Peace Flame Paul for the lantern and Watamu magic, Mannatech for nutritional and sport supplements, Brendan O'Sullivan for author photo, Tamsin for kind medical advice and supplies, Sheila for her shining heart, Gautam for website and techno-backup, Dungbeetle and the Norfolk Peace Climb team ...

Dan at Eye Books for his continued belief in me and for holding firm his glorious vision of sharing heart journeys – a dream that shines brightly making a difference for humanity. Martha for her editing wizardry and big heart; and Jenny for excellent book-midwifery.

Ivy Smith, her Wattle groups and Master Advarr for their dedication, loving guidance and radiant service given for the world expansion of light.

Those in spirit who hold my hand.

My grandchildren Elsie, Bess and Bodhi who remind me to see the love and perfection in all things.

ABOUT EYE BOOKS

www.eye-books.com

Eye Books is a dynamic publishing company that likes to break the rules. We publish books that truly inspire, by people who have given their all, triumphed over adversity, lived their lives to the full.

We are committed to ethical publishing and try to minimise our carbon footprint in the manufacturing and distribution of our books.

If you feel that you have a book in you, and it is a book that is experience driven, inspirational and life affirming, then please contact us. We are always open to new authors.

'Climb For Tibet' Tune-In

www.climbfortibet.org

We invite you to take part in our tune-in to help the peace and harmony of the Earth.

This is a peace focus which takes place for six minutes at 6pm (local time) on the sixth day of every month. People around the world simply hold thoughts for peace. It does not matter where you physically are, but a quiet mind concentrating for a few minutes contributes in a powerful way. It helps to think of the symbol of perfect harmony, the six-pointed star, sending out rays of light and peace to all beings.

Do join us.

"I am pleased to offer my prayers to 'Climb For Tibet' and all that it touches."

His Holiness the Dalai Lama

ABOUT THE AUTHOR

Tess Burrows was born in Southern England in 1948, educated at Bedales School and Edinburgh University in Ecological Science and moved to Australia to grow trees. In 1984 she returned as the mother of three young boys, motherhood being paramount. In 1990, hit by the realisation that it is possible to help the Earth and make a difference, she started climbing and using this medium for a number of unusual events to raise awareness and funds for charity.

In 1998 she founded the charity 'Climb For Tibet' with her partner Pete. Since then they have undertaken various 'Peace Climbs' and raised over £120,000 to build six schools for underprivileged children in Tibet as well as to support environmental charities.

She is the best-selling author of *Cry From The Highest Mountain,* telling of her attempted climb to the point furthest from the centre of the Earth and *Cold Hands Warm Heart,* that of racing on skis to the South Pole. A motivational speaker and a healer in the White Eagle tradition, she readily admits that her top job is being a grandmother. Her home is a cottage near Haslemere in Surrey, England.

She is a believer that we can, each one of us, reach up and touch the sky ...

www.climbfortibet.org
Facebook: tess.burrows   Twitter: @tessburrows1